THE BEST AUSTRALIAN
SPORTS
WRITING
2 0 0 4

THE BEST AUSTRALIAN
SPORTS
WRITING
2 0 0 4

EDITED BY GARRIE HUTCHINSON

Published by Black Inc.,
an imprint of Schwartz Publishing Pty Ltd

Level 5, 289 Flinders Lane
Melbourne Victoria 3000 Australia
email: sport@blackincbooks.com
http://www.blackincbooks.com

ISBN 1 86395 213 6

Cover image: Sport the Library
Book design: Thomas Deverall

CONTENTS

Sport, a Place Called Home Garrie Hutchinson ix

BEHIND THE LEGENDS

The Day Hookesy Passed His Test Peter Lalor 2

Four Minutes That Changed the World Stuart Rintoul 9

Never Again Gideon Haigh 16

In the Deep End: Swimming Upstream Nicole Jeffery 21

Under Lock and Key Jenny McAsey 29

STRONGER HIGHER OLDER DOPIER

How I Got Mistaken for a Korean Olympian Because of My Bad French Ian Hayward Robinson 34

Seared in the Memory Len Johnson 38

The Need for Speed Jacquelin Magnay 41

Modern-day Folk Hero Keeps His Cool amid the Maelstrom Peter Lalor 48

Let the Fully-drugged Games Begin! Stephen Downes 52

Good Sport, Bad Sport Julian Savulescu and Bennett Foddy 56

Bad Chemistry Robert Wainwright 61

ON THE EDGE

Middle Eastern Appearance Robert Drane 68

Partial Law, Mixed Feelings Robert Drane 77

Safari Politics Jesse Fink 82

Smoke on the Water Carl Hammerschmidt 96

WET WET WET

Sold to Soul Carl Hammerschmidt 108

Fifty-two Not Out Peter Lalor 119

Hell and High Water Leisa Scott 129

Sitting Pretty Richard Yallop 137

The Whole Hog Will Swanton 146

SEX, DRUGS 'N' FOOTBALL

Up Yours, Cazaly Philippa Hawker 154

Saints 2004: A Game, a Jumper, a Song Stephanie Holt 158

After Coffs: About That Night ... Christine Jackman 168

Mentality of the Pack Too Much for One Rookie Claire Halliday 186

Behind the Touchline Melissa Campbell 190

Why Football Needs Women Caroline Wilson 197

Professional Foul Neil Jameson 202

MEMORABILIA IS MADE OF THIS

The Sting in Memorabilia Jesse Fink 214

Funky Blue, Odd Balls and a Piece of Pitch Bernard Whimpress 226

A Memorabilia Idea for Tony Greig Tony Wilson 233

THE MEANINGS OF FOOTBALL

The Meaning of Football Martin Flanagan 238

Return of the Magnificent Six Roy Masters 243

The Chant of Jimmy Krakouer Martin Flanagan 246

How Rugby's Bid for Joey Was Sunk Greg Growden 253

Believing in the Impossible Tony Wilson 258

The Virgin Coach Paul Connolly 262

The Sport I Hate Anthea Henwood 268

The Game They Play in Sydney Gideon Haigh 272

World Cup Thoughts from the Sideline Michael Morley 274

ABOVE THE SHOULDERS, BETWEEN THE EARS

Andre the Mastermind Chip Le Grand 282

The Role of Sports Science in Australia's Sporting Success Matthew Ricketson 285

There Comes a Time When Too Much Sport Psychology Is Barely Enough Michelle Griffin 294

Leaps and Bounds Warwick Hadfield 301

BARRY DICKINS: A SPORTING YEAR

Grey Cup without the Crims and Fathers 314

Greyhounds with Chips Stop You Going to the Dogs 316

Courting the Good Old Days of Glory 318

The Remembrance of Wally Grouts Past 320

We Fought Them on the Beaches, and We Never Gave In 322

A Haircut, a Touch of Styptic and a Rocker Called Butch Gale 325

The Brat Who's Been Reincarnated as the Game's Great Listener 328

Ability and Humility a Doubles Team That Male Tennis Needs 330

The Boot That Sealed the Romance of the Roys 332

The Day Big Mick Conlan Barrelled the Vic Park Spit Brigade 335

Another Saturday at Auskick 337

THE PASSING PARADE

Unique Sportsman and Super Sports Scribe to Boot Ron Carter 342

A Game Well Played Ian Heads 346

Break Even Had a Winning Way Peter Lalor 349

SPORT, A PLACE CALLED HOME

Garrie Hutchinson

Princes Park, 21 August 2004. It was the last regular home game for the Carlton Football Club at the place the club has called home since 1897. While next year there might be a ceremonial finale, for most of us this was it: the last waltz, the final stanza of suburban AFL football. The game was confirmation that what had been for more than a hundred years a kind of medieval tribal battle between suburban statelets, was now mostly just a two-dimensional TV drama. The ancient rituals of going to the footy were at an end, replaced by decisions about whether to buy a seat at a sports theatre, or pay for a game on TV.

Football is like everything else in life and art, apparently. It's always evolving and, many argue, always progressing, improving, getting better. Once you've discovered electricity, there's no going back to steam power, whatever the consequences an insatiable demand for electricity might have for culture and the sustainability of the environment. So it is with Australian football. Many and loud though the lamentations are and have been over the disappearance of suburban grounds, there's no going back to suburban footy and the Coulter Law which saw players paid £3 a game. Now the turnover of clubs is in the tens of millions, and a no-gamer is paid more than a ten-year-veteran teacher. Next year all games in Melbourne (except perhaps Carlton's finale) will be played at two grounds, one of which is indoors. This will mean a loss of the variables that used to be a valuable asset of Victorian football, which was played in wind and rain, on different-shaped ovals and in front of different crowds of barrackers.

The national football game has at last gone genuinely national. If the formerly suburban clubs such as Carlton are to survive in the new media age they have to be fully involved in it, not nostalgically yearning for six games on a Saturday arvo, with every second one broadcast from the wooden press box that used to sit unsteadily in the outer at Princes Park.

Outside the ground some angry nostalgists were gathering names for a petition to call an emergency general meeting of the club in order to prevent the sell-out of the old home ground, and all that it represented. It's a sad thing. Like them, I much preferred footy thirty years ago, standing on the half-forward flank in the outer next to the press box, a gathering of footy mates bearing tinnies, barracking and listening, participating in the roar of the crowd as the big men flew, and Jezza, Big Nick and Tiger (and several generations of others) did the impossible on a regular basis.

We had our place in football then, in the outer, lefty and arty bohemians barracking for the club that boasted Menzies and Fraser as number-one ticket holders. In the fraternity of the outer, formal politics didn't play much of a part – there were days (of yore) when Bob Santamaria yarned with Manning Clark, and you could drink a can a quarter, and one for the win, and still get to work at the Pram Factory that night.

So I miss all that, as I miss a lot of the people from those days. But the outer disappeared long ago. In order to make way for a monument to himself, John Elliott destroyed the press box and our sacred spot at a time in the 1980s expunged from my memory. He built the so-called Legends Stand in the 1990s, which bore the name of no player, and pushed the club into the financial mess it is in now. With the outer gone, the experience of the game changed completely. Watching it sitting down, without rubbing shoulders and insults with barrackers from the opposition, just wasn't the same thing. Footy has changed, it's already largely a form of television entertainment, and you can't go back to the days of steam.

Reluctantly, and as much as I wish it was 1970 again, I didn't sign the petition, and have resigned myself to being part of my team's future, not its past. So it was a day of last rites: giving the Melbourne City Council one last opportunity to collect a parking fine (they didn't); a last walk up Pigdon Street to the accompaniment of demented lorikeets in the palm trees; the last purchase of raffle tickets outside the ground and last pies inside; the last feeling of contentment sitting in the sunshine watching the men and boys who have that immeasurable capacity to make you feel just plain old happy with yourself and the rest of the world. The Blueboys ran onto the velveteen surface through a garish banner to begin the unique warm-up antics of Australian football. Kouta, Kouta, Kouta, we cried.

Carlton looked like they always have, in old dark navy blue with the CFC monogram, the uniform for nearly a hundred years. The club dates back to 1864, and is older than just about every other football club in the world. But not older than the day's opponents, Melbourne, whose history stretches back to the beginnings of the game outside its own home ground in 1858. But modish Melbourne appeared in their 'away' jumper – bright red with the blue slash. Things had already changed, it was plain to see. The white mongrels were in yellow. And looking over from the Lower Pratt not-so-grandstand towards the scoreboard, there was no outer where we used to stand, even though John Elliott's name had been expunged from his edifice.

But some things had stayed the same. Supporters of both sides mixed together, and while there was vigorously insulting barracking to be heard, there was no segregation, fighting, streaking or smoke-bombing.

Carlton have been down near the bottom of the ladder for a few years, and the once mighty fortress of Princes Park has been breached more often than not. After a clean-out of players 2004 has seen better results, with fighting wins notably over Adelaide on their paddock and, always satisfyingly, against Essendon. Melbourne had been top of the ladder a few weeks before, but they'd lost a couple of matches. They haven't won a premiership since 1964, and they lost this game.

During the game the rackety old electric scoreboard (it hardly counts as electronic) flashed the note 'Jana Pittman wins in her heat'. A small ripple went around the Princes Park ground, which has its own Olympic history. The whole question of moving home games to the MCG would not have arisen if, in 1953, then-president Ken Luke's farsighted plans for the 100,000-seat Carlton Olympic Stadium and football headquarters had been allowed to come to pass.

As it was (and this is a true story), pressure by John Cain Senior's Labor government on the reluctant MCG Trustees forced the issue of the main 1956 Olympic Stadium. It was to be the MCG or nothing. International Olympic Committee president Avery Brundage had threatened to take the Games away from Melbourne (shades of Athens) if decisions weren't made and facilities built.

All Carlton presidents, from first to last, have had big ideas. Luke raised £300,000 towards the Carlton Olympic Stadium and said in 1953 that he 'always thought Carlton should be the people's ground'. Instead, the MCG adopted that slogan and through the Olympics, football and cricket, became the people's ground in fact. And 52 years after Carlton's failed bid, home games will be shared between the 'G' and the Dome.

Another finale. The last song was sung: we got to sing the song at the end of the game. Who knows whether Carlton will win the 'final' final game in 2005? I counted it as the last time that I could definitely sing, so I sang. I watched the players gather, and go into the rooms, and I reflected that I had watched a page of the footy record actually turn. I felt pretty good, actually. There's nothing quite like the feeling of satisfaction to be had from 'your' team winning. It sets up the rest of the week like nothing else, a buffer against misfortune. And a premiership, well, you get a whole summer and most of the next year out of that.

Next year football won't be the same, home games won't be at the old home ground. In the meantime we watched the Olympics, at home.

Going AWOL Over Sport

The passage of the year has, as usual, been punctuated by sport. Events in the sporting solar system roll around in accordance with their individual cycles: the football season, the Olympic quadrennium. Cricket has turned from a summer sport into an endless supra-seasonal event, and may pay for it. Our roster of champions and favourites has expanded after the Olympics – now there are many more out to battle for the Australian Way of Life (AWOL). Many of them are women. If ever there were an advertisement for AWOL, Jodie Henry, triple gold-medal-winning swimmer is she. If Jodie doesn't become the face of Australia, I'll go hee (or she). Amid all the po-faced professional seriousness and occasional macho bragging, Jodie was a beacon. It's just sport, have fun, win gold medals.

Appropriately for the Games played in the city of the goddess Athena, Australian women's sport seemed at last to have reached some sort of equality in appreciation and performance with the male variety. Perhaps it was the untimely and disappointing way Channel Seven telecast the Games, but for all the Australian success, and the dramas before the opening ceremony, there was a strong feeling that we're a bit over the Olympics. AWOL has moved on a notch, and in the age of terror, wallowing in blimpish one-eyed patriotism is not appropriate.

Not that I didn't enjoy winning.

The other side of the AWOL coin was the controversies over what it means to be an Australian, particularly in regard to Sally Robbins, the rower who gave up, or alternatively had given all she had, in the women's eights final. What was worse, letting your mates down, or complaining about it? The Australian ethical compass doesn't give much guidance in this. Sally had made a commitment. She had a history of hitting that uncharted interface where training, will and commitment meet emotion, lactic acid and a kind of collapse that overtakes everything rational and turns both mind and brain to the off position. It would have been better if the reality of this mystery had been acknowledged, and she had taken up an individual event. Her team-mates had every right to feel let down, and to say so. As Jane Fleming noted, 'At this level quitting isn't an option.'

There's always a moral aspect to this. These people are not only representing themselves, they are representing us, and, it seems, the AWOL. Mateship, in this context (and in the military context as well), does not permit letting your country down. Cynics and Skeptics (those old Athenians) may scoff, but defending AWOL is why we, as a nation, invest so much in sport. It's the most competitive we get, where we really punch above our weight. Roy and HG in their nightly medal count, using all sorts of measures of AWOL such as gold per head, conclusively prove that we are the world's best.

My new favourite sport, courtesy of the Tour de France and the cloudy mixture of news stories in 2004, has been cycling. It's been part of the AWOL since Banjo had Mulga Bill from Eaglehawk catch the cycling craze. As in the swimming, the women were fantastic. Anna Mears in the time trial, Sara Carrigan in the road race and Kate Mactier in the pursuit won gold, and Loretta Harrop won on the bike in the gruelling triathlon, heroic but pipped in the straight by a Geelong-born Austrian. Ossie Ossie Ossie Ja Ja Ja.

The men's team overcame the drug-injecting scandal and the disruption to the team in training to record far and away the best Olympic results ever. Robbie McEwen did enough in the Tour de France to finish high up in the road race despite sweltering conditions, but on the track was where the team really shone.

I loved it all – Ryan Bayley, the awesome teams-pursuit quartet Brad McGee, Graeme Browne, Brett Lancaster and Luke Roberts (or sextet, if you count the two champs who were unable to fit in the final team, Peter Dawson and Stephen Wooldridge), Stuart O'Grady in the kierin, even Tour de France hero Robbie McEwan on the road.

We invest a lot of money and emotional energy into the Olympics, proportionately more than bigger countries, and we do proportionately better than anyone. Is this a good thing? It's a fact, it's the way we present our national culture to the world, which I would characterise as inclusive, irreverent, successful, young and free. We do best in niche international sports suited to the AWOL – swimming and cycling – and less well in universal sports which don't require first-world infrastructure, such as track-and-field and soccer. Back in the avoirdupois

Olympic era of the Golden Girls and four-minute milers, it was the AWOL which gave us the interest and the advantage. Nowadays many other countries have discovered they can run fast or long and enjoy the benefits of Olympic success.

The Olympic Games are the culmination of the sporting year, and there was plenty to write and read about in the theatre of Australian sport, from Jonny Wilkinson's dramatic kick that won the Rugby World Cup, to Jana Pittman's soap-opera ending in the Olympic Games.

Individuals have done well, such as golfers Adam Scott and Rod Pamphling. However, the Davis Cup tennis team won the competition and then almost straightaway lost it.

Steve Waugh retired but the Australian cricket juggernaut rolled on under Ricky Ponting. The Brisbane Lions three-peated in 2003, and looked likely prospects to do it again. Despite the rise of the Saints though, it was Port Adelaide who ultimately ended the Lions' reign.

But both the AFL's and the NRL's macho football cultures were called into question with the emergence of lurid allegations against players in each code. So far no player has actually gone to jail, but the difference between what is permissible behaviour in the wider community, and among and between footballers, is very wide. The facts and issues are explored in these pages.

But in the end the players and clubs kept right on playing. Saints and sinners are in contention in the footy, in the Olympics, everywhere in the AWOL.

Garrie Hutchinson, September 2004

Acknowledgements
Thank to John Harms' email circle for valuable suggestions, Jesse Fink at *Inside Sport*, Michael Hyde at Victoria University for the opportunity to speak to his sports-writing class – one result is in this book. Readers and writers are invited to join the suggestion process at sport@blackincbooks.com.

BEHIND THE LEGENDS

David Hookes, Steve Waugh, John Landy, Ian Thorpe, Jana Pittman: the year saw new chapters added to their legendary stories. Peter Lalor's piece, my favourite of 2004, looks at David Hookes' 1977 apotheosis and his untimely death, while Stuart Rintoul takes the ever-modest John Landy back to his Olympian past and Gideon Haigh reflects on the career of the recently retired baggy green helmsman, Steve Waugh.

Ian Thorpe proved himself an Olympic legend in Athens, not least because of his new coach, Tracey Menzies, as Nicole Jeffery previewed. And Jana Pittman's journey to the 400-metre hurdles final was the biggest sporting soap opera since the life of Shane Warne, as explored by Jenny McAsey before the starting line.

THE DAY HOOKESY PASSED HIS TEST

Peter Lalor

He arrived at the Melbourne Hilton Hotel a 21-year-old with a kitbag full of attitude and little idea of what happened outside Adelaide's Thebarton.

He'd asked Gary Gilmour how to use the hotel shower. Sensing a new chum, Gilmour told him to be careful crossing the tram lines on the way to the Melbourne Cricket Ground because the electric current could kill a gullible kid from Adelaide.

The posh hotel seemed like 'the centre of the universe ... a fairytale' to the son of a tannery worker. Every face leapt out from the pages of the cricket books he'd devoured from a young age. Almost every living person who'd played a Test was there. There were cocktail parties and he was invited, but he fell asleep and had to rush to the first because he was late. When they sent him back for not wearing a tie, he ran all the way to the hotel to get it and all the way back, sweating even more. This was just like the recurring dreams in which he slept in before a big match.

He was relieved later when the Centenary Test started and the former captains of England and Australia paraded onto the ground. Ian Chappell was wearing a safari suit and no tie.

He'd found his mentor. He'd also found a sparring partner.

Settling in that night at the party, rubbernecking the crowd, shirt just dry, he heard a sensorious voice: 'Another left-hander who can't bat.' The South African accent left him in no doubt as to who it was – the abrasive English captain Tony Greig.

David Hookes was almost out first ball on the first day of his first Test and there were only about 90,000 people there to see it.

Playing back and across to Bob Willis he was hit on the pads and he knew he was plumb. It was a no-ball.

He'd just got comfortable and was on 17 before being caught by Greig off Chris Old. Back in the dressing room, management chastised him because he hadn't cleaned his sports shoes and the Adidas stripes had shown through when he sweated. Cricket had spent 100 years stamping out such crass commercialism. He put on another coat of white polish but was peeved that they'd do that during a game. The game went at a frenetic pace and life never seemed to slow down from that time.

*

Greg Chappell has had a lot of time to think since he was woken on Monday morning this week by Darren Lehmann. The big Test player was beside himself with grief. Inconsolable. Lehmann had been up all night near the hospital room where Hookes's body lay ventilated by a machine. Big, strong and boisterous just hours before, there were no signs of life now. Lehmann told Chappell their mate was going to die.

The former captain is happy to focus his mind back on the Centenary Test of 1977. It's a good way to remember David, he says. Sums him up in a lot of ways.

'We got, I think, 138 or something in the first innings and we bowled them out for 95,' Chappell says. Hookes had got his 17 but things happened so fast nobody noticed.

'We knew that if we bowled well we could probably restrict them to a modest first innings lead – to think that we finished with a lead of 45 is quite unbelievable,' he continues.

It had been a calamitous start, compounded by the smashing of Rick McCosker's jaw. The opener was helped off with Australia at 2/13. Chappell got a gritty 40. Rod Marsh recalls that he 'batted his arse off in the first innings, only got 28 or something, but I was in really good form at the time'. McCosker couldn't open in the second innings as his jaw was swathed in bandages, his head swollen.

Chappell didn't want to mess with the batting order too much. He turned to the young spinner Kerry O'Keeffe to open.

'I said, "I need you to play the innings of your life. I don't care how many runs you make, but you've got to get through the new ball."'

Former Test opener Ian Davis is the Australian sales manager of Dunlop Sport these days. Like everyone, he's had a bad week. 'It's an indictment on society as it is today. There's a hole in my heart.'

He's got an email Hookes sent him some time back. It opens with light-hearted abuse and ends with a request that they play a round soon. Davis will never erase it.

'We were the younger members of the side,' he says. Davis knew they had to knuckle down in the second innings. Hell, the Test hadn't even been going two days and the Queen was coming. 'O'Keeffe and myself struggled a bit – he got 14 or so, then I think we lost Cosier very early – oh yes, Greg first, then Gary. Two quick wickets.'

Chappell remembers going out. 'It pitched middle and hit middle. It was dead straight, but I was looking for something else. The bat got caught up in the pad ... anyway, I got out and Kerry got out.'

Davis was joined by Walters. 'I think myself and Dougie consolidated pretty well, because I think I went to bed on about 48 and Dougie wasn't far behind me and that was good because they bowled pretty well, the Poms. Bob Willis bowled fairly quick, actually.' The scorebook shows Davis had 45 and Walters 32. 'The next morning we started off okay, I ended up with 68 or so. I batted for 230-odd minutes. It was a long time, it was a grafter.'

And now Davis was out and Australia were 4 for 132 and Hookes was coming in, baggy green pulled down tight, shirt open, long blonde hair. Five 100s in the last six Shield games. Biggest Test match in history. 'I can't remember what I said to him, I used to always just wish them the best of luck and that's probably what I did ... I remember watching the innings and it was just brilliant,' Davis says.

Hookes took strike. Left-handed, looking over his right shoulder, feet wide apart.

Over in England this week former captain Bob Willis has been trying to deal with the news. 'He breezed out with a very positive attitude, almost with a hint of arrogance about him,' Willis recalls.

In fact, he'd breezed into the team like that. 'He had an aura about him that was unique,' Chappell remembers. 'There are few 21-year-olds who walk into the dressing room and bring that aura with them. There are many who slink in and hope that no one really notices, but bugger that, David bashed the door open and strode in and put his bag in the first empty locker and grabbed the first empty seat.'

Hookes figured he was as good as anyone. Max Walker says, 'most players come in to the dressing room and they sit in among the sweaty old shirts and they listen to the older players, and the odd bit of wisdom falls on the floor and [they] sort of tuck that one away, but a big breath of fresh air – David – walked in and probably took everyone by the scruff of the neck.'

On the field, Greig took up where he'd left off at the cocktail party. Bowler Willis heard it. 'Tony suggested to Hookes that his testicles might not have dropped yet and Hookesy was pretty quick to put a flea in Greigy's ear. He certainly told him to get lost in pretty few words,' Willis says.

Umpire Max O'Connell had stood in some of Hookes's South Australian games. He remembers the kid giving it back to the England captain.

Tom Brooks is 84 now. He stepped in from square leg. 'I just said "come on fellas" and they shut up.'

Chappell has his version. 'Greig put himself at silly mid-on and said to the young bloke, "How does it feel playing real cricket with the real blokes instead of with the boys?" and Hookesy, as ever, had an answer and on this occasion as usual it was spot on: "At least I'm an Australian playing for Australia, how are you going?"

'That summed Hookesy up, he was cheeky, he was brash, he was confident, full of bravado and that's the way he played his cricket.'

Hookes and Greig probably should have their say at this

stage. This exchange was done for the Nine Network's cameras – when they were older, wiser and still as competitive.

'Hookes arrives, I'll never forget it,' says Greig. 'Freckles intermingled with pimples … bumfluff and I remember saying something to the effect of "Ahhh, tell me Hookesy, have your testicles dropped yet?" and he looked around at me and as quick as a flash he said "At least I'm playing for the country I was born in."'

Hookes batted through to lunch, Chappell looking on and learning a lesson he would take to heart: ignore youth at your peril. 'It was just another game of cricket for him, he was full of life and not aware of what could go wrong. He was young and he was confident. He didn't see it as a pressure situation, it was a game of cricket and he'd played a lot of cricket and he'd made a lot of runs and why was this going to be any different?

'And here was Greigy, the big bloody tall streak of doo-daa that we all bloody used to love to hate and he'd started it with the verbal stuff. Hookesy's attitude would have been "Cop this you big Afrikaan prick – I'll show you what the young bloke can do", and it was a lot like his life: he met it head on.'

At lunch Hookes and Walters had put on 50 in 68 minutes. The kid had 20 off 40 balls. After lunch Walters went in the first over to Greig for 56. Marsh strode to the crease, bullish and determined to show the Poms what sort of form he was in. He was going to have to wait his turn.

Marsh has been with Terry Jenner in London this week. The former wicket-keeper is coach at the English academy. Strange how life changes. The last couple of nights they've been remembering their mate. Getting angry. Often sad.

'We've had a couple of nights where we've just sat around and had a beer on Hookesy and that's one of the things Terry said: "Hookesy said what a lot of people thought." He had the courage to say what a lot of people thought and I think that's a good man.'

Dennis Lillee is in Perth. He'd probably like to have a beer with Marshy and Jenner. Tuesday was rough and Wednesday he was starting to deal with it. 'I don't really want to talk about it

… you know? He was a good mate and if he's remembered for the way he played in the Centenary Test you are really remembering David Hookes the way he was in life.'

Back in 1977 Hookesy is about to let his bat do the talking. He and Marsh settle in together and in Greig's 13th over, the 52nd of the innings, Hookes begins to simmer. He fails to score off the first two balls. Then the world pulls focus on that patch of Melbourne turf.

Willis remembers: 'Greigy had had some success in the West Indies bowling his off-cutter-style delivery but it was still really in the experimental stage. Hookesy just climbed into him – he just backed himself.'

Hookes remembered the third ball. He was on 36. 'Greigy tossed it up and I thought "that's it" so I just hit it back over his head for four.' The crowd loved that.

'Because he's a medium pacer I premeditated the next shot,' Hookes continued, 'which you're not supposed to do, but I thought that he'd bowl a quicker delivery and that's exactly what happened.'

He turned it toward fine leg. Four more. The next one was a glorious drive over mid-off. The crowd was going mad. Hookes had raced to 48. The English captain was starting to get a little concerned: 'Three fours, the place is absolutely electric. There's no doubt that something special is happening here but it goes on.'

The fourth went for four to the leg side. The fifth copped the big cover-drive. Marsh, one of the hardest hitters in cricket, hadn't said a word. 'He just played five magnificent shots, all of them cricket shots, none of them were slogs, each of them I can remember thinking, "my God". I took off for a run each time because I'd never seen Hookesy bat before and I didn't realise just how sweet a timer he was.

'It was a hell of a big ground in those days, the fence was the boundary and all of them got there easily. If I hit a four I had to belt it, but he caressed those shots and it sort of put a different complexion on the game. It left an everlasting impression, that one over.'

Chappell was one of the players celebrating in the dressing room. 'I thought the on-drive was the best shot of the lot of them,' he says. Hookesy thought the cover-drive was one of his best.

On-drive. Cover-drive. Wouldn't have mattered if they were thick edges. He had five fours in a row. Of course, it was even sweeter that it was Greig bowling.

Greig was let off the hook when the last delivery, another strong drive, was well fielded. O'Connell thought that was the best shot of the lot and it should have been a sixth four.

Ever the showman, Greig snatched his jumper and cap from the umpire. 'Greigy said "give me my cap, I'm out of here,"' O'Connell remembers.

At the time the English captain did not understand the significance of the event. 'What didn't hit me at that stage was that I would be remembered for this every week of my life for the rest of my life – that all came later and had I known that at the time I would have thrown the ball to someone and got out of the place,' Greig said 20 years later.

Hookes was pretty happy just to be playing. 'For me, I was still a little kid facing the England captain – the stuff that dreams are made of as a youngster listening to the crystal set and reading books – it was still just surreal that I was there facing the English captain,' he said.

The five balls changed the Test match and would go down in cricketing history. 'It was just excitement, it got your spine tingling,' Ian Davis said.

Walker was amazed by what he saw. 'The sheer elegance and eloquence with which he went about the stroke-play was breathtaking,' he says. 'He didn't just plunder five boundaries, he went through the whole coaching manual. They were just five pieces of poetry, really.'

Derek Underwood came on the next over. 'He pushed at the ball and it held up and he was caught,' is all he recalls.

Chappell was still taking it all in. 'We thought, "shit, who is this kid?" We'd heard a lot about him, but there's a fair bit of cynicism amongst athletes – "oh yeah, he's made five 100s" but the Test guys are always, "so how good is he?" and then he walks out on the MCG and whoop, bang, thump. There was a fair bit of the "you bewdys" and "get up him" and "give it to the big ..." and then he was out and it was a bit of a shock, we'd had them on toast and he was gone. As it turns out, it's a metaphor for his life – just when he looks like he's on top he's gone.'

Looking back Chappell says something quite amazing. 'I would love to have batted like he did, I would love to have been that free to have gone out there and batted like that, but it wasn't my personality to bat like David did ... take it or leave it, that was the way he played and if you didn't like it, "stuff ya".'

And that kid from Thebarton is leaving the MCG, doffing his brand new baggy green, three days a Test cricketer and already one of the game's immortals.

The Australian, 24 January 2004

FOUR MINUTES THAT CHANGED THE WORLD

Stuart Rintoul

In the early morning light at Government House, Melbourne, John Landy, Governor of Victoria and sporting icon, has a slight frown on his face and a hint of agitation in his voice as he says, once again, that not being the first man to break the four-minute mile was not the end of the world.

Landy insists he never thought of it as something akin to the conquest of Everest, and while he might have preferred to have beaten Roger Bannister in the race they called the Mile of the Century (he shrugs), it wasn't to be.

He smiles wanly. The question of character has been Landy's cross to bear. He was brilliant, yes, and an Australian sporting hero. But did he have the killer instinct, the craving, the self-belief to change history? His one-time coach, the eccentric Percy Cerutty, from whom Landy split bitterly, didn't believe so. When asked at the time of his retirement from athletics what he lacked in big events, Landy himself said: 'A certain temperament, I suppose. I'm not quite as grim about running as some people. I feel lucky to have advanced as far as I have, really, because I'm not a natural runner. I don't really think I lack courage; I'd never quit to anyone on the track, I know. I guess I'm just not the blood-and-thunder type.'

It is 50 years this Thursday (6 May) that Bannister became the first man to run the mile in under four minutes. His time of 3:59.4 electrified the world, just as Edmund Hillary and Sherpa Tenzing Norgay's conquest of Everest the previous year had done. It was instantly interpreted as having extended the boundaries of human possibility.

There was a wonderful symmetry to the four-minute mile: four laps of the track at one minute per lap. It's an ordinary time now, of course. In 1999 in Rome, Morocco's Hicham El Guerrouj ran 3:43.13 and by then, almost a thousand individuals had run under four minutes. But 50 years ago, it was a very different story. No one could do it. Many believed it wasn't possible for a man to run so fast for so long. It was a barrier of body and mind that begged to be broken.

By 1954, three men on three continents were considered the most likely to break it: Bannister, 25, a medical student at Oxford driven by the need to atone for his failure at the Helsinki Olympics in 1952, a strong sense of history and the nobility of the pursuit; Landy, 24, a grammar school-educated agricultural science student in Melbourne who loved butterfly collecting, and hardened his body until it was machine-like by running barefoot in sand dunes, surf and bushland until late into the night; and Wes Santee, 22, a Kansas farm boy worked to the bone by his austere father, who believed he was just better than everybody else.

'It was a very simple sort of contest,' Landy tells *The Weekend Australian Magazine*. 'It wasn't confused by money in any way. There was no such thing as sponsorships; we weren't representing a firm. We were representing our countries, but we were also running as individuals. It was a more innocent age than it is today. Running then was a joy.'

But there was a great difference between Bannister and Landy. Bannister had followed Hillary's Everest expedition closely. He saw how England and her fading Empire rejoiced. He understood the importance of being the first to a summit. As Neal Bascomb writes in *The Perfect Mile* (one of three new books and a BBC documentary timed to coincide with the 50th anniversary): 'Compared to Landy, Bannister had a greater appreciation of the historical significance of being the first to run under four minutes, and he was not going to let anything stop him.'

'I never saw it in those terms,' Landy says, staring at his hands. 'I saw it just as a time. I never, ever, ever saw that. People for 20 years had been trying to do it and couldn't do it, and so it built up an equivalent, I suppose, to Everest, but it didn't appeal to me in the same way. I never saw it in those terms. I was interested in breaking the world's record, regardless of what it was. I'm not saying I didn't want to run four minutes, but I didn't see it in anything other than athletic terms.'

*

6 May 1954 was a bleak English day. It rained and the wind was blowing a gale. Bannister travelled up to Oxford from London with his coach, the Austrian Franz Stampfl (who would later emigrate to Australia), and laid his fears bare. 'Sure it'll be painful, but what's pain?' Stampfl said. 'If you forgo this chance, would you ever forgive yourself? Nobody knows what the future holds. Wes Santee or John Landy might do it first … There may never be another opportunity.'

There were six runners in the race, but only three that mattered: Bannister and the two 'rabbits' who would pace him, Chris Chataway and Chris Brasher (when Bannister had tried to break the barrier the previous June at a schoolboys' meet, he had used Brasher and the Australian Don Macmillan, who was studying in England and who agreed on the basis that if he couldn't help Landy it was better for an Englishman to break the mark than an American). Stampfl had plotted the pace Brasher and Chataway needed to set.

Bannister's memory of the race at the Iffley Road track, told in his 1955 biography, *The Four Minute Mile*, has lost none of its drama:

There was complete silence on the ground … a false start … I felt angry that precious moments during the lull in the wind might be slipping by. The gun fired a second time … Brasher went into the lead and I slipped in effortlessly behind him, feeling tremendously full of running.

My legs seemed to meet no resistance at all, as if propelled by some unknown force. We seemed to be going so slowly! Impatiently I shouted, 'Faster!' But Brasher kept his head and did not change the pace. I went on worrying until I heard the first lap time, 57.5 seconds …

At one and a half laps I was still worrying about the pace. A voice shouting 'relax' penetrated to me above the noise of the crowd. I learnt afterwards it was Stampfl's.

Unconsciously I obeyed. If the speed was wrong it was too late to do anything about it, so why worry? I was relaxing so much that my mind seemed almost detached from my body. There was no strain.

I barely noticed the half-mile, passed in 1 minute 58 seconds, nor when, round the next bend, Chataway went into the lead. At three-quarters of a mile the effort was still barely perceptible; the time was 3 minutes 0.7 seconds and by now the crowd was roaring. Somehow I had to run that last lap in 59 seconds. Chataway led round the next bend and then I pounced past him at the beginning of the back straight, three hundred yards from the finish.

I had a moment of mixed joy and anguish, when my mind took over. It raced well ahead of my body and drew my body compellingly forward. I felt that the moment of a lifetime had come.

There was no pain, only a great unity of movement and aim. The world seemed to stand still, or did not exist. The only reality was the next two hundred yards of track under my feet. The tape meant finality – extinction perhaps. I felt at that moment that it was my chance to do one thing supremely well. I drove on, impelled by a combination of fear and pride …

Bannister breasted the tape and collapsed, almost unconscious. The pain caught him like a vice. He felt 'like an exploded flashlight with no will to live'.

The announcement of Bannister's time was made by one of his friends and supporters, Norris McWhirter, later to become a right-wing political activist, writer, television presenter and co-editor of the first *Guinness Book of Records*, with his twin brother Ross, who was assassinated by the Provisional IRA in 1975.

He said: 'Ladies and gentlemen, here is the result of event number nine, the one mile. First, number 41, R.G. Bannister of the Amateur Athletic Association and formerly of Exeter and Merton Colleges, with a time which is a new meeting and track record, and which subject to ratification will be a new English Native, British National, British All-Comers, European, British Empire and World's Record. The time is 3 minutes, 59.4 seconds.'

The rest of the announcement was drowned out by cheering. 'Well, we did it,' Brasher told the *Daily Mail*. 'That means Landy and Wes Santee can never break the four-minute mile first.'

'Apres moi, le deluge,' Bannister said in the days following, quoting Louis XV, or perhaps it was Louis' mistress, Madame de Pompadour. 'You know, I think people have been frightened of this four-minute record. It's been rather like the sound barrier. Now it's been broken I'm sure others will break it too.' He was right. Landy was hot on his heels and many others would follow.

*

Landy was in a restaurant in Turku, the ancient capital of Finland, when Finnish runner Denis Johansson strode toward him holding a cable in his hand that announced Bannister had run the mile in 3:59.4. Landy had travelled to Finland for better competition and conditions before the Empire Games in Vancouver. Rather than the four-minute mile, he was more intent on breaking Gundar Haegg's 1945 record of 4.01.4, which he thought was more achievable.

Landy had hurled himself at the four-minute mark, but had been unable to penetrate it. By April 1954, he had run under 4:03 six times. After one race he had said: 'It's a brick wall.'

As he sat in the restaurant, he says he felt not envy, or great disappointment, but 'surprise and admiration, but also a feeling that I could also do it'. When he spoke publicly, he said: 'I'm sure that many more will achieve similar results now that the barrier is down. In fact, I feel as if a great burden has been taken off my shoulders.' Landy remembers that he and Johansson wrote a cable in the restaurant to send to Bannister. He forgets the actual words. It might have been 'great, great run, congratulations', he thinks.

Forty-six days after Bannister ran into the history books, Landy took his record away. With Chataway running against him, he ran 3:58 on the black cinder track at Turku. He said it was the best track he had ever run on. Bannister called it a 'wonderful achievement', but steamed. It set the scene for an epic clash between the two runners in Vancouver.

It was a race the *Daily Telegraph* in England called the Mile of the Century. The *New York Herald Tribune* proclaimed it the Miracle Mile. *Sports Illustrated* was launched to coincide with the race and millions of people around the world stopped what they were doing to listen on the radio. Landy ran from the front, as he had always done, intending to run Bannister into the ground if he could.

Down the back straight, he watched Bannister's shadow behind him. He lost it coming out of the final bend and looked over his left shoulder to see if he had finally shaken Bannister off. 'It was a look of hope,' he says. As Landy looked to his left,

Bannister hurled himself around on Landy's right in two long strides. It was a crystalline moment in sport. Bannister breasted the tape at 3:58.8 with Landy running 3:59.6.

Later it was learned that the day before the race, while jogging barefoot in the early hours, Landy had cut his foot on a photographer's flashbulb. Those few who knew were sworn to secrecy. Landy made no excuses.

Bannister ran only one more race and then retired from athletics to devote himself to medicine, becoming a neurosurgeon. Landy returned to Australia drained, retired to teaching at his old school, Geelong Grammar, but came back in 1956. He continued to run sub-four-minute miles but, running with injury after promotional races in the United States, was placed a disappointing third in the 1500 metres at the Melbourne Olympics. Neither Landy nor Bannister nor Santee ever won an Olympic gold medal.

But Landy etched himself into his nation's heart with one more defining moment in sport. At the Australian Championships in Melbourne the same year, a young Ron Clarke fell to the track and Landy, after gashing Clarke's shoulder with his spikes, stopped to pick him up before chasing down the leaders and winning the race. It was a moment of sublime sportsmanship. But as he sits in this room at Government House, surrounded by portraits of former governors, Landy is again just slightly irritated, saying it was no more than instinctive 'good behaviour'.

'It's most unfortunate that it has received the publicity it has,' he says. 'I did it instinctively. I'd sooner forget it.'

Would his life have been any different had he been the first man to break four minutes? He pauses, and after a while says: 'I don't know. I've had a terribly fortunate life, a very happy life. I've never regretted it, I've never let it interfere, I've never made excuses, or said what effect it might have had on my life. I've never thought of it in those terms. I've had an extraordinarily interesting life and I just leave it at that.'

The Weekend Australian Magazine, 1 May 2004

NEVER AGAIN

Gideon Haigh

No Regrets. Never Satisfied. Never Say Die. Over the last few years, the titles and themes of Steve Waugh's enduringly popular tour diaries have explored a strangely similar set of ideas – of negation, prohibition, even downright refusal. Was there in the works, one wondered, a book called *Never Retire*?

Waugh would never have made so bold. Yet he has been a poignant sight in recent seasons. He has stirred from his team cricket of an increasingly hectic and relentless brand, as though at the head of a Zulu *impi*. But he has also been on his own path, each innings a little essay in resistance: against age, rivals, critics and selectors, as well as opponents. His individual performances have become a story within the story of Australian cricket, a subplot assuming proportions menacing to the triumphant principal narrative. The foreshadowing of his retirement on 26 November came, therefore, as a relief as well as a sadness, freeing admirers to contemplate what he has done rather than dwell on what he might.

In fighting on, of course, Waugh was doing what he always had. The best of Waugh's innings had tended to involve fighting back rather than leading a charge. Australia were 73 for 3 when he began his Test-best 200 at Sabina Park in April 1995; 42 for 3 and 39 for 3 respectively when he began his two-part solo, 108 and 116, at Old Trafford in July 1997; 48 for 3 when he wrested control of the World Cup Super Six game against South Africa at Headingley in June 1999. 'In many ways, the delicate situation has always been the one I play my best cricket in,' he writes in his latest book – a remark akin to Yehudi Menuhin saying he quite liked a bit of a fiddle. Waugh seldom, moreover, abandoned any innings prematurely. It used to be an old cricket truism that batsmen were vulnerable immediately after scoring centuries, relaxed and disarmed by the landmark. Waugh

scoffed at the idea. His average Test hundred, inflated by undefeated innings, was 255 – greater than any other batsman, Don
Bradman and Sachin Tendulkar included. A memoir of his batting alone would be called *Never Enough*.

This was not always the way of it. When 20-year-old Waugh
made his Test debut at the MCG against India on Boxing Day
1985, he was chosen for his eye-catching strokes in the lower
middle-order, handy change bowling and, above all, youth. It
was an investment in style, with the hope of substance, that did
not bear fruit at once. After 52 Tests Waugh was averaging in the
mid-30s with the bat and more than 45 with the ball; take away
the three prosperous Ashes Tests in 1989, moreover, and his batting average shrank to less than 30. He had already spent one
season, 1991–92, by the wayside; he had not, the following summer, made the number three position in the Australian XI quite
his own. It is arguable that Dean Jones, who in his own 52-Test
career was averaging almost 47, would have been the better bet
in England 10 years ago; disgruntled Victorians muttered darkly
about the New South Wales hegemony in Australian cricket.

It was this 1993 tour, however, that marked the turning point
in Waugh's career. That it was the first on which he kept a diary
– an idea which he came up with himself rather than having it
put to him by a publisher, and to which he applied himself with
scrupulous care – strikes one as more than a coincidence. A cal-
culating cricketer had always lurked beneath Waugh's natural
talent; from childhood, for example, he had always counted his
runs while batting, and he never lost the habit. Now that cool,
rational, meticulous cricketer began to crystallise. A glimpse of
the Waugh to come was seen at Headingley when he batted most
of the second day in partnership with his captain Allan Border.
'Batting with Border always makes you concentrate that little bit
extra,' Waugh wrote, 'because you can see how much it means to
him to give his wicket away.' He admitted to having consciously
'set my sights on getting a big hundred' – there were, he had
come to understand, 'so many tough times in cricket'.

Border was 175 and Waugh 144 at the close of the day's play,
but Border surprised Waugh by batting almost another hour the

next morning, explaining his desire to 'cause further mental and physical disintegration'. 'Mental disintegration', of course, is the expression Waugh has used in recent years to describe the psychological pressure his team exerts; Border is, perhaps, its intellectual godfather.

In some senses, too, it was the end of Border's career in March 1994 that prepared for Waugh the role he would fill: that of the immaculate bulwark. Under Mark Taylor's captaincy, Waugh turned seven Test centuries into 17. When his twin brother Mark was at number four, Steve's sternness at numbers five and six seemed particularly pronounced: Mark batted as if in a dream, Steve as if in a trance. After watching his 170 and 61 not out at Adelaide in January 1996, indeed, two Sri Lankan players asked Waugh if he meditated; he seemed, they insisted, to be on a different plane of consciousness while batting.

This entailed sacrifices. Some of his boyish brio disappeared; he ceased to hook and seldom pulled. Again, though, this brought out qualities in him rather than suppressing existing gifts. He had, in that pinched face, those gimlet eyes, that low-slung stance, the elements of an aura – and he used it. He would come out to bat quickly to 'own that space in the centre'; he tugged his old Australian cap low, as if to draw strength from the tradition of which he was part. His back-foot drive was executed like a sock to an opponent's jaw, his slog-sweep like a haymaker to the solar plexus.

That self-absorption was held against Waugh when Taylor announced his retirement in January 1999. Neither Waugh's succession nor his success was preordained; when Australia drew Test and one-day series in the West Indies that they had been expected to win easily, then went to the brink of exiting the World Cup, his aptitude seemed in doubt, not to mention his attitude. When he had Australia inch to victory over West Indies at Old Trafford in an unsuccessful effort to exclude New Zealand from the tournament's Super Six stage, he was coldly dismissive of criticism: 'We're not here to win friends, mate.'

Australia, of course, won the Cup – and Waugh, architect of the triumphs against South Africa at Headingley and Edgbaston, so much more. Waugh's attitude to winning friends underwent a subtle transformation too. The first group were in his own dressing room. Waugh as captain reminded me of a resolutely self-contained man surprised to find a new world opened to him by fatherhood. From the rises of Brett Lee and Adam Gilchrist, and the resurrections of Justin Langer and Matt Hayden, Waugh derived as much satisfaction as from any personal landmark; from instilling in his team his own ethos of continuous improvement, he created a culture that outlives him. Remember when you were a kid, looking up to and wanting to join the toughest gang in town? This Australian team is that gang. It has its own codes, creeds and customs. It assimilates newcomers, largely because they wish to be assimilated. And it speaks with one voice, that of its captain. As Stuart MacGill once put it, its prime directive has been: 'When in Rome, do as Steve Waugh.'

Waugh has also acted like the peasant who accompanied Caesar's men on their triumphal processions through the streets of Rome whispering, 'Remember, you are dust.' During the Test at Hamilton in March 2000, for instance, he donned the cap he had worn during his first series against New Zealand, when Australia had been beaten – a warning against complacency. Likewise, before the Edgbaston Test in July 2001 he gave a brief but heartfelt address about what it was like to lose an Ashes series – something only he could recall. Waugh's captaincy was almost – but not quite – a personality cult. Not quite because the loyalty of his players reflected his loyalty to them. The Australian team psychologist Sandy Gordon once asked team members to complete a questionnaire which included identifying scenarios they found 'particularly mentally demanding'. Waugh replied without hesitation: 'Selection meetings – having to leave out players.'

In one aspect of the Australians' approach, too, Waugh was able to win goodwill as well as games: through 2001 (3.77), 2002 (3.99) and 2003 (4.10), his team's scoring rate increased, until they seemed to be playing cricket on 45 rpm while opponents remained grooved at 33 rpm. As *Inside Edge*'s Chris Ryan has commented astutely, the effect has been a kind of cricket with only two possible outcomes: victory or defeat. On only five occasions in Waugh's 53 Tests have his teams been stalemated. Guaranteed an outcome, Australian Test audiences have risen from 411,335 in 1999–2000 to 568,324 last summer; everywhere they go now, the Australians are feted for their enterprise. To beat them is to beat more than a team; it is to thwart a method.

In another respect, sadly, Waugh did not quite deliver on his promise. For one who prided himself on his historical awareness, he condoned in his team a very modern truculence. This did not do him justice: he was an exceedingly generous opponent off the field, and an uncommonly charitable man away from the game, as evidenced in his patronage of the Nivedita House orphanage in India. Yet, Waugh's innate resistance, his ability to shut out doubt and discord, became a shortcoming. He conspired, unwittingly, in the idea that Australia win Tests by intimidation rather than excellence – an idea willingly taken up by teams that have tried to adopt the air of Waugh's team without their skills. He failed, in this case, to harness his stature for the good of all cricketers.

For his stature grew and grew. In the final stages of his career, Waugh reminded me of Swede Levov, the Jewish athlete in Philip Roth's *American Pastoral*. 'I have to tell you that I don't believe in death, I don't experience time as limited,' Levov says. 'I know it is, but I don't feel it.' His final Test appearance in England, after a severe calf injury, seemed to symbolise his indestructibility: an unbeaten 157 on one leg, like an old man toying with children in his backyard. The summer of 2001–02, however, was a *memento mori*. In nine Tests against New Zealand then South Africa at home and away, Waugh cobbled together only 314 runs at 24.15. A few years earlier, such a streak would barely have occasioned comment; in a 36-year-old, it was interpreted as the last beats of a fading heart.

Waugh's Test captaincy was protected by the selectors' Napoleonic faith in lucky generals, but the form lapse cost him the one-day job. This, Waugh told Greg Baum of *The Age* recently, was a greater blow to him than he realised at the time: 'You put up a brave front and say you're going to get back in here and fight hard ... At the end of it, I was at the crossroads, wondering if I should retire or play on.' A timely century against Pakistan at Sharjah in October 2002 silenced doubters; his stunning hundred against England at Sydney a year ago turned them back into stark raving fans.

It passed without remark at the end of November that Waugh's designation of 2003–04 as his valedictory summer is without Australian precedent. Ian Chappell, Border, Taylor, Ian Healy, Geoff Marsh, Waugh's own brother Mark: none of these sought or were rewarded with last farewells. Greg Chappell, Dennis Lillee, Rod Marsh, David Boon: these had a Test to say goodbye, but either wished or were granted no more. Bradman received his three cheers, of course, but even then nobody knew if the innings would be his last. Steve Waugh has been a cricketer *sui generis*. The future biographer even finds their title ready-made: *Never Again*.

Wisden Cricket Asia, January 2004

IN THE DEEP END: SWIMMING UPSTREAM

Nicole Jeffery

'There goes that girl,' says an unknown voice, and Tracey Menzies braces for what might come next. In the 22 months since Ian Thorpe announced he was leaving his childhood coach, Doug Frost, to work solely with Frost's hitherto unknown assistant, Menzies has heard it all: 'It's your fault he's not swimming the 400 metres ... you've cost Australia a gold medal ... you're the worst mistake he's made ... you should put glue on his feet.'

That sample comes from the days after Thorpe's 'oops' moment at the Olympic trials when he fell into the water before his 400-metre freestyle heat, disqualifying himself from his gold-medal event. It hasn't all been abuse, but the comments have been mostly negative. Every punter, from the supermarket to the swimming pool, has felt free to give unsolicited advice. 'Everyone's an expert,' she shrugs.

If Menzies didn't realise what she was taking on when she agreed to become the guardian of Australia's favourite sporting son, she does now. One day she was a 29-year-old suburban high-school art teacher, coaching swimming part-time, doing wedding photography on weekends and planning nuptials of her own. Then the telephone rang – the world's best swimmer, fresh from winning six gold medals at the Commonwealth Games in Manchester, was calling to say he was leaving his coach. Menzies didn't understand at first that Thorpe was offering her the job – she thought he needed a confidante and counselled him accordingly. Then he called back and dropped the other shoe. 'I'd really like you to be my coach,' he said.

Menzies was flabbergasted. She had known Thorpe since he was a student and she was a casual teacher at East Hills Technical High. She remembers him as 'a nice polite boy who never gave you any grief if you had to take relief class'. But on this day in August 2002, he threw her life into turmoil. She was flattered, daunted, worried about the effect such a move would have on so many lives. Frost in particular would be devastated to lose the athlete for whom he had spent a lifetime preparing – he was a prickly personality, set in his ways, sensitive, protective and rightly proud of the work he had done with Thorpe.

Thorpe's decision to leave Frost for Menzies meant that their tight little unit at the Sutherland Leisure Centre, in Sydney's south, would be torn asunder. At the behest of the local council, she took over the elite senior squad and he worked with the elite junior group. Their training times did not coincide, but it remained an exceedingly awkward situation. 'In many ways it was upsetting,' Menzies says. 'I had trained with Doug as a swimmer, and he had trained me up to be able to do the job as a coach; he had given me a lot of the qualities as a coach that Ian saw in me. It was hard. But he was supportive of me – he wished me well, and he wished Ian well.'

After a year, Frost left to start afresh. He is building a new squad at Southport on the Gold Coast. Menzies says their relationship is strained but not broken. 'I still speak to him. We don't go out for coffee, but there is and always will be a respect between us.'

Frost was deeply hurt by the split but he has maintained a dignified silence in public. 'I am not happy about the way it transpired, but I don't want to talk about it,' he said recently.

'I felt completely honoured,' Menzies says of Thorpe's proposal. 'But the other side was, "God, can I do this? Have I got the courage and the skills to do this?" But [Ian] was 100 per cent behind me and had 100 per cent faith in what I could do as a coach. It was really nice because I didn't think that anyone had seen ... I had never envisaged myself being at that level now. He saw something in me that I didn't even know was there.'

Still, Menzies didn't say yes right away. She spent days thinking about it, seeking counsel from her family and her fiancé, Jason Stegbauer. They offered their complete support. Then she questioned Thorpe closely about what he wanted from her, what he thought she could do for him. And eventually she agreed. 'There have been incidents in my life where things have happened and I have thought, "You really have to screw up your courage. You have to pull this together, Trace. Get a grip."' As the news of this risky new alliance spread, Menzies was sucked into a whirlwind from which she is yet to emerge. Young, inexperienced and female, she was suddenly charged with guiding the career of the world's best swimmer. To use one of her beloved art analogies, it was like being asked to touch up the Sistine Chapel. No such thing had ever happened in swimming.

'She was a demure young lady thrown into the savage world of coaching jealousy,' says Don Talbot, Australia's most respected swimming coach. 'It's everyone's dream to have a swimmer of Ian Thorpe's calibre. There's no one who wouldn't want to be coaching Thorpie, and the egos of coaches are among the biggest in the world. And there were some coaches who felt she got in under Doug's guard.'

Thorpe denies this, insisting the switch was his doing entirely, that he had lost motivation and needed a change if he was to keep swimming. Others say Frost had not heeded the signs of Thorpe's discontent, had failed to recognise that the boy was now a man and that their relationship needed to find a new balance.

In Talbot's opinion, there is no hotter seat in world sport than the one Menzies now occupies. Thorpe is a national treasure – every poll suggests he is our best-loved sportsman – which makes Menzies the keeper of a country's dreams. If they don't return from Athens with a fistful of gold, people will be looking for someone to blame, and it won't be 'our Thorpie'.

By Talbot's reckoning, Thorpe must win both the 200- and 400-metre freestyle before Menzies earns even 'begrudging credit'. If he can win the 100 metres, 200 metres and 400 metres – no man has ever done it – and set a couple of world records in the process, people might start thinking she's a good coach. A 40-year veteran at elite level, Talbot cannot predict which way it will go.

'Ian going to Tracey surprised everyone, including me. I still don't know if he made the right decision. The biggest test she's ever going to have is these Olympic Games. At least in the 200 metres and 400 metres, if there is anything less than gold, there is going to be a lot of criticism in the field in Australia.'

*

The most remarkable thing about Menzies is that she is utterly normal. And she treats everybody around her that way. No wonder Thorpe likes her style: in the abnormal world of Ian Thorpe, Inc. – famous at 14, world champion at 15, Olympic champion, millionaire and globetrotting star at 17 – normality is the thing he craves.

Yet Menzies is an oddity all the same. In the ego-driven world of elite coaching, she is warm and humble, more interested in people than athletes, slightly lacking in self-confidence. 'That's something I have to learn to do more of, to believe in myself,' she says. Her gentle touch is seen as softness, her willingness to listen to others as indecision, her readiness to allow Thorpe an opinion as weakness. She knows other coaches see her philoso-phies as 'airy-fairy', but she is standing strong.

Tracey Menzies has been with the Olympic team for only a year, but she knows the names of every swimmer's nearest and dearest and asks after them. She treats birthdays and milestones as important and doesn't care if other coaches think she mothers her swimmers. 'They are human. They do have emotions. They are not machines; they are not robots. One of the things I have tried to do is know each of them not just as a swimmer, but as a person.'

When Michael Klim was asked about Menzies at the time of the switch, he said facetiously that his mum could coach Ian Thorpe. Now, after spending May and June working with Menzies at a high-altitude camp in Arizona, Klim is an admirer. 'She's a little bit different,' he says. 'She's really emotionally involved and she really cares about the person's feelings when she coaches, and she thinks a little bit laterally about technical things.

'It's more a friendship thing with Ian and Tracey. She's softly spoken. It's not in her character to be authoritarian, which is why I think she was misunderstood. Ian is a talented swimmer, but Tracey gives him guidance and they share a lot of ideas. Her success will be to keep him motivated and in the sport. With him having achieved so much, that's hard to do.'

Thorpe has said repeatedly over the past year, when called on to defend his coach, that Menzies is keeping him in the sport. He says he is comfortable with her and likes her approach to her work. 'I have worked with other coaches as well in a small way, but I looked at Tracey's attention to detail ... what I like is her [training] program and her eye for my stroke.'

But the impression persists that Thorpe's program is 'athlete-driven', a cardinal sin in the coaching world.

'I think that Tracey is very aware of that criticism and she has to make sure she makes the decisions,' Talbot says. 'I don't think it's an athlete-driven program, but Ian would be unhappy if he didn't get to give his opinion. If a coach has any brains, he will listen to that, but he may need to moderate it.'

Talbot believes women tend to have 'too much compassion', which makes them better people but poorer coaches because there are times when a coach has to come down hard on an athlete to achieve the right result. 'I think there's much more determination in Tracey than is apparent,' he concludes. 'She's tough-minded, she's sure of where she's going, but she's also open-minded about the program and she accepts input.'

Says Menzies: 'I have come across a lot of people who challenge my way of coaching and my philosophy – that I shouldn't allow an athlete to have so much say, that I should be more forceful in my approach to him. But he is a man. He's gone from a boy into a man. There's a lot of things that he's taught me and things that I've taught him – that's what makes our relationship good. In some ways he's my teacher and in other ways I'm his teacher. When it comes to coaching, I have the final say.'

*

It is just before 5 a.m. Dawn is two hours away as Menzies arrives at the outdoor pool at Sutherland. Steam rises where the heated water meets the chill winter air. By the time the birds wake and the sun peeks over the horizon, Thorpe will be more than halfway through his morning workout. Some might complain about the early mornings but Menzies loves them, particularly in winter. 'I see the sunrise every morning, so there couldn't be a better job than that,' she says. An early start is essential to pack in the hard work and the rest required to recover between sessions.

Thorpe and his training partners swim from 5.15 a.m. to 7.30 a.m., six mornings a week. On three days they do a gym session afterwards to build their core (torso) strength. After Saturday morning's session and on Monday afternoons, Menzies joins her swimmers in running five to seven kilometres. Thorpe swims again four afternoons a week, adding yoga on Tuesdays and Thursdays. On Friday morning there's a boxing session. The morning swims are for the hard slog – slower, aerobic work to build up endurance – while the sharper race-pace work is reserved for the afternoons.

Menzies participates in most of the dry land work, but when Thorpe swims she watches every stroke. If he is training alone, she paces every metre that he swims, a lone sentinel in track pants and a baseball cap. She gives him the thumbs-up when he gets the pace exactly right (and he frequently gets it right to a tenth of a second). She reminds him of his posture, corrects his chin position. She sets him little challenges for every set of laps, making sure he never feels that he is out there alone.

On reflection, she says the worst day of their two-year partnership was the first, when Thorpe made the announcement. 'To be put on the arena and judged and viewed – people making judgements of me as a person when they didn't even know who I was ...' By comparison, the 400 metres disaster at the Olympic trials was 'character-building – you have to be strong, even though you feel hurt for him. You have to show courage; you have to show that leadership, that we need to move on from this, we need to go forward.'

Even discounting the circumstances, they haven't had an easy run together. Until 2002, Thorpe's career soared with barely a hitch. But unexpected setbacks have come with daunting regularity over the past two years. On her first international trip with Thorpe – to the World Cup circuit in Europe in January last year – Menzies was stricken with a stomach bug. The day before his first race in Paris, she was 'hurling into a garden bed' outside the pool. By next morning, most of the Australian team had gone down with the same illness. Menzies was too sick to leave her bed as Thorpe swam his first international race under her tutelage.

A month later, in the lead-up to his first national trials under Menzies, Thorpe became seriously ill with viral encephalitis. He recovered, qualified for the world championships and went to Barcelona, where the zipper on his black suit broke ten minutes before the 400-metre final – his first championship race with Menzies. 'As I went to do up the zipper, he jerked and it busted,' Menzies recalls. 'We had to put a new suit on and I got the giggles because we had to try and get this suit on in ten minutes. He was saying "don't laugh", but it's in situations like that that you've got to laugh and you have to make him relax.' Thorpe went on to become the first man to win three consecutive world titles in one event, adding a second 200-metre title for good measure.

But neither of them could raise a smile when Thorpe was disqualified from the 400 metres at the Olympic trials in March. Craig Stevens' eventual decision to step aside put Thorpe's Olympic campaign back on track. Menzies believes they are both stronger for the experience. 'When hurdles come, it makes you a better person and you learn from those things, and you are never going to learn if you don't make mistakes or things don't happen. In 19 months, I think Ian has developed a lot as an athlete, but he's certainly developed a lot as a person.'

As has Menzies herself. She's still uncomfortable with the cameras but is learning to be more assertive. At last month's international meet in California she castigated a US college coach for suggesting that Stevens had been paid to step down from the 400 metres. 'People cast a judgement of Stevo when they don't even know who Stevo is,' she says. 'You probably wouldn't get two more close-knit guys on the Australian team.'

*

This is not the life that Menzies envisaged for herself. By 31, she expected to be married with children and have a life much like her parents, Rex and Jennifer. 'I had a perfect childhood,' she says of growing up with younger sister Natalie in Sydney's southern suburbs. 'Mum's the peacemaker of the family. Dad is fiery but he's a real teddy bear inside – always looked out for my sister and myself.'

Her life plan has been substantially modified but she did squeeze in her wedding to Stegbauer after last year's world titles, and they intend to have children after the Olympics. 'That's something I said to Ian, back before we even started. That it is something I want in my life. "I want children, I want to be married, and that's going to work, and you have to fit in with that." And he's extremely supportive of those aspects. That's what he wants for me – he wants me to be happy as well.'

That has been her solace through the storm. Happiness for Menzies is not about acclaim. As long as she is appreciated by Thorpe and by her family, friends and peers, she is satisfied. 'Just a simple thanks, that's all I need. I don't need a banner to display that I'm the coach. For me, it's not about ownership, of having that athlete, and that's my gold medal. That's not my gold medal at all. All I've done is help him achieve a goal that he has set for himself, and if that's a gold medal or a world record, that's my job to do that.

'If you are humble, and you can walk out of the sport and still be respected and people hold you in really high esteem, I think that's far better.'

The Weekend Australian Magazine, 31 July 2004

UNDER LOCK AND KEY

Jenny McAsey

Jana Pittman had been told in no uncertain terms: 'You can't do any training, no stretching, no sit-ups, no sprinting, nothing, unless I'm there supervising.'

It was an emphatic order 10 days ago from her coach Phil King. He wanted to put her on a leash, to curb her tendency to over-train following a series of minor niggles that were threatening to derail her Olympic campaign. The mishaps had occurred while Pittman, who is more energetic than a cordial-charged toddler, was exercising alone, without him as watchdog.

Then last Tuesday at Olympic Park, while King was busy away from the track for a few minutes, the world 400-metre hurdles champion couldn't resist the urge to get started. Even though she had a thigh problem, the ever-exuberant Pittman tore off, doing a 60-metre sprint down the red tartan as King came outside.

'I saw it and said to myself, "Oh my God what is she doing?"' recalled an exasperated King. 'She was kidding herself that she was in a state of fitness to do that, living in fantasy land thinking she could do a 60-metre sprint.'

Pittman pulled up in obvious distress, the damage done. 'I ran when I possibly shouldn't have,' she said sheepishly this week after scans revealed she had a strained right quadriceps muscle.

The injury means she is almost certain not to run at the Olympic trials in Sydney in two weeks. Fortunately, Athletics Australia has a flexible selection policy, and as one of the country's main gold medal hopes she will still be on the team to Athens, although possibly not until July after she proves her fitness.

It's not time to panic but the setback has prompted King to tighten the reins and contain Pittman's wild ways to get her back on course. She has moved out of the Mornington house she was sharing with two girlfriends, and into the nearby home of King and his wife, 1988 Olympic 400-metre hurdles champion, Debbie Flintoff-King, and their three children.

'I'm like their fourth child,' Pittman laughed. 'Debbie is cooking for me and I haven't missed taking a vitamin pill since I moved in. I'm stretching with Debbie and doing meditation and getting to bed early. I've never lived so well. I wanted them to help me lead the lifestyle they led in 1988.'

King said Pittman, being a busy 21-year-old who didn't have the word relaxation in her vocabulary, needed guidance. 'Because she is a genuine medal contender and because time is so short, we really have to put her in a padded corral and point her in the right direction,' he said. 'Her only crime, so to speak, is always wanting to do more. But she needs to be locked up at certain times. She is like a super-super talented filly and if you put her out to graze with the flock she will want to do everything that every horse in that flock is doing.'

The first sign of trouble for Pittman began in January, when she pulled out of the A Series meet in Brisbane at the last minute with knee soreness. The following week she withdrew from a scheduled 400-metre hurdles race in Canberra, then hurt herself two days later while training on her own in Sydney, where she was filming a pet food ad. She came back to Victoria and sat down for a serious talk with King.

'Jana came to us with a cry for assistance. She said she'd been a bit wayward, not in terms of her social life, but not doing the little things. She wanted to get herself sorted out,' King recalled. 'I said to her, "Jana, sack yourself as coach, and shut up and do what you are told for seven months." Because more is not better and harder is not smarter,' said the straight-talking King, who has a close bond with his highly charged athlete.

For several months Pittman had been privately challenging herself with exercise sessions, including a sit-up routine and boxing devised by world junior welterweight champion Kostya Tszyu.

King believes those extra sessions were the root cause of the instability in her back and pelvis that led to the recent leg injuries. 'Instead of being a 10-minute thing it had extended to a 40-minute ordeal,' he said. 'So it is part of our new agreement that with every physical activity she does, because of her exuberance, I am going to be there to control and monitor it and make sure she doesn't hurt herself.'

It's been a roller-coaster ride for Pittman and King since she moved from the Australian Institute of Sport to Victoria 18 months ago after asking him to coach her.

The likeable, good-humoured Pittman is a unique package. She has a big, strong body and a personality to match. A heady blend of high spirits, enthusiasm and boundless energy, mixed up with wildly swinging emotions.

On Tuesday, she was in tears at the track, aware she had done the wrong thing and aggravated her leg injury. By Thursday night, when the A Series meet was held at Melbourne's Olympic Park, the bubbly, social Jana was back, on a high as she greeted fellow athletes with hugs, mobile phone always to hand as she text-messaged friends and happily signed autographs.

Her positive nature and effervescence help make her the champion athlete that stormed home to win the world championship 400-metre hurdles final in Paris last August. A few weeks before the titles she was grief-stricken when she heard that Russian rival Yuliya Pechonkina had broken the world record in a time that would put her 12 metres in front of Pittman at the end of the most gruelling lap in the sport. The next day, her self-belief had returned. She knew she could still beat the Russian tank and she did.

But, like many 21-year-olds, her excitable nature can also lead her to make rash decisions. 'Change is her middle name,' says King, who reckons he has gone grey since he started coaching her. 'If you give her an hour of free time it is free for 30 seconds because out comes the mobile phone and the SMS starts and there is two hours of activity put into that one hour. Debbie is insisting Jana does meditation because she is like a car that is on top-level revs the whole time. Debbie believes when it comes to the crunch at the Olympics she is going to need a vehicle like meditation to be able to wind herself down and almost remove herself from the occasion.'

Pittman is a smart young woman who understands the need to be more patient, hard as it might be. 'I do things to the extreme and it is possibly what makes me good on the track, but it is also what I have to watch for the next couple of months,' she said.

David Culbert, chairman of AA's selection committee, is disappointed Pittman won't be competing at the trials. A huge admirer of her talent, Culbert says she has to take control of her life over the next few months.

'Jana's weakness is that she is so desperate to be successful and that desperation means she pushes the boundaries of what her body is capable of,' Culbert said. 'Her exuberance is a quality you'd like to bottle up and give to all athletes, but you've got to sip at it in measured doses.'

The Weekend Australian, 14 February 2004

STRONGER HIGHER OLDER DOPIER

*Australians participate in the Olympic Games in different
ways, as athletes, volunteers, TV viewers and flame carriers.
It was ever thus. Ian Hayward Robinson infiltrated the
Melbourne Games by accidentally impersonating an athlete
with a passing resemblance to Peter Sellers. Ron Clarke
memorably carried the flame into the MCG to light the
cauldron in 1956.*

*Athens itself was cruelly marked by drugs scandals, not
least among the athletes of the host nation. The Australian
male track cyclists maintained a high degree of drama up
to the start of the games, as Jacquelin Magnay and Peter
Lalor report. The cyclists' record six gold medals was a
triumph of the team ethos over doomsaying controversy.
However, drugs were surely never far from the minds of
Games watchers. Stephen Downes imagines a competition
between fully-drugged athletes, while Julian Savulescu,
Bennett Foddy and Robert Wainwright examine the
science behind drug detection.*

HOW I GOT MISTAKEN FOR A KOREAN OLYMPIAN BECAUSE OF MY BAD FRENCH

Ian Hayward Robinson

Weighing in at a solid 15 stone and 5 foot 10 inches, with reso-lutely Caucasian features, no one could possibly mistake me for a Korean. But at the 1956 Olympic Games that's exactly what happened, and it was all because I couldn't speak French.

My lack of facility in what are these days quaintly called 'languages other than English' is legendary. In successive years I failed Year 11 French, Year 12 French and French 1A (the easy one!) at Melbourne University until finally the Alliance Française gave me a certificate for perseverance and politely asked me to pick on someone else's language for a change. Out of some kind of perverse and masochistic whim, I picked on Chinese for six months, to little effect on my linguistic skills, before deciding to give the whole foreign language thing a miss and stick solely to the Mother Tongue. (Later, in 1968 I did manage to convince the Professorial Board at Melbourne University that *Psychology One* was a language other than English, but that's another story.)

In 1956 I was a Year 11 student at a secondary school not far from the Olympic Village in West Heidelberg, and an avid sports fan to boot. I attended a number of Olympic swimming and athletic events and I saw Hec Hogan and Betty Cuthbert compete in the sprints. I saw the famous high jump leap-off between Chilla Porter and Charlie Dumas, which was fought on into the fading light of dusk. I saw the great Vladimir Kuts blitz the field in the longer distances. I also dabbled in sport as a participant, being full-forward in the school footy team and a member of the school athletics team. In fact I had just won the combined schools hurdles race so I thought pretty highly of myself as an athlete. I suppose it was some compensation for my manifest failure as a linguist.

In those days we used to train for a few hours after school every day, and one day we decided it might be fun to go for a training run up to the Olympic Village for a change to see if we could meet any of the Olympic athletes we so admired. We were all dressed in our tracksuits and runners and I also wore a little knitted navy-blue beanie not unlike the ones the Hungarian athletes were fond of, so I suppose it shouldn't have come as the surprise that it did, but as we got closer to the village and began running past the many sightseers and fans making their way towards the gates, rather than seeing any famous Olympic athletes, we began being mistaken for them. People stood aside for us and looked at us in awe, clapped us and cheered us on. We felt strangely exhilarated.

Of course we realised that our new-found fame would be short-lived because as soon as we reached the gates of the village we would have to turn around and run back again and the illusion would be broken.

But when we reached the gates, they turned out to be nothing more than a single hand-operated boom gate controlled by a couple of young fresh-faced uniformed AIF privates. In an unpremeditated act of bravado, one of our number – if memory serves me correctly it was Rodney Allen – ran straight up to the guards and rattled off a stream of absolute gibberish. Lo and behold one of the guards immediately lifted the boom gate to let us in and, so as not to create any suspicion, we all had to keep running, through the gates and on into the bowels of the Olympic Village. It was that easy.

You have to remember that this was Melbourne in the '50s. You couldn't buy a strong drink after 6 p.m., you couldn't buy anything at all on Sunday and everything was taken at face value. If you looked like Olympic athletes out for a training run, you were Olympic athletes out for a training run and the thought didn't cross anybody's mind for a second that you could be anything else. You didn't even need a letter from your mum.

So there we were, inside the inner sanctum, the Holy of Holies, the Olympic Village. What did we do now? The answer soon became obvious. Drink, of course.

One of the interesting things about the Olympic Village in 1956 was the fact that every purveyor of so-called 'health drinks' had a roadside stall, from which pert young women dispensed these elixirs to the athletes. Free. They were all there: Ovaltine, Milo, Cadbury's Bourneville Cocoa, Bonox, the lot. None of them had aggressive reptilian names ending in '-ade' but they were all, by their own admission, very, very good for athletes, and, as voracious teenagers who had just run about three miles to get there, we were of course quite thirsty. We tried them all. More than once. We had a field day. Or should I say, a track and field day. As well as free drinks, there was the opportunity to strut your stuff on the Olympic quality training track. After staring for a while at the genuine athletes going through their paces, I had a bit of a run over the hurdles and my friend, distance runner Ian Downie, actually ran a few laps with the legendary Emil Zatopek. We were in sports fan paradise.

But like all good things it had to come to an end. We could not stay in the village all night, even sustained by Milo and Ovaltine, so we reluctantly made our way to the exit gate and, unbeknownst to us, the supreme ordeal of our quest. Getting out the gate was not a problem; a short burst of gobbledygook and the boom obediently opened and you were outside the village. It was here that the real problems began, because outside the gate were hoards of schoolgirls and fans in general hoping to get not just a glimpse of an athlete, but an autograph as well. As soon as we stepped into the real world, a dozen autograph books were thrust into our hands, followed by a dozen biros. What could we do?

If we didn't stop and sign a few books we would surely seem surly and unfriendly and bring the Olympics into disrepute. These were after all the 'friendly games'. So there was nothing for it but to put pen to paper. Of course we couldn't sign our own names, could we? After all, we were posing as foreigners.

Because of my unrequited love affair with the French language, I decided to be French. But I thought it was only fair to give the unsuspecting autograph collector at least some kind of convoluted inkling that not all was kosher with my signature; not knowing the French for 'bullshit' I did the next best thing and signed with the French word for spade – L.A. Bêche – which was as close as my limited knowledge of the language could take me. It seemed to work like a charm and there will be many autograph books of that time that bear the signature of that famous Gallic athlete. However, success breeds complacency and I was about to be brought up with a jolt.

A well-dressed gentleman approached me and asked in a foreign accent: 'What country you from?' If my French had been better I would have picked the accent, but, as we have already established …

Without thinking I replied 'France' and went on signing L.A. Bêche in some schoolgirl's autograph book.

'Ah, bon', he exclaimed, 'moi aussi!'

Sensing the danger, I tried to edge away, but he stayed with me and uttered some gibberish: 'Keskaspaw? Keskaspaw?'

'Oui,' I said, hoping he would go away. I tried to find some other books to sign. But the man had now attached himself to me like a long lost friend. He kept repeating this mantra 'Keskaspaw' over and over again and over and over again I replied dutifully 'Oui.' I was hoping he would get bored by this charade and go away. Just as I began to sense that he was getting a bit frustrated, if not downright tetchy, at my taciturnity, it dawned on me what he was saying: something like 'Qu'est que sport?' What sport?

This insight was a huge step forward in our blossoming relationship, but any ecstasy I felt was short-lived as I very soon realised I didn't know the name of one single Olympic sport in French. I was cornered and was beginning to panic.

My companion was getting more and more irritated by the apparent brush-off he was getting from a fellow countryman and I could see that things could get nasty. I dredged the deepest caverns of my memory for one French word for a sport, at first with no success. Then I had it. From way back in first year French I remembered that we had conjugated the French word *courir*, 'to run'.

'Courir,' I announced triumphantly, 'courir.'

My tormentor's face lit up with understanding. He smiled knowingly at me. I breathed a sigh of relief. Then ...

'Ah,' he said, 'you come from Korea! Pardon. Bon soir.' He disappeared into the crowd.

And I lived to sign autographs another day.

So that's the story of how during the 1956 Melbourne Olympics I was mistaken for a Korean athlete because I couldn't speak French.

In hindsight I wished I had signed my name Kow Poo and told anyone who asked that I was Chinese. At least my compatriots would have been a lot easier to spot in advance.

SEARED IN THE MEMORY

Len Johnson

According to Olympic legend, Ron Clarke almost gave his right arm for the honour of carrying the Melbourne Olympic torch on its opening ceremony lap and lighting the Olympic cauldron.

Fragments of magnesium spitting from the flame singed his arm and burnt holes in his white T-shirt. The combination of that and what Clarke insists were the overzealous ministrations of a first-aid attendant in bandaging his arm from wrist to elbow led to the conclusion that he had suffered far more serious burns than he let on.

The fact is, says Clarke, he would have given his right arm to run in the 1956 Games. An ill-timed three-month stint of national service duties deprived the then world junior record-holder for the mile from making a stronger bid to make the team as an athlete. (Clarke went on to run in two Olympic Games when he revived his career as a senior athlete.)

'It was a great honour to be selected as the final torchbearer,' says Clarke, now Mayor of the Gold Coast. 'It was very exciting, but I would have given my right arm to be there as a competitor.'

The identity of the final torchbearer is traditionally shrouded in secrecy. Clarke was whisked away from work in an official car eight days before the opening ceremony to be told he would be the one to carry the flame around the MCG before more than 100,000 spectators, until Sydney in 2000 the greatest number at an Olympics.

Not even Clarke's family were to know. He kept quiet as they made arrangements to watch the ceremony with relatives who had a television set. Only on the day 22 November 1956 was he allowed to tell them that he was taking part and that he had VIP passes for them.

Still, Clarke reckons some guessed. For one thing, like many athletes at the time of the Games, his club was allocated spots in the torch relay. Clarke, who then ran for Melbourne High School Old Boys, was down to run a leg between Echuca and Seymour a couple of days before the ceremony.

Clarke did not think he should take two bites of the cherry and deprive someone else of an opportunity. He told his club that one of his parents was ill. 'Alan Middleton, the club president, reckoned he guessed I was carrying the torch,' he says.

More of a worry, Clarke was also identified by a media outlet. He rehearsed his role at 9 a.m. on 22 November. The time had been chosen because the media would not yet be in the stadium and to maintain the secrecy he wore a balaclava.

A Melbourne broadcaster, Norman Banks, was at the stadium early to check on facilities. Banks, who broadcast football, knew Clarke and his brother, Essendon's star player Jack Clarke, well enough to see through the disguise. Clarke reckons he put it to air, but it was only hours before the ceremony and news did not travel as quickly in the pre-internet, pre-hourly bulletin days.

When he entered the arena, Clarke spotted two mates: 'There

were a couple of players from Essendon sitting right near the ʼ
entrance tunnel. One was Paul Doran, and you can see him
getting excited on all the official films.'

The teams were massed at the centre of the MCG. Then, as
now, athletes were not supposed to record any of the ceremony.
'Athletes weren't supposed to carry cameras,' Clarke says, but
only the Australians, perhaps constrained by a sense of host-
nation propriety, observed the ban. 'They all smuggled them in
under their blazers and broke ranks to run over and take pictures
as I ran.'

The cauldron was on a platform between the northern stand,
built for the 1956 Games, and the old southern stand. To get
there, Clarke had to run up an enclosed stairwell, disappearing
from view and reappearing at the top. An official was stationed
halfway with a spare torch in case Clarke's went out. 'He was
near the top of the stairs with the replacement torch,' says
Clarke. 'He went to light it, just in case, but he was shaking so
much that there were matches going all over the place.'

The other bit of planning for the worst-case scenario almost
cost Clarke more burnt skin. A technician was supposed to
turn the gas on gradually. Instead, he turned it on full. Clarke
plunged the torch towards the centre of the cauldron and
recoiled as flame instantly filled the bowl. He leapt back from
the stool on which he was standing, fortunately away from the
edge of the drop into Yarra Park.

*

Clarke broke many world records in his running career and won
an Olympic bronze medal. He acknowledges that his greatest
slice of Olympic history is lighting the Melbourne flame, and
reckons people would not remember the name of the final torchbearer had he not gone on to later success.

'I'd be telling everyone about it,' he says. 'No one would have
remembered. It was only that I came back into the sport that
caused me to be held in some awe. Otherwise the name of the
man who lit the flame would have been a great Australian trivia
question.'

For the 1956 Melbourne Olympics, equestrian events were held in Stockholm because of quarantine problems. Accordingly, the flame also visited Sweden that year.

The Age, 3 June 2004

THE NEED FOR SPEED

Jacquelin Magnay

Cyclists are supposed to be super-human. They climb torturous mountains at a frenetic pace, day after day, month after month, or whip around the track at 70 km/h. There is the Giro d'Italia, the Tour de France, the Tour of Germany. The very reason for their lauded heroism is their hard-to-attain physical state. They are the gods of Europe and Japan.

In the past week there has been a collision of worlds: the cycling world's extreme measures and an unsuspecting public and its shock. There has long been a culture within road and track cycling to do nearly anything that will produce a better performance and help them conquer Mont Ventoux, Alp d'Huez or even Mt Hotham or clock a super-slick time on the Dunc Gray velodrome.

Cyclists are determined control freaks. They strictly monitor their diet, they undergo intense training, sometimes for eight hours a day, they have intravenous fluid replacement, they pop and inject supplements, head for the Alps for altitude training and even shave their legs to make massages easier.

But Senator John Faulkner's claims that five elite cyclists used room 121 at the Australian Institute of Sport's Del Monte headquarters in Adelaide as a 'shooting gallery' set alarm bells ringing. Whether, and if so, just how a third of the institute's team were able to inject unknown substances into their veins and muscles for months on end without detection will be part of the urgent inquiry headed by the retired judge Robert Anderson, QC.

*

'Soon after moving to the AIS Del Monte I discovered a culture among athletes to inject vitamins and supplements as part of a regime of maintaining their general health in the course of extremely rigorous training,' the banned 19-year-old cyclist Mark French said this week. He said the use of supplements was an 'open secret'. 'It is visible to those involved but hidden away from those who did not take part,' he said.

A family friend told the *Herald* that French was so terrified of needles, his father, David, had to drag him screaming to the dentist. Mark's older brother, Luke, had an illness which required intravenous drips and regular injections, which had left a mental scar on the young boy.

For decades cycling has been at the forefront of getting an edge, whether it be by legal means or illegal use of drugs, for the sport is surrounded by big money, the lure of superstardom and a professional climate. Illegal drug use among the professional trade teams is rife, with undetectable growth hormones, insulin and EPO (erythropoietin) most popular.

Cyclists are quickly introduced to the ideas of super-supplementation and massive vitamins as a legal way of helping recover from the rigours and demands of training. Whether they then progress to the illegal substances appears to depend on which team they become linked with. But even if the institute tries to quarantine itself from such murky practices, the cyclists are exposed to European ways from an early age. For several years the Australian junior road team (under-23) was based in Italy.

The trade teams in Europe all have medical personnel permanently attached to the team. A coach in another sport said nearly all of the distribution lines of drugs into international track and field and swimming came from cycling. 'Those guys [cyclists] were the guinea pigs because if it didn't kill them and it appeared to work, everybody else was trying to get some of the stuff,' he said.

As soon as new drugs were at the medical research stage, they nearly always found their way into the hands of cyclists, willing to try anything that is undetectable to gain a performance edge. In 1998 the red blood cell drug interleukin-3 was just being researched, yet sources claimed it was already being abused on the professional cycling circuit.

Back then, the Australian cycling head coach, Martin Barras, rated the success of drug testing worldwide at five or six out of 10, but that was 'compared to a zero a few years ago'.

And the institute team manager, Michael Flynn, said on the eve of the Commonwealth Games then: 'The Australians are clean – if one of ours are positive you can send me home butt naked. But I would be amazed if everyone felt that [international] cycling was relatively clean; it is naive to think that all sports here are clean.'

But French claims that he was so seduced by his role models at the institute, he overcame this terror in the pursuit of faster times, even though he said he nearly fainted when he was first injected with vitamin B by another cyclist. French, who was a four-time junior world champion and one of Australia's most exciting talents, has admitted to injecting carnitine (which aids in energy production), vitamin B and C and Testicomp, which he claims he had been told by other cyclists, and he believed, was a legal homeopathic remedy.

Within cycling circles Testicomp is touted as a substance to stimulate the production of testosterone – it was one of the 37 different substances found in the boot of the car owned by the disgraced and banned Lithuanian cyclist Raimondas Rumsas just after he finished third in the Tour de France in 2002. French's admission that he used Testicomp was one of the doping breaches that resulted in his two-year ban from the sport and a life ban from Olympic competition.

But it is the existence of 13 empty vials of equine growth hormone found in the sharps container in the bottom of French's wardrobe by a cleaner that is at the heart of the drugs scandal.

Somebody was using a banned poison designed for a horse in the strong belief that it helped performance. French claims anybody could have had access, in addition to the other cyclists he says used the room to inject vitamins – none of whom he has accused of using anything illegal.

The Adelaide manufacturer of the equine growth hormone, Bresagen, says one vial is enough for a 500 kilogram horse. It is a drug to promote growth. Institute staff say they are devastated at the French evidence.

Sources claim that the names French provided to the Court of Arbitration for Sport include several athletes very unlikely to take such a risk, and Del Monte cyclists are furious that 'a convicted drug-taker's evidence' is being used to slur their reputations. The Australian Olympic Committee is pressing the cyclists to reveal more to the Anderson inquiry, given that their Olympic selection is on the line.

There are clear processes at the institute for cyclists, particularly emerging ones like French, to obtain permission for injecting vitamins. Some cyclists have previously obtained official approval for injection of legal substances. The fallout from the French case resulted in two other cyclists being severely reprimanded by the institute for not notifying medical authorities that they were injecting vitamins.

French's evidence reveals his sheer trust of his peers. 'I accepted without question what I was told about these substances, that they were harmless and legal. I looked up to these other cyclists ... as my role models; I had no reason to feel that I was being misled in any way ... I wanted to learn from them.'

What does it take to be like them? These are elite athletes who train for six to eight hours a day at an intensity that sees superfit athletes throw up. It is not unusual for cyclists around the world to wolf down substances like colostrum and creatine and lie in bed at night enveloped by an 'oxygen tent', which manipulates the oxygen levels of the air to encourage the body to produce more red blood cells.

The benefits can be financial. One of the reasons for the delay in the arbitration court's hearing in the French case, apart from the Australian Sports Commission wanting it to be heard after the Athens Olympics, was the unavailability of French. He spent 10 weeks in Japan in the lucrative kierin series, where cyclists are treated like greyhounds, shut away from the big-punting Japanese before competing at night. In each of five kierin races French was up against seven Japanese and he won the series overall. Sources claim he earned about $100,000 in that short time.

*

Defining the line between acceptable ethical practices and illegal cheating is not so easy. Six years ago, the institute's cycling team was part of a university study to determine the effectiveness of colostrum, but one of the high-profile cyclists of the time, Lucy Tyler Sharman, refused to take part. Since then, research has shown that colostrum does produce elevated levels of a banned hormone, insulin growth factor-1, but it has not yet been banned. Now even one of the youngest members of the Australian Olympic team for Athens, swimmer Jessicah Schipper, regularly takes it, her coach believing it helps ward off colds and flu.

Nor is it easy for the athletes to comprehend the new world order in anti-doping. No longer is it sufficient for the drug testers to take urine samples, have them analysed and the laboratory uncover any murky goings-on. Nowadays the biggest drugs scandals around the world centre on circumstantial evidence and a new cooperation between law enforcers and sports bodies: the 1998 French border check of Festina manager Willy Voet uncovered a stash of growth hormone and EPO, both undetectable drugs at the time, and testosterone which revealed how dramatic the systemised drug-taking of the elite road cyclists was on major tours.

Earlier this month, on the eve of attempting his sixth Tour de France victory, Lance Armstrong was implicated as a drug-taker in a book, *L.A. Confidential*, written by journalists David Walsh and Pierre Ballester. A former US Postal team official, Emma

O'Reilly, claimed in the book that Armstrong used EPO; that he asked her to dispose of syringes at the 1998 Tour of Holland; and that she was sent to Spain to pick up drugs for him during his 1999 Pyrenees training camp. A furious Armstrong is suing the authors.

Lately there has been the Balco drugs controversy in the US, where evidence seized during a federal government raid has been turned over to the country's anti-doping agency. The computer files and calendar notations have resulted in drug charges laid against the world's fastest man, the 100-metre world record holder Tim Montgomery, as well as three others. They face a lifetime ban.

Evidence from that raid shows that being a sports cheat doesn't come cheaply – a five-month regime of a designer steroid THG, EPO, testosterone and growth hormone, with medical supervision and regular blood and urine screening, cost more than US$20,000 (A$28,600).

At the moment the institute cyclists are preparing to move to Rockhampton for warm weather training. In Adelaide they have been assailed with comments from car drivers and questioned by family and friends. They are eager to escape the intense scrutiny to prepare for the Olympic Games.

'We are committed to competing drug-free and we are extremely disappointed and angry with ill-informed recent comments and innuendo, which have cast a slur on our sport and us as individuals,' seven of the cyclists said in a statement this week.

More than Pedal Power in Play

'There is political warfare above our heads; we are the football being kicked around,' says a person closely connected to the Mark French drug allegations.

What is obvious is that the cyclists at the heart of the matter – those that have to prove their innocence before the Australian Olympic Committee president, John Coates, will ratify their selection for the Athens Olympics – feel they are being harshly treated. They say they are being singled out, not for any behaviour that has been looked at by two investigators already, but for political point-scoring.

And here is why. Coates is president of the AOC, but is also a board member of the Court of Arbitration for Sport and an International Olympic Committee member. He has long held strong anti-doping views and before the Sydney Olympics encouraged the toughening of the Customs Act to prohibit the trading of sports drugs. But Coates is at odds with Peter Bartels, chairman of the Australian Sports Commission, and Mark Peters, its chief executive. The ASC oversees and funds the Australian Institute of Sport.

Central to their power dispute is the $100 million the AOC accumulated as part of Sydney hosting the 2000 Olympics and its reluctance to use the money for anything other than sending away future Olympic teams. But there is debate about who should get credit for Australia's Olympic successes.

They have been taking pot shots at each other for quite a while – last year it was over childhood obesity and the Athens medal predictions. Now it is centred on how Senator John Faulkner got hold of a Court of Arbitration for Sport judgement into the French case.

Coates is linked to Faulkner through Labor Party associations, while Bartels is very much tied to the Liberal Party.

Coates says he just wants to protect the reputation of the Australian Olympic team, of which only fit and proper people should be members. Peters says there has been reckless use of information which appears to be driven by rumour and selective quotation out of context.

Coates's threat could lead to very ugly scenes. Observers think we are not even at half-time in this clash.

The Sydney Morning Herald, 26 June 2004

MODERN-DAY FOLK HERO KEEPS HIS COOL AMID THE MAELSTROM

Peter Lalor

For a time the Yeti lived in a cave, although some said it was a bear or a bandit in there. Whatever it was, it was big, it was hairy and it could be horrible.

Sean Eadie got the Yeti nickname at the track cycling world championships in Copenhagen two years ago. He got the cave as reward for being mad enough to throw in his modestly paid job as a kindergarten teacher at Villawood in Sydney. It was part of the reward package for being an Olympian and a world champion: no job, no money, nowhere to live but out the back of Mum and Dad's in the caravan.

The thousands of fans chanting 'Eadie ... Eadie ... Eadie' as the Australian powered his 98-kilogram frame around the velodrome in Denmark in 2002 had no idea about his domestic arrangements, but they loved the 33-year-old hairy giant (in those days the outlaw beard was even more luxuriant than today's modest chin mullet).

Coming into the final race against 20-year-old South Australian Jobie Dajka, Eadie had it all on the line and maybe the crowd sensed it. The year before he'd finished 10th in the sprint event and figured maybe it was time to give up. In November he was about to pack his bags and leave the Australian team because he felt he didn't fit in under coach Charlie Walsh. Martin Barras took over the job just as Eadie reached the end of his tether – it gave him the chance he needed to hang in and he grabbed it with both paws. 'Otherwise I might have to retire and get a real job,' Eadie said at the time.

He hadn't had a beer for six months going into the world titles in Copenhagen. He was totally committed. He not only gave up the grog, he gave up shaving and sex, too. 'I just wanted to get the beard on the podium,' he told *The Weekend Australian* this week. 'Whatever it took, it was about getting the beard up there.'

Dajka won the first of the three heats in a photo finish, was beaten in the second and led Eadie all the way to the home turn in the last 'heavy metal' encounter. The pair crashed, crunched and jostled to the line. Each riding at 70 km/h.

It was another photo finish. The crowd gave them a standing ovation as they awaited the decision and got even louder when they heard their favourite – the Yeti – was the new world champion.

The past couple of months have been the hardest, dirtiest and most controversial of Sean Eadie's life. Derailed by injury, he stared down mortality in a do-or-die ride-off against Ben Kersten for a place in the Olympic team and made it by a fraction of a second. Then came the Mark French scandal at the Adelaide AIS, closely followed by news he had been sent some strange nutritional supplements five years ago.

He was thrown off the team before any evidence was heard and denounced widely as a drug cheat. There was so much mud thrown you would expect Eadie to come out the other end of it the most unpopular man with a beard this side of Osama.

But no.

Everywhere you go you hear people say 'It's hard not to like Sean Eadie.' Maybe it's the way he's looked the world in the eye, faced the cameras and the courts square on and said 'this is just another hiccup, another hurdle … it's something else we'll work through, then we'll go back and get down to the business which I do, riding my bike.' When it appeared natural justice was thrown out the window and he was thrown from the team, he didn't bleat, didn't miss a beat. Just got on with it and got his name cleared. Eventually.

One thing's for sure, if Hank had been around, things might have been a bit different. Hank? He's the bloke you might have seen simmering on a plastic seat before the event in Copenhagen. He was at the Dunc Gray Velodrome in Bankstown last month when Eadie had to beat 18 seconds to make the Olympic team.

Hank was the evil man with a beard, listening to what Eadie calls 'murder, death, kill music' on the iPod. Hank usually hasn't had sex or beer for months and would eat his own if that's what it takes. Hank is angry and hungry.

He comes in handy, even if he frightens his manager. 'I stay well clear of Sean before a trial,' Kerry Ruffles said this week. 'If he asks a question I answer it, if he wants to talk I talk, but generally I keep well out of his way. It's the safest policy.'

Eadie says that scary bloke is not him, that's Hank. 'I let Hank out at the time trials, he's my alter ego, he comes out when I need him,' Eadie said with a laugh. 'I can turn him on at will, but sometimes I have trouble turning him off. Hank's been under lock and key lately; he could have been totally out of control in those situations.'

Eadie was born in April 1969 and is one of seven children raised by Barry and Barbara Eadie. They're a rolling, generous family whose door has always been open to others less fortunate.

They're close, too. Barry, Barbara and Sean's younger brother Michael were in Copenhagen for his win and will be joined by his teenage sister Cherie in Athens if they can find accommodation.

Eadie took up cycling in the early 1980s when he and a brother went to the local track for a bit of fun. 'I was absolutely hopeless, but I fell totally in love with it,' Eadie said.

It has been a long, slow uphill grind since. Eadie started to hit his stride in the 1990s. Every year he got a little bit better and by 1995 he had developed enough to win the Oceania sprint titles and come second in the Australian titles, but these were the days of Gary Neiwand and Darren Hill and there was not enough room at the top for everybody. So Eadie pushed himself harder and harder.

Friend, former Australian junior champion and elite coach Peter Bundy met Eadie in 1982 and says he has always been extraordinarily committed. 'He's really done it the hard way, but he's always had that determination to get through,' Bundy said. 'I have never known a rider to train as hard as Sean does and I've seen a lot of riders. He's sacrificed everything for his sport and there's no one who works as hard.'

Early in 1996, Eadie came off the bike in South America and ended up at home getting a bone grafted from his hip and a pin put in the collarbone. Bundy, who runs Peter Bundy Cycles in Sydney's Riverwood, remembers Eadie checking out of the hospital and, despite being warned by the doctors, going straight to the gym. 'He was straight back into the squats at full weight,' Bundy said. 'He still had the bandages on and there was blood coming through them.'

Cycling News's Gerard Knapp reckons there's a charisma about Sean Eadie that is enough to fill any sized velodrome and defy any crisis. 'He's very focused at the big events, but at the country carnivals he is king of the kids, they can't get enough of him,' Knapp said. 'He's always been a really good ambassador for the sport and you can see the way he's handled this pressure that he is a man of great character.'

Knapp has seen a shaved Eadie ride in Tasmania with his face painted in ridiculous colours. At a washed-out carnival in the country the crowd had stayed until it was dark but the meeting was eventually cancelled. When it did stop raining, Eadie got the kids to tape fireworks and sparklers to his bike and rode exhibition laps with the things fizzing and exploding away on the frame.

It could well have been a metaphor for the big fellow's lead-up to Athens. As of last night, Eadie was nominated by Cycling Australia to ride at the Olympics but was waiting on an appeal by Kersten.

The Weekend Australian, 24 July 2004

LET THE FULLY-DRUGGED GAMES BEGIN!

Stephen Downes

I've had a gutful of drugs in sport. Apart from a Friday beer – or several – as I chat up a barmaid, I try to keep them separate. It's not that they're hand-in-hand all the time that irks me. It's the hypocrisy of just about every commentator, sports official and competitor when he or she opines on the most effective and fundamental of human symbiotic relationships. The match of pharmaceuticals with running, jumping, peddling bikes and pumping iron is made in heaven. Nothing could be better.

What I want is *more* drugs in sport! Many more! And more of them in quantity. Not less. Or, heaven forbid, none at all. I clamour for wholesale use of drugs in sport. I want to see a cocaine-fuelled 100 metres. (On a track or in a pool.) I'd like to watch a heroin high jump and a steroid steeplechase. Unimpeded use is what I want to witness. Free use! I want to see chemical cocktails enhancing sports performances like never before. We're mugs if we don't adopt such a policy.

Using drugs freely in sport – openly – has many benefits. First, it would at last kill stone dead the hypocritical rantings of those who declare their opposition to the idea. Drug-taking in sport is already rife. Legitimising it would have an important moral consequence that I'll come to later.

Secondly, in the drugged championships I envisage, enhancement would be controlled under expert supervision. Even in what I call the transcendental events, in which teams and athletes would have open slather and would not have to declare the drugs they were using or their quantities, doctors and pharmaceutical specialists would be in control.

Wouldn't the result be great for TV! Imagine the audience a network would attract if there was a good chance a 10-metre long jump or a tonne-and-a-half clean-and-jerk would be coming up after the break. And the enormous wealth the television industry would extract from fully-drugged sport would inevitably be churned back – at least in part – into sport itself, the promotion of physical activity, which would benefit the community, and, of course, the development of sport's natural partner, drugs.

Here's how it would work. Fully-drugged sport would be sponsored by the drug companies themselves. They already siphon billions of dollars into the pockets of doctors and lobbyists, into political chicanery and bureaucratic manipulation. I'm sure, bearing in mind the terrific exposure they would have worldwide, that they would leap at the chance to back individual athletes and even whole national teams. GlaxoSmithKline gains gold for Guatamala! Beiersdorf backs Bulgaria!

And for the drug companies it would be a boon. Sanctioning pharmaceuticals in sport, beginning with the Olympics, would be bound to mean more effective testing of new potions, pills and products. Why? Because athletes would assay them under extreme new conditions. I would not go so far as to say that more money would, by necessity, be spent on drug research, although that might very well be the case. But I am saying that a new way of widespread drug-testing under a revolutionary set of conditions presently denied drug companies would be immediately available. With any sort of luck at all, this would be of enormous benefit to the pharmaceutical industry as a whole and eventually, therefore, world health. Discoveries would be made. Treatments and perhaps cures would follow. And not just human health would be graced. Enough athletes are taking drugs made for lesser animals such as horses and greyhounds that all God's chillen – even those with cloven hooves and eight legs – would finally benefit.

What would this mean, too, to the present enormous illicit trade in performance-enhancing drugs? Well, it would stop it overnight. Whack criminals and sharks with an invisible bullet. Immediately.

And what of records. Wouldn't they tumble! Can man run 100 metres in six seconds? Sure he can if he's doped with 10 milligrams of this two weeks before his final and 20 milligrams of that five minutes before and 5 milligrams of this other stuff as he takes his blocks. Can't you just see the drug companies working over their boiling cauldrons? Coming up with a batch of perfect recipes and regimes specific to an event and even to an athlete. Schedules would vary between even, say, freestyle and butterfly swimmers.

And the athletes themselves? Well, because sport would be awash with even more money than the tides of it that flood in now, sport's financial rewards would be beyond belief. Talk about money! And sponsorships! Free track pants, swim goggles and sets of runners would be superseded entirely. Athletes could for the first time afford to buy their own gear, which would add greatly to their self-esteem.

They would have to be adults, of course. And their pharma sponsors would no doubt want them to sign liability waivers in the event of serious injury or death. But it would not be in the interests of drug companies to kill off their athletes. On the contrary, they would take the utmost care to dose their charges with only substances and amounts that would return performances, not fatal accidents.

It's true that there might still be drug cheats, the sort who would secretly dope beyond levels specified for an event, say. Freelancers, who go it alone outside the factory teams. But under controlled use and backed by drug companies with vested interests in precise dosing to optimise performance and not kill or maim, I imagine the fly-by-needles might be few. Just as they have in motor sport and yachting, the amateurs would fall away, the big money and technology take over. And there would be, of course, open-slather events in which athletes and their backers would be allowed carte blanche doping for those willing to take the greatest risks. (I envisage many events in which only specified amounts of specified drugs would be allowed.)

Legitimising drugs in sport would also mean the enormous amount of time and millions of dollars wasted in randomly testing for drugs would be saved. Controls would be up to the drug companies themselves, which would eliminate public expenditure altogether. Run through a kind of all-party test panel, it would be in the interests of the pharmas to play ball with each other, to see that the game is played.

Are you concerned for the athletes? Don't be. On the surface, open-slather drugs in sport appears to be disastrous for them. I don't think so. Don't forget no one would be forced to participate in drugged sports. Athletes would participate of their own free will. And danger? Let's not forget one of the most dangerous sports is that genteel business of sitting on a fractious nag that doesn't want to jump high fences or descend vertical cliff-faces. And who stops the Moto GP riders from straddling their machines on the grid? Athletes drugged under stringent medical and pharmaceutical supervision, in my view, could expect to be among the 'safest' of participants in physical activity. Supported by governments and not even a sport, taking the drug nicotine has killed millions. How does the occasional woozy faint or tummy upset of a runner or swimmer compare with that?

But it's all unlikely to happen, we've got to admit. It disappoints me even that I have to write much of this piece tongue-in-cheek, as if sport is too dear to our hearts to be subjected to serious moral scrutiny. Because a rigorous think through the ethics of the present situation, of widespread illicit drug-taking in sport, reveals several moral discrepancies.

The first is the denial by sports personnel – athletes, trainers and officials – that it takes place when they know very well that it's rife. To take a moral stance and admit the use of performance-enhancing substances would be an adequate first step and give a global fill-up to ethical quotients.

The second and most obvious moral problem is the advertisements for cheating promoted by this denial. Athletes of world acclaim, held in esteem and awe by millions of lesser mortals, loved by many, it appears, find it natural to be dishonest so long as they don't get caught out. Ditto their backers. What does that say to the rest of us in our ordinary lives? We should cheat, too, because our greatest heroes do it. It's OK.

Thirdly, the whole logical basis on which the self-righteous no-drugs-in-sport rhetoric is based is wrong. We don't want drugs in sport, say the moralising, because they give unfair advantages to those who take them. How long have these people been around? Where have they lived? The *whole of life* is unfair. What's fair about Ian Thorpe's magnificent triangulated body, which didn't come about by training, huge hands and feet, which allow him to apply more force to the water, compared with mine? What's fair about the central African distance runners who are naturally built like sticks and are nurtured in rarefied air so that when they descend to an Olympics at sea level they're ahead of the pack and over the horizon? What's fair about sprinters and weightlifters with more quick-fire muscle strands than the rest of us? Nothing. It's called life. The best athletes have always had unfair advantages over their opponents, whether physical or mental. So to carp about drugs giving unfair advantages is logical nonsense.

Finally, what would controlled drugs in sport do for drug-free athletes? Would they not be lauded to the heavens? Would they not be ennobled more than ever? What a wonderful moral consequence that would be.

GOOD SPORT, BAD SPORT

Julian Savulescu and Bennett Foddy

Scandals are already rocking the Olympics and the starting gun hasn't even fired. Long gone is the romantic ideal of Pheidippides running barefoot from the village of Marathon, demonstrating a test of brute human endurance, courage and spirit. The reality is that many athletes now compete on a drug cocktail. Performance-enhancing drugs, however, have been around a long time. Early Olympians used extracts of mushrooms and plant seed. In the modern era, chemistry has helped the cheats. It barely raises an eyebrow now when some famous athlete fails a dope test.

Attempts to eliminate drugs from sport have patently failed. And will fail. The drive to perfect performance is irresistible. In the late 1990s, *Sports Illustrated* reported a survey by Dr Robert Goldman of past and aspiring Olympians. Goldman asked athletes if they would take an imaginary banned drug if it was guaranteed that they would not be caught and that they could win. The results were compelling – 195 said they would take it and only three said they would not.

In 1997, Dutch physician Michel Karsten, who claims to have prescribed anabolic steroids to hundreds of world-class athletes, told *Sports Illustrated* that very few athletes can win gold medals without taking drugs. 'If you are especially gifted, you may win once, but from my experience you can't continue to win without drugs. The field is just too filled with drug users.'

Drugs like Erythropoietin (EPO) and growth hormones occur naturally in the body. As technology advances, drugs have become harder to detect because they mimic natural processes. In a few years, many will be undetectable. The goal of 'cleaning' up sport is hopeless. And further down the track the spectre of genetic enhancement looms dark and large.

So is cheating here to stay? Drugs are against the rules, but we can redefine the rules of sport. If we made drugs legal and freely available, there would be no cheating. But would that be against the 'spirit of sport', as Raelene Boyle has said? The Athenian vision of sport was to find the strongest, fastest or most skilled man.

Drugs that improve our natural potential are against the spirit of this model of sport. But this does not need to be the only model. We can choose what kind of competitor to be, not just through training, but through biological manipulation – that is, by taking drugs. Far from being against the spirit of sport, biological manipulation embodies the human spirit – the capacity to change ourselves on the basis of reason and judgement. When we exercise our reason, we do what only humans have the ability to do.

Taking drugs would make sport less of a genetic lottery.

Winners would be those with a combination of the genetic potential, training, psychology and judgement with performance enhanced by drugs – the result of creativity and choice.

Unfair?

Carl Lewis once said, 'To be the best, work the hardest.' Wouldn't it be wonderful if the fairytale were true? Sadly, it is not. Sport discriminates against the genetically unfit. Genetic tests can already identify those with the greatest potential. If you have one version of the ACE gene, you will have endurance. Another gene will predispose you to win at short events. Black Africans, for example, generally fare better at short-distance events because of biologically advantageous muscle type and bone structure.

Sport is the province of the genetic elite, or freak. The starkest example is the Finnish skier Eoro Maentyranta. In 1964, he won two gold medals. Subsequently, it was found he had a genetic mutation that meant that he 'naturally' had 40 to 50 per cent more red blood cells than the average competitor. Was it fair that chance gave him a significant advantage?

The ability to perform well in sporting events is determined by the ability to deliver oxygen to muscles. The more red blood cells you have, the more oxygen you can carry. EPO is a natural hormone that stimulates red blood cell production, raising the haematocrit (HCT) – the percentage of the blood comprised by red blood cells.

EPO is produced in response to anaemia, haemorrhage, pregnancy or living at high altitude. At sea level, the average person has an HCT of 40 to 50 per cent. HCT naturally varies – 5 per cent of people have a HCT above 50 per cent.

Raising the HCT too high can cause health problems. Your risk of harm rapidly rises as HCT gets above 50 per cent, especially if you also have high blood pressure.

In the late '80s, several Dutch cyclists died because too much EPO made their blood too thick. When your HCT is over 70 per cent, you are at high risk of stroke, heart and lung failure.

Use of EPO is endemic in cycling and many other sports. In 1998, the Festina team was expelled from the Tour de

France after trainer Willy Voet was caught with 400 vials of performance-enhancing drugs. The following year, the World Anti-Doping Agency (WADA) was established as a result of the scandal. However, EPO is extremely hard to detect and its use has continued.

Members of the Chinese swim team, which won four swimming gold medals at the 1992 Barcelona Olympics and then took 12 of the 16 women's titles at the 1994 world championships, have used EPO (along with testosterone, anabolic steroids and growth hormone).

In addition to trying to detect EPO directly, the International Cycling Union requires athletes to have a HCT no higher than 50 per cent. But 5 per cent of people have a natural HCT greater than 50 per cent. Athletes with a naturally elevated level of HCT cannot race unless doctors can prove their HCT is natural.

Charles Wegelius was a British rider who was banned and then cleared in 2003. He had had his spleen removed in 1998 following an accident – since the spleen removes red blood cells, this increased his HCT.

There are other legal ways to increase the number of red blood cells. Altitude training can push the HCT to dangerous, even fatal, levels. More recently, hypoxic air machines simulate altitude training. The body responds by releasing natural EPO and growing more blood cells, so that the body may absorb more oxygen with every breath. According to Tim Seaman, a US athlete, the hypoxic air tent has 'given my blood the legal "boost" that it needs to be competitive at the world level'.

There is no difference between elevating your blood count by altitude training, by using a hypoxic air machine or by taking EPO. But the latter is illegal. Some competitors have high HCTs and an advantage by luck. Some can afford hypoxic air machines. Is this fair? Nature is not fair.

Ian Thorpe has size 17 feet which give him an advantage that no other swimmer can get, no matter how much they exercise. Some gymnasts are more flexible, and some basketball players are seven feet tall. By allowing everyone to take performance-enhancing drugs, we level the playing field. We remove the effects of genetic inequality. Far from being unfair, allowing performance enhancement promotes equality.

Should there be any limits to drugs in sport? Yes, the one limit is safety. We do not want an Olympics in which people die before, during or after competition. Rather than testing for drugs, we should focus more on health and fitness to compete. Forget testing for EPO; test for HCT. We need to set a safe level of HCT. Currently that is 50 per cent. Anyone above that level, whether through the use of drugs, training or natural mutation, should be prevented from participating on safety grounds.

If someone naturally has a HCT of 60 per cent and is allowed to compete, then that risk is reasonable and everyone should be allowed to increase HCT to 60 per cent. What matters is what is a safe level of EPO (or other hormones) – not whether that is achieved naturally or artificially.

We need to take safety more seriously. In Goldman's survey, athletes were also asked whether they would take a banned drug if it was guaranteed that they would not be caught and that they would win every competition they entered for the next five years, but then die from the side effects of the substance. More than 50 per cent of the athletes said yes.

We should permit drugs that are safe, and continue to ban and monitor drugs that are unsafe. This would be fairer in another way: provided a drug is safe, it is unfair to the honest athletes that they have to miss out on an advantage that the cheaters enjoy. Taking EPO up to the safe level, say 50 per cent, is not a problem. This allows athletes to correct for natural inequality. However, we should focus on detecting drugs like anabolic steroids because they are harmful – not because they enhance performance. Far from harming athletes, paradoxically such a proposal may protect our athletes. There would be more rigorous and regular evaluation of athletes' health and fitness to perform. Moreover, the current incentive is to develop undetectable drugs, with little concern for safety. If safe performance-enhancement drugs were permitted, there would be greater pressure to develop safe drugs.

We have two choices: to vainly try to turn the clock back, or to rethink who we are and what sport is, and to make a new twenty-first-century Olympics. Not a super-Olympics but a more human Olympics. Our crusade against drugs in sport has failed. Rather than fearing drugs in sport, we should embrace them. Performance enhancement is not against the spirit of sport; it is the spirit of sport. To choose to be better is to be human.

The Age, 3 August 2004

BAD CHEMISTRY

Robert Wainwright

There is a dark secret locked away in the records of the Australian Government Analytical Laboratories in Pymble. The identity of seven likely Olympic drug cheats, outed by science but protected by legal opinion and a cloud of bureaucratic doubt, remains hidden four years after the most successful Games in history.

Their names are concealed by code, as are the sports in which they competed. Their nationality and gender will never be known, nor if they were medallists or merely competitors in this most elite of athletic endeavours.

It is equally unlikely they will ever face justice, despite the fact that the evidence could be unlocked simply by comparing records kept by the Australian Sports Drug Testing Laboratory, which holds the coded results, with the Lausanne offices of the International Olympic Committee (IOC), which can match the codes with the name of an athlete.

As the controversy over the cycling and weightlifting teams for Athens threatens to envelop the entire Olympic team, a scientist at the forefront of anti-doping tests in the lead-up to the 2000 Olympics has revealed the untold drug story of the Sydney Games.

Robin Parisotto was the lead scientist from the Australian Institute of Sport (AIS), which developed a blood test used during the Games to identify athletes taking Erythropoeitin (EPO), a powerful performance-enhancing drug that stimulates the red blood cells that deliver oxygen to muscles.

The test was hailed as a major breakthrough in the fight against doping but it was approved only in part. The IOC agreed to an 'on' test, which would identify an athlete currently using EPO, but was worried about the legal ramifications of an 'off' test, which would identify an athlete who had been using EPO in the weeks leading up to the event.

During the two weeks of competition in September 2000, 2758 athletes (roughly a quarter of competitors, including all gold medallists) gave blood and urine samples for drug tests such as steroid use. Of these, 310 were drawn at random to test for EPO. None returned evidence of drug use during the Games.

But the 'off' test, done as an unofficial data collection exercise, returned alarming results. There was clear evidence that seven of the 310 athletes had been using EPO in the lead-up to the Games. Parisotto and his colleagues were stunned, realising that it was possible that 60 or more Olympic athletes might have been caught if all 2758 samples were tested.

'It was the sort of result that would have brought the Olympics to its knees,' Parisotto says. 'Imagine if the off test had been approved and the results published.'

Instead, the scientists were told the results would be forwarded to the individual sporting federations of the exposed athletes. It would be left to the federations to take action. To this day, he doesn't know if they were sent let alone acted upon.

'We didn't do the tests and we were never told their identity,' he says. 'We presumed the individual sporting federations would take their own action, but if the results were ever passed on then nothing was done, at least publicly.'

Parisotto says the incident is indicative of attitudes to drug testing. Though much has been achieved, the issue remains a

Pandora's box that bureaucrats would much rather avoid than confront.

Parisotto has a particular axe to grind with officialdom. He is still seething about a decision made by the federal government just six months after the Games to shut the research team operating out of the AIS.

Overnight the team, which had been lauded for its work in establishing the EPO test, was disbanded because of a decree that it was 'inappropriate' to have a body involved in drug research and the preparation of elite athletes. The decision was roundly criticised by several leading sports administrators, including Jim Ferguson, the former chief executive of the Australian Sports Commission, and John Boultbee, a former director of the AIS. The outspoken president of the World Anti-Doping Agency (WADA), Dick Pound, also questioned the move.

Five of the scientists, including Parisotto, left the AIS within months. A group, including Parisotto's colleague, Mike Ashenden, have since set up their own private research facility – Science and Industry Against Blood Doping – which has successfully developed three new blood tests under WADA's financial patronage.

Ashenden argues that in hindsight the IOC's decision not to sanction the 'off' model was correct, although the seven athletes were probably guilty. The test has since been refined and is now recognised by the International Cycling Union, which has banned three riders for returning positive results. Ashenden says the 'off' model should be adopted across all sports.

'Of course Australia could improve the way it tackles the problem of drugs in sport, but then so can every country,' he says. 'I think that attacking Australia is missing the point that world sport itself has a long way to go to get on top of the problem.

'Australia's testing regime is not sophisticated enough to catch the cheats. Mass, random and unannounced testing is too scattered and does not properly target elite athletes who may be using drugs while preparing for important events.'

Ashenden says he is not impressed by the raw data of testing. 'The emphasis seems to be on the number of tests being done and not on the effectiveness of the regime,' he says. 'When somebody says that 4000 tests have been done it means nothing to me without knowing who was targeted and how.'

Parisotto says there is a continuing cultural problem among elite athletes in their use of legal drugs. The breadth of the issue was borne out in the results of a survey done during the Sydney Games and published, without fanfare, two years later.

The *Herald* has obtained a copy of the report – 'Medications used at the Sydney Olympics 2000' – which remains the biggest survey of elite athletes ever conducted.

Athletes were asked to detail what legal medications they had taken over the previous three days. Almost 80 per cent admitted taking 'a large number and variety of medications and supplements'. Although most took one or two different substances in a day, 542 of those surveyed took five or more, including one athlete who took 26 and four others who took 20.

Almost a third of the athletes also admitted using anti-inflammatory drugs, 'often in inappropriate doses and for a prolonged time', while the rate of asthma had sky-rocketed with 15 per cent of Olympic athletes reporting exercise-induced asthma.

At the 1996 Atlanta Games, 383 athletes were registered as asthmatics. In Sydney in 2000 the number had jumped to 607. Statistics for the Australian team, alarmingly, were even higher. At the 1988 Seoul Olympics, 21 team members (7 per cent of the squad) were diagnosed asthmatics. In Sydney 12 years later, the number had jumped to 128, or almost 21 per cent of the squad.

The report's authors, Brian Corrigan, a consultant with the NSW Institute of Sport, and Ray Kazlauskas, director at the Australian Sports Drug Testing Laboratory, pulled no punches in their conclusions.

'The trends point to a dangerous overuse of nonsteroidal anti-inflammatory agents and an unnecessary overuse of vitamins in this population, while pointing out the increased prevalence of asthma and the dangers of drug interactions,' they wrote.

'The question should be not why athletes are taking vitamins but why they are taking them in such huge quantities. We are not alone in suggesting that this inappropriate dosage is a problem – authorities on this topic who agree hold up their scientific hands in dismay. It seems, on the basis of the evidence of this survey, that vitamin use has become an unhealthy fixation amongst athletes who have developed the same mind-set about vitamin supplements as they have about anabolic steroids, believing their use is beyond question.

'The scientific message is clear – genetic endowment, appropriate training and adequate diet are the cornerstone of athletic excellence. This is a message that needs to be reinforced but it has been stated so many times by so many experts that the problem has become that we are preaching to the converted. As shown in this survey, this message is not getting through to athletes or their coaches.'

Corrigan says that the IOC has shelved the report: 'They commissioned it but when we finished they simply said thanks very much and did nothing. It was very disappointing.

'The results were shocking and I don't think anything has changed since. We must tackle the psychology of legal drug use in sport if we are going to beat the problem of illegal drug use. Somebody has to put an end to this bullshit mentality about injection.'

The Sydney Morning Herald, 17 July 2004

ON THE EDGE

Sensitive sports fans might find boxing, fighting to the death or near it, hunting and attempting world speed records extreme, but these are nevertheless part of the wide landscape of sport. Robert Drane's hard-edged and controversial accounts of Jeff Fenech and the boxing milieu in Sydney, and the dangerous business of no-holds-barred fighting, go to places where few journalists have been before. Jesse Fink takes a look at sustainable hunting, and Carl Hammerschmidt at life on the edge of the world speed record attempt.

MIDDLE EASTERN APPEARANCE

Robert Drane

Intriguing stories unfold inside the blue-and-yellow walls of Jeff Fenech's gym in the inner-western Sydney suburb of Marrick-ville. The former world champion has returned to his old head-stomping ground as a boxing educationalist, his nursery for world-class fighters stacked with talent: Danny Green, who has just brutally acquired the interim WBC super-middleweight title from Eric Lucas; brothers Nedal (Skinny) and Hussein (Hussy) Hussein, for whom the plum of world-title glory is tantalisingly within reach; and Vic Darchinyan of the Armenian diaspora, one of many well-turned former 'Iron Curtain' ama-teurs now transforming the fight game. As Vic and Hussy both have the stuff of world flyweight champions, their paths may cross one day at the big intersection of world boxing. But for now they spar routinely, showing enough of their fighting form to leave the ravenous gym gazers satiated.

It's a rare situation. Seldom does this country accommodate two championship-calibre fighters in the same division; never the same gym. As with Green and Mundine, one might soon block the other's path. Unlike Green and Mundine, neither wants it. Who'd want to face his moment of truth with a friend in the opposite corner? World-rated brothers are only a little less common. The Waters and Sands families immediately spring to mind.

Fenech occupies the centre of this talent maelstrom. His pater-nal presence commands the sort of loyalty he craved from the Australian public when he was a fighter. And gets it.

It's a tribute to his status that his fighters all seem to introject something of him. Hussy's intonation and expression in particular are pure Fenech. The 'ehms', 'ahs' and 'y'knows'. The locutions like 'simple as that'. The tone of his utterances, like protests tempered with hard-gotten understanding. The inflections, barely raising the pitch a semitone above the rapid monotone. The way the last word of a sentence dips. Mate.

It's only natural that Fenech would attract the misunderstood, the disaffected, the minorities; not just because he is, after all, Jeff Fenech, but also because he is a boxing trainer, and that's what boxing is all about. An unknown sage once said, 'If I woke out of a coma after 50 years and wanted to know which ethnic group was at the bottom, I'd just ask who the heavyweight champion was.' That aphorism says plenty about boxing's place in our society. Many an ethnic group has gained legitimacy in 'Australian' eyes through boxing. Each has had its peak time. Until the post-war immigration boom, fighters such as Paddy Slavin, Les Darcy, Fred Henneberry and Jimmy Kelso all had keen followings among poorer Irish-Australians. Aboriginal fighters – Ron Richards, Elley Bennett, Dave Sands, Lionel Rose, Tony Mundine, Hector Thompson – boxed their way out of impoverished and dishonoured circumstances, and their participation peaked in the 1950s, '60s and '70s. In those same decades, Italian boxers, sons of market gardeners, labourers and factory workers such as Rocky Gattelari, Rocky Mattioli and Paul Ferreri, rose to prominence.

Today's Muslim Arabs live outside the existing social order's 'accepted' values, afflicted with the sort of social disadvantage that produces boxers. September 11 and subsequent events have knocked them back to the Dark Ages in the collective western mind, whose totem of terror is no longer the anarchic gangsta rapper but the dark, scowling, implacable fanatic willing to die, even if it means taking you with him.

In Australia, mischievous sections of the media have been busy appealing to the debased patriotism that prevails at times like these, subtly turning the headscarf, turban, beard and mosque into tokens of an unwillingness to assimilate. During a gang-rape trial in 2002, a photographer from Sydney's *Daily Telegraph* persuaded a group of Lebanese school kids to look as menacing as possible for a front-page story entitled 'DIAL-A-GUN: Gang says it's easier than buying a pizza'. The resulting image and story helped perpetuate the cycle of mistrust.

In this setting of jingoism and paranoia, Nedal and Hussein Hussein's achievements – on behalf of Australia – have been largely overlooked by sporting fans and our Prime Minister, who used to be in the habit of sending telegrams to Aussie world-title contenders. When Hussy and Skinny fought for their respective titles, neither got the exposure that was important to them and their community. The opportunity has passed for now. We can debate the merits of sportspeople as role models, or the transforming properties of sporting success, but in very difficult times for the broader Arab-Lebanese-Muslim community, one vacancy screams out for fulfilment: hero required.

*

It's a discordant experience to interview a boxer – and to remember that he is a boxer – in a Muslim home where the women wear the traditional *hijab* and every framed Arabic prayer tapestry shares a wall with 50 boxing trophies. The Husseins are a Muslim family, a Lebanese family, but also a boxing family.

They kept a respectful, noisy distance in the entrance area of their small home in Sydney's fibro belt, the day *Inside Sport* (*IS*) arrived to interview Hussy Hussein. In three days he was to be married to the beautiful daughter of family friends, and there was excitement in the air. His mother, Wafa, who looks too young to be his mother, was prudently hospitable. A glass of Diet Coke appeared in front of me. Then, two small but dense date cakes, elegantly wrapped in wax paper. From a distance his father, Mustafa, seemed expansive and ebullient. Two of their precious sons are world-ranked boxers. Another, Billy, trains his brothers under Fenech.

The tale of Lebanese-Australian kids in Sydney can be told statistically: the number of them on the wrong side of the NSW judicial system; the dearth of academic achievers. 'A lot more are in boxing because they're aggressive. But you get a couple in the gym and they tend to bring a lot with them,' Hussy tells *IS*. He believes, as many fighters do, that boxing will teach these youngsters things that school cannot, and his aim is to divert the typical trajectory of the bored Lebanese-Australian teenager.

'If someone came to me and said, "Mate, let's do something for these kids," I'm volunteering, first one,' he says. 'They think, "I'm a hard bastard. I wanna be cool. I wanna be this rapper, that gangsta." We're copycats, mate! Whatever America does, we do. They want to be respected. Someone's got to be there to tell them what's right and wrong. Parents don't know what their kids are doing.'

The portrayal of the Lebanese-Australian community in parts of the media, particularly after the gang-rape trial of 2002, rankles with the normally placid and humble Hussein: 'It comes down to individuals. When a Lebanese bloke rapes someone, it's not Ahmed so-and-so. It's a Muslim man. People judge the whole culture. What are they saying? That *I'm* a rapist? I don't even know the guy who did it. My community needs one good spokesman to stick up for us – in a respectable way; don't get me wrong. A lot of Lebanese sportsmen are doing well, but not many get in the papers. The image that gets most publicity is bad. Look, opinions are like arseholes. Everybody's got one. But [the media] shouldn't disrespect people.'

Hussy and Skinny were bored and aimless Belmore kids until their father pointed them in the direction of the Police Boys' Club. Boxing's routines and its culture can be powerful magic for a kid seeking focus. They loved the encouragement and self-esteem it brought, says Hussy: 'I became a trophy collector. "Gotta have more fights, more trophies."' Sometimes all three Hussein boys would bring home a trophy. Hussy was a very good amateur, unlucky at times. One loss, at the 1997 world champs in Budapest, was as outrageous as Fenech's at the Los Angeles Olympics in 1984, when the judges' decision in the Australian's favour (against the eventual silver medallist) was overturned by a 'jury'. But at least that happened on the night of the fight. In Hussy's case, the decision – over a Hungarian fighter – was overturned a day later, as he was preparing for the next bout.

Hussy's discipline was respected by his classmates at Belmore Boys' High School. 'I finished school and rushed to the gym,' he says. 'Then I went home. These kids had nowhere to go so they hung around buses, took the bus down to the station; [had] nothing to do for three or four hours. I stood my ground and kids respected that. One kid offered me a smoke and a mate said, "Mate, he doesn't smoke. He's a fighter." That saved me. I was dying to go out sometimes but I couldn't.'

His religious upbringing and that early self-control armed Hussy with the sword and shield of integrity. Now he happily shoulders the burden of example, 'for my culture. My religion. We need role models. You don't even realise there are people who look up to you. The amount of e-mails I got before the title fight, I was stunned. They want to see you succeed and care about what you do.'

The chicanery of boxing merely offends Hussy, whereas it infuriated his mentor, Fenech. Because of the orchestrated misfortune he sometimes endured, the Marrickville Mauler became a symbol for those who hate the abuse of power and authority. He was our irrational response, punching and shredding his own route through the injustices that life threw his way, never sacrificing his pride. Hussy's moral sense is affronted more than anything: 'Because I don't get involved [in the seedier side of boxing] I don't expect no one to [exploit] me. I could say people are against me and get cheap publicity. I couldn't live with it, mate. Simple as that.'

*

The title fight, last November against Thailand's Pongsaklek Wonjongkam, was held at Lumpini Stadium, a mephitic hellhole with a dank, steaming interior, nauseating with the stench of urine, sweat and decaying matter. Amid the fumes, the airless humidity and the ceaseless skirling of *klui*, local flute-like instruments, gamblers scowl behind barbed-wire cages. Arising out of the centre of the chaos is the reason for its existence: the

organised spectacle of Muay Thai. As soon as the priestly rituals finish, carnal concerns take over as a fight begins. Money
changes hands; the crowd snarls.

Hussy's fight – the main event – was the only boxing match on
the card. No foreigner had ever fought a Thai champion inside
this Malebolge and emerged victorious. The trump of outrageous home advantage was played expertly. Already, the Thais
had unnecessarily deferred the fight, without informing the
Fenech camp. Their motive became clear when they insisted on
a date during Ramadan, knowing this would give any decent
Muslim three choices: to withdraw; to fast anyway and try to
train for a world title; or to shun Ramadan altogether and risk
personal and, possibly, social consequences. Hussy chose the
latter. After all, he'd postponed his wedding twice and trained
for one fight, one opponent, one style, for ten months. 'They
knew. They're not stupid. They've got Muslims in Thailand,' he
says. At the pre-fight press conference, with no chair in sight,
Hussy stood for three hours. If the Fenech camp hadn't made its
own arrangements, it would have had a 100-minute drive to the
gym; no sparring; no air-conditioning in a no-star hotel. Then
the final, devastating ploy: the fight was moved forward four
hours, into the middle of a Bangkok afternoon. Still, Hussy
entered the hostile shack feeling sharp. But after being called
from his dressing-room, he endured the introduction from the
ring of an endless procession of local dignitaries for 45 enervat-
ing minutes. When his edge was blunted, a fresh Wonjongkam
entered the ring.

Hussy would have a big round, then ease back in a vain effort
to save energy, keep the hard-punching southpaw off, and still
score enough to win. In the 11th, the Australian went down for
the first time in his career. Yet he almost stole the diadem in the
last as he expended his remaining energy punishing the fading
Thai, cutting him up.

Misfortune dogs Fenech's fighters right now. You'll hear a lot
about them padding their records with 'Indonesian cab drivers'
and unknown Filipinos with big claims and uncheckable
records. But they have attained world rankings and kept

Australian boxing – partly due to Fenech's promotions – alive at a time when Australia's dollar and distance have been disincentives to the best Americans and Europeans. As they won't come here to give Fenech's boys experience, they've had to brave hostile worlds and barefaced bias. Glen Kelly, Adam Watt, Shannan Taylor, Danny Green, the Husseins.

When Nedal Hussein fought for the international superbantamweight title against Manny Pacquiao, a dramatic Filipino with a spectacular punch and just enough crockery in his chops to make his fights interesting, he had similar luck. In round two, Skinny found the china with a shattering left. Pacquiao crumbled unconsciously, and stayed that way long enough for two countouts, but the referee, Carlos Padilla (of 'Thrilla in Manila' fame), faffed around until he struggled to his feet. Pacquiao held desperately for the rest of the round, until Padilla found an excuse to penalise Skinny for holding, denying him the round as well as the fight! Eventually Skinny, his brow badly lacerated, lost.

'Padilla done everything he possibly could to make Pacquiao survive,' Hussy says now. 'Whenever they got in close, he broke them up. If Pacquiao started fighting he let them go. If Skinny started fighting, break 'em up. *You-should-win-and-lose-a-fight-in-the-ring.* They should be respectful to fighters who train hard. I'd hate to win that way. Like Beyer against Green. I'd be too ashamed to call myself champion. Too a-shamed! To get your arse beat and end up with a belt around your waist – I'd be saying, "Hold the belt, I'm not a champion, mate. I'll fight him again."'

Recently, Pacquiao moved up, took on Marco Antonio Barrera – considered a featherweight great – and stopped him. People now see Skinny's electrifying effort against the popular Pacquiao in a different light. The unfairness of it all doesn't worry Hussy, though. It offends him. It makes him indignant. *Losing* worries him. Harsh places? He knows them well.

*

The Hussein family left the northern port city of Tripoli, Lebanon, to escape the troubles of 1973. They were there for a holiday in 1982 when Israel invaded. This time they were caught. Bombs constantly shook their residence. A rocket came through the roof but didn't explode. They slept in underground car parks converted into bunkers. 'At night you'd hear *buh-buh-buh-bah!*' Hussy tells *IS*. 'They're echoing from here, then from the opposite end and you'd know you're in crossfire. You'd turn on the radio to find out if someone's invaded. Someone was shot in front of us, on his balcony, and he tumbled out his window to the ground. Y'know it was disturbing, mate. We were only kids.' Two years they were trapped there. 'That's what woke me up in the first place.'

As a practising Muslim – and an Arab – he's had his share of recent hardships. Travelling overseas, especially to the US where the finer distinctions of Middle East politics are not the stuff of daily news, the Hussein brothers might as well have been Uday and Qusay. Hussy has copped the most, as though his name is a double affirmation of his terrorist status: Hussein Hussein? Saddam Saddam? You tell me, boy – what's the difference?

'I get continually searched,' he says, ruefully. 'I went over to watch the Lewis–Tyson fight. Skinny was fighting on the night and we got a domestic flight. The woman [at the airport ticket counter] said, "The computer won't let me access your seats." Her supervisor came over and said, "It's in the FBI's hands. You'll have to wait until they question you." The FBI guy pulled out a badge and it was like some movie. He was asking me silly questions, y'know: "Are you a terrorist?" "Do you know any terrorists?" "Do you know anyone in the Middle East?" Then before I get on the plane, I get searched again. If they wanna be strict, I've got no problem. I wanna be safe on the plane too! But there's a limit.'

Above Hussy's head, in the lounge room of the Hussein residence, the dramatic Arabic script vividly announces itself. 'It's a strong prayer – a protection prayer,' he explains. Another tapestry says 'Mohammed'. Another, 'Allah'. His family prays before he fights. 'We're believers, you know? You believe in something, you follow it.'

*

Vic Darchinyan – the Raging Bull – will be the next Team Fenech fighter to enter a world-title ring. He's more mantis than bull, reminiscent of another Aussie southpaw named Vic – Vic Patrick, the great World War II lightweight and welterweight. Like Patrick, he extends his right arm, waving it languidly in front of his man's face. It might suddenly change direction like a heat-seeking missile and cause damage and dismay, or it might serve as guide for a left cross that can knock a man across a ring and through the ropes. His hands are heavy and fast, his demeanour cool and concentrated. He and Hussy know each other's styles intimately, yet those gym gazers will have to dine out on dreams, because, according to Hussy, they'll never fight.

'I got too much respect for him. He's very moral, very respectable – he's a great bloke,' he tells *IS*. 'We've got so much in common, like [the Armenians'] way of living's very much the same as Arabs.' He smiles at the thought of his stablemate. 'He doesn't think he can lose. You tell him, "You're gonna fight this guy," he shrugs his shoulders. "I fight him. I beat him."' He laughs as much at his own high-pitched staccato imitation as Vic's blunt manner. 'Not a care in the world. Like Kostya. Strong-minded, don't fear nothin', you know? Even at golf. Guy can't hit a ball but he says, "Come on, I can beat him." He's been a real plus for us at that gym.'

Darchinyan trains in anticipation of a fight with Colombia's unbeaten WBA champion Irene Pacheco – probably the best of a batch of very good flyweight champions. Fenech watches. It seems he's had to traverse the circles of hell to become the Jeff Fenech God intends him to be. Wealth and success are good outcomes for an ex-pug, yet he has more reasons to curse his luck than ever. But today he has the patience of a man who has faced foes he can't punch and shred – the last thing he needed as a fighter, when his bright, intense star came and went quickly. Now, patience fills his gym like the scent of lavender.

Hussy knows now that his loss to Wonjongkam was important. He learned that the pace of a world-title fight is hot; that his left rip can be nullified against good southpaws; that he doesn't want to go backwards. 'It'll wreck me to go back,' he says. 'I've done it 17 years now. I'm sick of it, mate.' But impatience is the last thing Hussein needs as a fighter. 'The good thing is that I've got a loss on my record. Now they'll say, "He got dropped," whatever, and they'll want to fight me, mate.'

Only a lack of world-class opposition can contain the burgeoning talent in Fenech's nursery. 'Yeah, y'know it'll come,' he says, sounding remarkably like Hussy Hussein. 'It'll come.'

*

Two weeks after *IS* was at his gym, Jeff Fenech was attacked by four men. His face was slashed with the jagged edge of a broken bottle. The situation had a terrible irony for Fenech and the Husseins: the men, initially described as being of 'Middle Eastern appearance', were, indeed, Lebanese.

Inside Sport, May 2004

PARTIAL LAW, MIXED FEELINGS

Robert Drane

George Foreman once said that boxing is the sport to which all other sports aspire. He was wrong. This is. At least it could be. That's if Foreman meant that, if not for the rules that restrain them, or their own physical limitations, the purest reaction of all sportspeople would be to take their, say, hockey stick or cricket bat and, when competition is at its most heated, bludgeon an opponent over the head.

This could become the ultimate realisation of all those desires. This – not boxing. The 'noble art' is violence, but it is violence modified. This, 'No Holds Barred', or mixed martial arts, is conducted under rules loose enough to admit every form of fighting, yet tight enough to prevent men being killed. Mixed martial arts has been condemned as barbaric in Victoria by the Australian Medical Association, but it holds a fascination for a large part of the population. Keilor International Basketball Centre holds 1500 and tonight it's full. In May, the great Randy Couture filled the 5000-seat Melbourne Convention Centre to capacity.

There's no ignoring it. With this 'reality' fighting, all those pub rows would seem to be brutally settled; arguments about which style of fighting is better, or whether a 500-pound wrestler – say, Andre the Giant – familiar with every means of grappling a man into screaming submission, or unconsciousness, would beat a smaller man – say, Bruce Lee – who knew seven different ways just to rip out a man's jugular, and similarly traumatise any other part of the body. But the sport has a dilemma. It has strict rules designed to stop it becoming itself. If it becomes what it can become, it'll be banned immediately. If it doesn't, its mass appeal might wane – unless there are rule changes. It's a strange cocktail. These men are capable of crippling an opponent. So it seems at times the equivalent of a balance of terror. When contestants are on their feet, there's not a lot of action. They don't seem to punch or kick much, despite the huge diversity of martial arts backgrounds. Each fighter wants to wrestle his man to the ground, and then attain either a submission, or sit on top of him and beat his face with his fists until he submits or the referee stops it. Until this happens, each fight typifies the strange banality violence can sometimes attain, like watching elephant seals bump against each other: a ritual that must be got through. There's a lot of grim grappling; a lot of static action – pardon the oxymoron – but at any time, the grounded grunt 'n' groaners might explode in frustration or anger and start throwing real punches. When this occurs, the man on top invariably wins.

It will be interesting to see what other rules they come up with. Maybe the first half of every five-minute round should be fought with standing techniques. Still, men like this are brave. In boxing, or wrestling, or martial arts, you get a small percentage who genuinely want to take on any man, anywhere; men not afraid of the unknown, or even of ultimate, public, failure.

They will gravitate towards NHB. They're the most fearsome men in the world, because they're the most fearless. Unless you're prepared to die, you don't dice with them.

NHB fighting was always going to happen. Go underground, and the fights are more vicious still. Some involve life and death. Above ground, NHB enjoys a degree of mainstream acceptability. People love it, or love the thrill of knowing what it could become. It's for the masses. After all, we live in a generation that allows its mind to go places it would never once have allowed it to go. Well, not since just before the fall of a certain great empire. The small leather gloves the competitors use – open at the fingers and palms – resemble the cestus.

Keilor International Basketball Centre fills up with interested onlookers, plus the usual floating population of gym rats, chop-socky kids, hardcases, imitation hardcases and gum-chewing, rumbustious local legends of the suburbs and their flocks of flunkies, all of whom limber up even as they converse. Bandannas, earrings, piratical headscarves, tattoos, muscle shirts and shaven heads. A hard knot of squat and muscular men gathers at the door – a pyknic's picnic interrupted only by the sudden, towering presence of Hawthorn's Peter 'Spider' Everitt. Joe Cursio and John Donohue, the promoters, might be thinking this will be a dangerous crowd, judging from the amount of security guards here. But surprisingly, they're completely well behaved.

Tonight's bouts are to be conducted under Shooto regulations, which determine winners by combining boxing and wrestling rules. There are points decisions, submissions, count-outs and three-knockdown rules. The fights have a very different feel to boxing. The fighters look as though they've walked in straight off the street, or been picked from a willing crowd of scrappers.

A lot of them don't resemble boxers – they're tough, but mostly fresh-faced. Each fight invariably ends on the ground. Faces get redder. The bouts come to resemble street fights. Punching upwards, twisting, bridging. Headlocks. Furious punching exchanges on the ground – most harmless as the fighters strive for leverage. Legs scissoring heads. Some of the fighters have grappling as their strength. Others strive to attain that street-fighting position of superiority, astride their supine opponent, punching downward. The standing action is designed to get a man down by upsetting his leverage: hurtful knees to the thighs, stamps with the heel onto the foot. They finish a round soaked in sweat.

The most curious fight this night features Chris Brown, a multiple Olympian for Australia in wrestling who retired and came straight into NHB. He says his jiujitsu is 'improving every week'. It seems that some knowledge of jiujitsu is compulsory among this brand of fighters. His opponent, Jun Kitagawa, is an inordinately respectful Japanese fighter who seems torn between awe of Brown's reputation, his own desire to win and a strange compulsion to look up at himself on the big screen whenever the slightest opportunity presents itself. In the first round, he pokes his mouthguard out, then paws with tentative lefts. Brown throws punches and kicks only as feints, his real purpose being to get close to Kitagawa.

When he finally succeeds in getting him down, Kitagawa resists being locked into a submission hold by squirming, bridging, twisting and, when he can, punching. In frustration, Brown stands up quickly, and gets a kick in the face for his trouble. Brown locks Kitagawa's legs under his arms and attempts to twist him over, Boston Crab-wise. Again he fails. Back on the floor, he throws a few short-arm jolts at his recalcitrant opponent. As the Japanese rises, his face is covered in blood from a forehead gash that looks worse than it really is. But there are many opportunities to rip open a wound like that in this sport, and therefore it must be seriously looked at. Kitagawa attempts to kick Brown, and when he fails, his plan 'B' is to run away. His comical flight is made more amusing by the fact that Brown doesn't know how to cut off ring space or throw punches – he's trying to catch him so he can wrestle him. He ends the round on his back because Kitagawa suddenly stops, hooks his foot behind his back leg and pushes him to the floor. As Kitagawa walks to his corner, he checks out his bloodied face on the screen.

Brown, muscular and athletic, chases his awkward foe around

the ring in round two, finally wrestles him to his knees, then manages to stand up, get behind Kitagawa and punch him repeatedly with his right hand to the side of the head. When the referee breaks them up, the narcissistic Kitagawa stands and glances up at the screen again. His face is a mask of blood, and, after Brown again assails him on the ropes, the referee steps in and stops the fight. The crowd boos: 'Ah come on, ref, give the bloke a go!' Kitagawa reels, slumps and staggers around the ring crying, protesting, sneaking little glimpses of himself on the screen. His corner men follow him around with a towel while he reels just out of their range inconsolably, in a scene strangely reminiscent of James Brown's cape routine for 'Prisoner of Love'. Eventually he makes his way to Brown's corner, gathers himself with a steel-jawed dignity, as though he's made up his mind to commit harakiri with his next action, then he sighs a resigned, determined sigh and jumps through the ropes before his seconds can get to him, and disappears into his dressing-room, bowing, crying and bleeding at the crowd all the way. Great Japanese theatre.

The main bout features Soa Palelei, a monstrous Samoan from Perth with a jiujitsu background who wants to make it to the top; in Japan, they get crowds of 80,000 to these events. Two things are certain: when Palelei gets his man on the ground, on his back, he is going to win. And, unless he runs into a man who's bloody good with his fists and knocks him unconscious before that happens, then it will happen. Christian Wellisch is a well-proportioned all-American wrestler. No midget at 100 kilograms, but outweighed by 28 kilograms.

The entire bout is concerned with Palelei cornering Wellisch and leaning on him, and Wellisch trying to wrestle his way off the ropes to stay upright. He slams his heels onto Palelei's enormous feet. When Palelei does grapple him down, Wellisch quickly finds the ropes and they resume, standing. Neither is good at boxing, but Wellisch knows Palelei will give him the mother of a thumping if he gets him on his back. Wellisch has the skills, and the cunning to stay near the ropes, but Palelei is sheer strength. Both men stand in the corner trying to manoeuvre the other into a submission hold. Those heels to Palelei's feet only serve to make him angry. At the end of the round Palelei seems the more tired of the two – although both sweat heavily. When Wellisch attempts a punch, Palelei pokes his tongue out and hisses aggressively, Maori haka style, swinging slow, low, roundhouse rights that might fell a building.

Through sheer attrition, Palelei finally gets his man in that inevitable, unenviable position, and we know it's over. He looks out to the crowd and exhorts them to cheer and bay for blood. Then he drops the heavy weight of his tired, heavy arms, fist first, onto Wellisch's head. Wellisch doesn't look too hurt when the referee steps in; it's just that the referee knows the pounding isn't going to stop until he's a 300-metre strip of transparent rolled meat. Violent? Yes. A spectacle? NHB has some way to go. It's exciting at times, but its inherent thrill depends on how close it's allowed to get to its horribly violent potential, and that's entirely up to us.

Inside Sport, September 2004

SAFARI POLITICS

Jesse Fink

Sport likes to think of itself as the great leveller. For all the global inequity in wealth, weapons, manpower and resources, in the elite competitions of the world, the assorted World Cups and the Olympics, it all comes down to whoever is fastest off the starting blocks, whoever cracks the winning run, whoever drills the ball into the back of the net in the dying seconds. Sport respects no racial or socioeconomic boundaries; it makes heroes of men and women who ignore the bum hand that life has dealt them and rise up through all manner of adversity to become winners, whether they happen to come first or not. Competition is what matters; that, and sheer exhilarating unpredictability. It's what sport is all about. Or at least that's what it's about most of the time.

For on the fringes of that great amorphous category of human activity known as 'sport', there are pursuits that some would argue are not sporting at all. Such as hunting, the only sport on this earth in which the ultimate aim is to kill something. After all, just how much competition can there be between a high-powered $200,000 Holland & Holland 'Royal' .700 Nitro Express double rifle and a lumbering African elephant with a cranial diameter the size of a small car? The outcome is usually depressingly predictable.

Certainly it would not be a stretch to call hunting the most maligned sport in the world. Its list of critics makes the anti-boxing lobby look like a Country Women's Association meeting. Which is why hunting is having something of an identity crisis. For centuries it was the gentleman's sport; the very word 'sport' a byword for a man who knew how to handle a firearm and dispatch a pheasant, tiger or fox and return to the club in the evening to smoke a pipe and imbibe some Courvoisier.

But today hunting sits uncomfortably in the sporting community, a sort of evil second cousin the rest of the family simply shuns or hopes will go away. The talk among hunters now is not of their pursuit as being sport, but of existing for nobler, even higher motives. Calling it a sport just doesn't cut it any more and killing for killing's sake is a hard sell in anyone's language. In the twenty-first century, more creative ideas are required. And a few friends in high places.

*

Today's archetypal hunter is not the drooling, gap-toothed yokel of the backwoods country in *Deliverance*; he's professional, well heeled, well travelled, law-abiding and, above all, political.

Hunters surmised long ago that changing social mores had the potential to threaten the very existence of their sport, and drastic action was required: to survive, hunting needed to serve another purpose than merely adding more stuffed heads to lounge-room walls; and blasting away at anything that moved wasn't doing anyone any favours, least of all hunters. Some serious image massaging was called for.

If any one group can be said to have characterised the ensuing dramatic transformation of hunters – and hunting – in the past two decades, it is Safari Club International. Founded in 1972, the 40,000-member hunting organisation based in Tucson, Arizona, which claims to represent 45 million hunters worldwide, has long preached the benefits of 'wildlife management', in which the primary motivation of hunting is not sport. Rather, it is the very future of wildlife around the world. In SCI's eyes, animals are of no inherent value just gambolling about. But give them a dollar value, and that changes everything. By putting money from trophy fees back into wildlife conservation programs and local communities, a kill is no longer merely a kill. It's both a conservation measure and an economic incentive. When a deer is slaughtered for its antlers, leaving its carcass to rot on the forest floor is not effective use of the animal. But by handing the meat over to hungry people, that's charity. And instead of just rushing ahead and mounting all those heads in the den, call yourself a 'curator' and turn your house into a museum. That's education – and an effective tax deduction.

The math is irresistible. Hunters become humanitarians. Aggressors become angels. Butchers become benevolent sportsmen. Which all adds up to more dead animals – with more spare change.

Not that SCI hunters need to start penny pinching. More than half the membership earn US$100,000-plus a year, and the 13 million or so hunters in the US, which make up six per cent of the population, spend some US$20.6 billion on their sport each year. The average SCI hunter spends about US$15,000 a year. The average joe in the woods, about a tenth of that.

With such clout, SCI hardly needs to curry favour with American politicians, even though it has funnelled US$700,000 in political donations to Republican candidates since 1998. And it certainly doesn't need to buy influence when it can count the nation's political heavies as supporters.

President George W. Bush's father, former president George Bush, is SCI's celebrity *capo di tutti capi*, but other Republicans are prominent members. These include former vice-president Dan Quayle, former commander of Allied forces in the Gulf War General Norman Schwarzkopf, current Homeland Security chief Tom Ridge, and current deputy director of the US Fish and Wildlife Service Matthew J. Hogan, himself a former SCI government affairs manager. Even President Bush was the recipient of SCI's 'Governor of the Year' award for his 'outstanding record of wildlife conservation', which made the former Texas governor 'a favourite among hunters'.

It's no surprise, then, that with such high-profile spruikers, and with such a voice on Capitol Hill, American hunters are enjoying halcyon days. Barely a year after donating US$53 million to saving forests in west Africa, the Bush Administration attenuated the very piece of legislation protecting most of Africa's and the rest of the world's rarest wildlife from trophy hunters, the US *Endangered Species Act*. The Administration's proposed amendments would allow hunters, circuses and the pet industry to kill, capture and import a number of endangered animals from developing countries.

The 'pay their own way' mantra of SCI had been adopted as policy by the most powerful nation on earth.

*

Hunters style themselves as 'real' conservationists, arguing that traditional forms of conservation – protectionism – don't work.

They have some grounds for thinking this way. Programs such as the Migratory Bird Conservation Fund in the US and South Australia's Watervalley Wetlands are held up as proof of what hunting can achieve for conservation.

The hundreds of millions of dollars earned from hunting licenses and other taxes, which goes straight back into purchasing and rehabilitating wetlands, has certainly provided food for thought for the anti-hunting lobby. Yet when wildlife management in developing countries is on the table, the jury is out.

CAMPFIRE (Communal Areas Management Program for Indigenous Resources), a scheme operating in southern Africa that provides villagers with funds from trophy fees, as well as the sale of hides, meat and other animal products, mainly from elephants, has long been seen by SCI and other hunting groups as the way of the future in big-game conservation.

But according to Wayne Pacelle, senior vice-president of the Washington, DC-based Humane Society of the United States, CAMPFIRE has been an unmitigated failure and has not delivered the promised payday to local communities.

'Number one, it was a program subsidised by the US government; it was not self-sustaining. If it was successful it shouldn't have needed US$28 million from American taxpayers to prop it up,' he tells *Inside Sport* (*IS*). 'Number two, larger political issues have overtaken circumstances in Zimbabwe. It's not even a program that's operating any longer – it's not happening. The people enriched are mainly the guides and outfitters and other people tied in with the safari industry; the local people don't get much. You also have government officials skimming from the till. There's just not much evidence that there are any practical benefits for the animals in the wild.'

This is not the lone cry of left-wing, vegan conspiracy theorists. Even SCI's African chapter's own newsletter, *African Indaba*, has revealed that half a dozen safari companies are being investigated by the Zimbabwean authorities for failing to declare $10 million worth of trophies. Corruption among the country's park rangers is also rife, with many charged with abusing licenses and allowing illegal hunting.

In Zimbabwe's neighbour Botswana, trophy hunters also are under attack for seriously depleting big cat numbers, mostly because they seek out mature, or 'primary', males with large manes. A recent estimate of lion numbers Africa-wide was put at 20,000, down from 230,000 in 1980. Lions are not just dying from hunting, but also from a rare form of lion HIV, lion lentivirus, as well as being killed by poachers or captured by wildlife smugglers to feed the rampant black market international trade in animals, said to be worth some $10 billion a year. This is just what's happening in Africa, where trophy hunting is still a relatively new industry. In Canada, where it is an enshrined family tradition, scientists have found that 30 years of hunting has dramatically altered the genetic variability of bighorn sheep, because trophy hunters shoot males with big horns before they have mated. There are fears the same thing will happen with Africa's elephants.

*

None of this, however, has made the slightest difference to SCI. In January at SCI's 32nd Annual Hunters' Convention in Reno, Nevada, regarded as the biggest hunting show in the world, it was business as usual. Each year, 16,000 cashed-up hunters from all corners of the globe gather to browse five-and-a-half hectares of exhibitors' stands, offering everything from the latest laser-sighted handguns to bear-hunting travel packages in Russia's far east. Also during the four-day event, auctions of 'donated' hunts take place (this year the big-ticket item was a permit to hunt an endangered wild sheep called argali in western Mongolia, value US$100,000) and awards are bestowed upon members for accumulating trophies. 'Grand Slams' are earned for hunting various species, such as the Africa Big Five Grand Slam (lion, leopard, rhinoceros, Cape buffalo, elephant), the Bears of the World Grand Slam (polar, grizzly, Alaskan brown, Eurasian brown), and so on.

Once each Grand Slam is earned, hunters ascend to the 'First Pinnacle of Achievement' and upwards until they reach the 'Crowning Achievement' for killing 138 animals native to their specific territories. There is also an 'Inner Circle' in which hunters ascend in Copper (seven or eight species killed), Bronze (12 species), Silver (10 animals from 10 species), Gold (12 more trophy animals) and Diamond (18 more) rankings. There are 29 Inner Circle categories, including 'Trophy Animals of the South Pacific' and 'Spiralled Horned Animals of Africa'. To get all 29, an SCI hunter must kill at least 322 species.

Many of the aforementioned 'harvested' animals are recorded for posterity in SCI's *Official Record Book of Trophy Animals* (RRP US$200). The next edition, a three-volume leather-bound set, is due out in 2005. The aim of every SCI hunter is to get one of his or her kills in the book.

Yet it is this very award system – of treating animals as notches on a belt – that makes it difficult to take seriously the green credentials of SCI hunters. Many in the Australian hunting community find it distasteful and downright offensive, as well as counterproductive to the interests of hunters' public image. Others claim the award system is fuelling the very thing the hunting community claims it is against – unsustainable destruction of endangered, and hence more expensive, wildlife. But, paradoxically, many of those same hunters remain members of the American organisation.

It pays to have the big guys behind you.

*

In Australia, the number of hunters has been put at anywhere from 600,000 to two million. Clearly for the major parties, like their American cousins, these men and women represent an important constituency, and accordingly various attempts have been made by state and federal politicians to make life easier for hunters, even though a grab bag of state-based recreational hunting laws has largely curtailed the growth of the sport and the development of a big-game hunting industry.

Everywhere except the Top End, where Darwin International Airport sees regular arrivals of US, British and German hunters, all keen to bag a water buffalo, banteng (wild ox), or feral pig. 'It's pretty well recognised that the safari industry is an essential part of the tourist industry in the Territory,' says Brian Dudley of the Northern Territory Firearms Council. 'The government supports it.'

It sure does. A Northern Territory Parks and Wildlife Service draft management plan released for public comment late last year called for 25 crocodiles of more than four metres' length to be shot or harpooned by trophy hunters, out of the annual quota of 600 killed for their skins by Aboriginal enterprises.

The plan requires approval by the federal government. According to the plan, the inclusion of crocodiles as game animals will 'attract greater interest from international clients', and 'abundant populations of crocodiles should be maintained for their ecological and economic value'. The proposal is geared as a financial godsend to Aboriginal communities, which, with the plan in place, will have an increased 'incentive ... to protect crocodiles and crocodile habitats'. In motive, strategy, framework and language, the whole document could have been written in Tucson.

But Mike Letnic, wildlife management officer for the NT Parks and Wildlife Service and the document's author, says the plan has been driven by home-grown concerns, primarily economic: 'It's largely been driven by landowners in the Territory who want to diversify their incomes ... we haven't received particularly strong lobbying from safari hunting groups, but a lot of them are naturally supportive of it ... [the plan] has also looked at overseas situations, and how crocodiles are managed overseas. For example, in the US they have safari-style hunting of alligators as part of the management strategy. It's another way of saying, "Look, hey we can do this in the Territory."'

So how much will it cost to bag a croc? 'In terms of the landowners and operators, they're going to try to maximise their cash return. That's something the market will determine ... we're talking roughly about $3000 to $12,500, but I'm unclear whether that's the trophy fee or the package fee.'

*

Ray Hammond, a plumber from Guyra in the northern tablelands of NSW, is president of SCI Down Under, formerly SCI South Pacific. The biggest SCI chapter in Australia (a smaller Victorian chapter is headquartered in Clarkefield, north of Melbourne), it has more than 100 members and donates 30 per cent of any monies generated through its biggest fundraiser each year to Tucson. In late February it will have its annual conference at Novotel Opal Cove Resort in Coffs Harbour, 'a group get-together of all the hunters from virtually all around Australia', where hunting outfitters and firearms companies will exhibit their wares alongside the nation's top taxidermists. Hammond is an avowed devotee of SCI's trophy culture, something that contributed to SCI South Pacific splintering into the two new chapters and giving rise to a third group called Australian Hunters International.

Though the main causes of the break-up were financial, AHI's Robert Borsak told *Inside Sport* that the Tucson group was 'degenerating into a hunt 'em, shoot 'em and collect 'em organisation'.

The criticism bothers Hammond, who by his own reckoning has 'the biggest trophy collection anywhere in Australia ... life-size grizzly bears, lions – bigger than any museum'. But he's not advertising the fact. 'I usually don't give interviews because a lot of times you see the stuff [in print] and it comes out totally different,' he says. 'I want to be put in [*IS*] as a conservationist, and I believe that we've got to look after these animals, that we won't have a lot of them to hunt; and I believe genuine hunters are right in the forefront of protecting a lot of these animals.'

Despite the grisly reputation of his sport, Hammond says hunters are making great strides with their public image, particularly after the Strathfield and Port Arthur massacres saw a massive shift in public opinion about the need for Australians to own guns.

'Years ago it was like if it moves you shoot it, if it grows you cut it down,' he tells *IS*. 'That mentality's gone now. A lot of the hunting clubs are getting much better educated, much more conservation-minded, because they want [game] to be around for their kids ... we've got more game around now than there was 20 years ago.'

Robert Brown, an SCI member and chairman of the newly formed NSW Game Council, certainly holds to that view. 'One of the problems hunters have had, whether it's because they perhaps don't have the professional PR capabilities to be able to penetrate the broad-scale magazine market, for instance, is you don't see stories about hunters in *Australian Women's Weekly*. Well, the Game Council is going to change that, I can tell you that right now,' he says.

Brown has reason to be cheerful. In 2002 the NSW Upper House passed the Game and Feral Animal Control Bill amid much protest from Greens and Independent senators and opposition from community-based groups such as Gun Control Australia, the National Parks Association, the Australian Conservation Foundation and WWF Australia.

The Bill, championed by NSW Shooters Party MP John Tingle, an SCI 'International Legislator of the Year' award winner, allowed for the creation of a hunter-dominated 16-member council that would control the issuing of game licences and allow hunters to shoot game such as deer, quail and hare, and feral animals such as pigs, dogs, cats and foxes on public land – a massive achievement for the gun lobby, which has long cited feral animal control as a strong reason for gun ownership.

Yet unusually for a man in his position, and for a representative of a community group struggling to gain public acceptance, Brown sees the Bill less as a death sentence for feral animals in the state and more as a unique opportunity for developing hunter tourism. This even though the Act's stated objectives are 'the effective management of introduced species of game animals' and 'to promote [their] responsible and orderly hunting'.

Peter Hall, the National Party member for Gippsland, was so impressed by the Council, he issued a press release saying a similar initiative in Victoria would afford 'great opportunities to bring international visitors' to the state. Brown sees no problem with that at all. 'That would be a good thing, wouldn't it?' he says. 'In fact the [Council] regulations are going to make allowances for licenses for those particular types of purposes.'

*

On the Council, the only statutory body of its kind in Australia, are eight representatives of Australian hunting groups appointed by the Carr government. A number of these hunters are members of SCI. However, the eight does not include former SCI South Pacific scientific adviser Max King, one of the Council's two government-appointed wildlife management scientists.

In '97 the federal Senate-appointed Rural and Regional Affairs and Transport References Committee heard submissions from a range of anti- and pro-hunting lobby groups, including SCI South Pacific, on the subject of the Commercial Utilisation of Australian Native Wildlife. King, a population biologist and former honorary senior research fellow at the Department of Genetics at La Trobe University, told the committee: '[SCI] oppose protectionism and preservation as conservation principles because habitat becomes valueless to primary producers under this approach. We want wildlife to become a valuable and sustainably harvested asset.' One example he proffered was the critically endangered Siberian tiger, which numbers only 350 to 400 in the wild: 'You put a very large trophy fee on them and make sure that the people in the area where the tigers come from get 75 or 80 per cent of the trophy fee ... normally the [local] people who are in a financially depressed state ... go out and poach the tigers to sell on the illegal drugs market for the Chinese medicinal trade.

'[If] there are only one or two trophy tigers to be hunted, the people in the area will go out and protect those animals to the nth degree because they know they will get a hundred times more than their previous income.'

Even coming from a hunter, let alone a wildlife management scientist, shooting a Siberian tiger seems extreme. Had King changed his mind since then? When *IS* contacted him at his farm in the Riverina town of Balranald, 910 kilometres west of Sydney, he didn't want to respond to any questions regarding his time representing SCI South Pacific.

'I'd prefer not to,' he said, though he did confirm he was no longer a member, but a member of AHI. Asked to account for his comments, King responded: 'I don't want to answer any questions about anything, really. See you later,' and hung up.

However, Wayne Pacelle was happy to express an opinion on the matter: 'The best predictor of future behaviour is past behaviour. If [King] is advocating such an extreme course, trophy hunting Siberian tigers … that's probably the most extreme type of trophy hunting in the world. It's a majestic big cat, nobody eats the meat of these animals. It's one of the rarest animals in the world, facing all sorts of continuing pressures.'

So does Robert Brown see any issue having King, a hunter, on board as a wildlife management scientist? 'That's what he is,' he responds matter-of-factly. 'Dr Cilla Kinross [environmental management lecturer at the University of Sydney's Orange campus, and the Council's second wildlife management scientist], I won't call her an animal rights activist, does that mean she should disqualify herself because of her personal interests? There's no doubt about it, the hunters control the Game Council because it is in the best interests of achieving the aims of the Act to have it so.'

But Andrew Cox, executive officer of the National Parks Association, who has called the Council a 'one-sided, hunter-friendly shooting regime', strongly disagrees: 'I don't believe the best way to do feral animal control is to let hunters run it … we want to make sure in the interests of everybody in NSW that it's being done from a biological and animal welfare point of view, and it's not just solely focused on sport.'

Brown is unfazed by all the fuss. 'The problem I've got with people like the NPA and all the animal liberation groups is that they are more inclined to want to legislate their beliefs to the point where it stops someone else doing what they want,' he says. 'Most of the things that hunters have ever done, I have to say, are defensive things. The Game Act is a defensive position. No doubt about that. It's been done to try and draw a line in the sand and make a stance and say, "We're entitled to do what we want to do, provided we do it within the law."'

*

Despite all the laws in the land, though, some hunters will flout the rules. And as *IS* can reveal, even the most professional hunting outfitters are doing just that. Handgun hunting is outlawed in Australia, yet the popular international big-game hunting website huntingreport.com, 'The Newsletter Serving the Hunter Who Travels', which publishes elite trophy hunters' tales, documents that in October 2000 Paul Dachton, a resident of Saint Augustine, Florida, participated in a then legal handgun hunt for feral pig, goat and banteng with Australian Big Game Safaris, based in the Northern Territory. In June 2002 he followed it up with an illegal handgun hunt at Marble Island, Queensland, with outfitter Kingham Safaris, hunting for deer. Kingham Safaris was an exhibitor at the 2004 SCI Convention in Reno.

Dachton travelled far and wide to hunt with a handgun. In his own words, he leaves 'every three weeks for a hunt'. Records from the *Hunting Report* show that outside his Australian excursions he hunted with a handgun in Argentina in October '99, South Africa in June '01, Spain in December '01 and the US in January '02. His most recent recorded hunt was with a rifle in New Zealand in May and June '03.

According to Dachton's own report about the Marble Island hunt, in which he shot two rusa deer, one sambar deer and one red deer, the highlight of the trip was 'Taking all game with a handgun. All should be #1 [trophy ranking] with a handgun. Two should be top 5 overall.'

When *IS* contacted Dachton while he was on holiday in Georgia in the southern US in late December '03, he admitted he had never had a problem using a handgun in Australia. But after the issue of the Kingham Safaris hunt was raised, he clammed up: 'I'm not going to give information out about any of my hunts ... any information as far as hunting in Australia like that, I'm not talking [and not giving out] any information about it.'

Dachton did say, however, that he planned to return to Australia this year. 'I'm well aware of what the laws are,' he said, but would not comment about whether he intended to use a handgun in Australia again.

Andrew Webster of Kingham Safaris was more forthcoming to *IS*, but similarly shaken by our line of questioning. Webster said the type of handgun used by Dachton, a client, was 'single shot, with a scope on them; they're high calibre but I think on the danger scale they're fairly limited' and claimed that its use by the American hunter had been lawful.

'There's a few licenses you can get to use a handgun … I'm just going off the top of my head here,' he began. 'We've got primary producers' permits. If you're helping someone in primary production, you can use their handgun in Queensland. What [the government did] to limit the number of licenses, with a family, they wanted to limit one to a property – yourself, or your family, or people helping out on the property can use them as well.'

Webster said Kingham Safaris 'don't encourage' handgun hunting and 'don't advertise it … it's a very rare occurrence', but that the Floridian's handgun hunt was for 'management purposes … our main business is all rifle shooting, so it has happened once. We don't encourage it, because the circumstances in which you can do it are fairly limited.'

However, Mike Crowley, acting inspector for Queensland Police's Weapons Licensing Branch, confirmed to *IS* that handgun hunting was outlawed in his state – 'It doesn't happen. Banned.' – and any use of a handgun by a foreign tourist was illegal under Section 54 of the *Weapons Act 1990*. The only primary producers allowed to use handguns are agents (managers of the properties), employees or members of primary producers' immediate families.

'People try to put their own interpretation on things,' he says, of Webster's defence. 'The only person who can interpret the legislation to determine whether they are meeting that requirement or not, is a magistrate … an overseas person is not eligible to obtain a licence here. Therefore they don't fall within the criteria to start with.'

*

One of the most confounding aspects of the hunting movement is that it doesn't seem to know what it stands for. While groups like SCI talk of conservation and wildlife management, other hunters speak of their civic duty to hunt. Then there are those who paint hunting as an economic cure-all for impoverished indigenous people, a means of spiritual enlightenment, a vocation, a sport, a provider of food, or, as is now the vogue, an expression of repressed Anglo-Celtic culture.

Whatever it is, one thing is certain: hunting cannot be sold to the general public on its own terms – killing for pleasure – and hunters know it. They will use whatever excuse they can, whenever it is available, to legitimise and defend a pursuit that to many is indefensible.

But do hunters need an excuse? Is the problem not with them but the hypocrisy of people who happily buy KFC or Red Rooster products made from broiler chickens, yet wave their fists in outrage at the sight of a stuffed head on a wall? Or with lawmakers who decree that it's OK to kill an animal with a rifle, bow or harpoon, but not with a handgun? There are no easy explanations. Says Robert Brown, cutting through the subterfuge: 'Every hunter does it for enjoyment. Is there anything wrong with enjoyment?'

If only we could talk to the animals. Then we might just have the answer.

Inside Sport, March 2004

SMOKE ON THE WATER

Carl Hammerschmidt

They've tried and died. World records are set to be broken and Ken Warby, the fastest man on water, wishes someone would break his – or at least that the men who give it a go stop killing themselves in the process.

In 1978 Warby out-thought and out-muscled physics to set the world water speed record of 317.6 mph (511.11 km/h) in his jet-powered hydroplane, *Spirit of Australia*. It was on the Blowering Dam in southwest NSW. He blasted through the magic 300 mph mark. He smashed the previous record. No other man has gone there and lived.

'When you've got an 80 per cent death rate, you don't exactly get people lining up to have a go at it,' says the low-key 64-year-old.

Those that did – Lee Taylor Jnr on Lake Tahoe, California, in 1980 and Craig Arfons on Lake Jackson, Florida, in 1989 – died, airborne, somewhere approaching half the speed of sound, in a shower of exploding water and disintegrating machinery. They were spectacular and grim ends in a discipline with a spectacular and grim history.

The two decades before that were owned by legendary Brit Donald Campbell. He cheated death in his iconic *Bluebird* by breaking the record seven times between 1955 and 1964 (as well as the land speed record). That was before his luck ran out one glassy morning in 1967 on Coniston Water in the British lakes district when his boat left the water in what has become one of the most examined maritime accidents next to the *Titanic*.

Before Campbell, three other men of resolve and ambition died hoping to be called the 'fastest man on water'. One was Henry Segrave who, in 1930, in *Miss England II*, tried to top 100 mph (160.9 km/h) and hit a submerged log. In 1941 another Pom, John Cobb, hit the 200 mph (321.8 km/h) mark on his first run, but crashed and died on the mandatory second. Previous holders and contenders have included inventor Alexander Graham Bell and professional soldier and adventurer Thomas Edward Lawrence – aka Lawrence of Arabia.

'Over the years, I have desperately wanted someone to break the record. That way we would have something to strive for again,' says Warby. But instead, 25 years later, on the anniversary of his achievement, Warby has naught else to hit out for but his own benchmark. So he's going to make an heirloom out of it.

When *SoA* flies again, it's going to be a father-son double-act.

In a tradition of homespun powerboat mechanics and design that makes him unique in the world of speed records, Warby Snr has built *SoA II* himself – just as he did with the original boat. His son David is going to drive it.

'I was 10 when dad set the record,' says the 34-year-old social worker and champion powerboat racer from Newcastle. 'The boat was always in the backyard. It wasn't any different to your dad owning a truck. As a kid, when you see your father do something like that, it's what you want to do.'

*

A sense of occasion is one reason for the Warbys' second tilt at the record. Another is the two rival teams – one American, one British – that are both talking loud about taking the record home 'where it belongs'. They have daredevil drivers, huge technical teams, impressive websites and big corporate backing. Both teams, however, are yet to build a boat.

Nigel Macknight is the ex-aviation and motoring journo at the controls for the British *Quicksilver* team. With what appears to be a sense of duty to the Empire's proud history of great feats, he plans to hit the 400 mph (643.6 km/h) mark back on Coniston Water.

'There's unfinished business at Coniston,' the 48-year-old told the BBC during a press spree for the launch of the *Quicksilver* attempt in 2001. He was referring to Campbell, whose headless torso was only pulled from the bottom of the lake and given a decent burial in the past 12 months. He came up when they raised his boat's wreckage.

'We are making the risks more acceptable by applying modern technology to the age-old problem of going quickly on water,' Macknight said about his craft, which looks like a cross between a top-fuel dragster and a *Star Wars* X-Wing fighter.

Chief designer for *Quicksilver* is Ken Norris, who co-designed Campbell's *Bluebird*. In 2001 they were claiming the boat – or models of the design – had undergone years of extensive development, including wind tunnel and water tank tests, and computer simulations.

Two years on, team *Quicksilver* still talks of the great achievements to come, but work is yet to commence on building the actual boat.

'If Campbell had modern technology it would have saved him,' Macknight said. 'Sensors would have warned him that the boat was close to taking off. A speed of 300 mph is borderline. If we're to get to the next level we have to understand what happens at the interface between water and air.'

A man who believes he knows more about the 'interface between air and water' than most is Russ Wicks. Wicks is the face of, voice for, and driving force behind the Seattle-based *American Challenge* team.

The 40-year-old grew up on a farm and raced motocross in his youth. He became a fully sponsored professional by 15, good enough to become a factory rider for Honda. He attended race-car driving school in France. As a result, he has driven for Formula 2000, Formula Super Vee and Indy Car teams.

On 15 June 2000, after only two weeks driving hydroplane powerboats, he got behind the controls of *Miss Freei* and set the world record for a propeller-driven boat: 205.494 mph (330 km/h). The Warbys claim he promoted himself as the fastest man on water, until it was pointed out that he hadn't done anything to quantify that statement. He now refers to himself as a 'world speed record holder'.

Wicks made a fortune in marketing during the internet boom. He offers his services as a corporate speaker and says the *American Challenge* team has 'a team of engineers and scientists who are experienced leaders in both aerospace and marine technology'. It was sheer force of cash and self-promotion that got Wicks behind the wheel of *Miss Freei* (Freei was a Seattle-based free internet service making $150 million a year). He bases himself out of the home of an IT millionaire and markets himself not just as a water-speed record aspirant, but as a one-man speed record-breaking juggernaut.

Both Wicks's and Macknight's teams expect to burn through around A$10 million on their record attempts. Space age technology and computer modelling doesn't come cheap, especially when you hire the best people in the biz. With those overheads, the two teams seem as focused on business and sponsorship platforms as they are on making boats that go fast. The fact is that while they may be going for one of the heaviest achievements a man can chase down, they still have a hard time raising a fraction of the dough generated by, say, an average Indy Car team.

*

As far as speed records go, there are only two that count: the fastest man on water, and the fastest man on land. Anything else is B-grade. But for all the extreme sports glamour these records would seem to have in an X Games, go-fast fizzy-drink world, where a man's sporting achievements are often measured by how hard he falls, Ken Warby's story had humble beginnings: in the coal town of Newcastle, NSW, where he grew up, and later, the backyard of his home in Concord in Sydney's inner-west.

That was where Ken built the original *SoA* – once he'd designed it on the kitchen table. It had been a long time in the making. Ken decided to break the record when he was 13. His hero was Donald Campbell. He built his first speedboat when he was 16. His father was a truck driver. *SoA* took eight years to build. The second-hand jet engine cost $65. Without sponsorship, it cost around 10 grand all up.

He sold bush landscape oil paintings in the local shopping mall to support his family. 'The first boat, I sat down on a Saturday night with a pencil and a piece of paper and I designed it on the kitchen table,' Ken says. 'I had three kids and a rented home and the boat was built in the backyard under a tree.'

He broke the world record for the first time on 20 November, 1977, on Blowering Dam. On that occasion he reached 288.60 mph (464.35 km/h). He often slept in his car instead of a motel in between a day's runs in order to save money. When he broke the record it was indeed, he says, a childhood dream come true – which is probably the most romantic thing you will ever hear the practical Warby Snr say.

'It took us a couple of years to get the first record,' he says.

'The main reason was because there was no money. On the first boat we had the whole of the jet engine hanging out in the breeze and my head three feet in front of the intake. As money became available we kept adding pieces to the boat.'

On the back of the first record, swimwear company Speedo gave Ken $30,000 to do it again. He did, less than 10 months later, in his red one-piece racing suit, with his full, orange beard hanging 'out in the breeze' underneath his crash helmet's visor. David, the youngest of his sons, wasn't there to witness it 'just in case something happened'.

The Queen gave Ken an MBE. The federal government gave him $140,000 to take *SoA* to the States to showcase Australian technology. There he met drag racer Craig Arfons. They started building and running funny cars together. Ken decided to stay. He has lived in Cincinnati, Ohio, for around 20 years.

SoA lives in the Australian Maritime Museum at Darling Harbour, Sydney. Warby is proud of his place in history. He's confident in his hands-on approach, and has never been backwards in sharing his thoughts about rivals. He says he pointed out the flaws in Arfons's boat before the fatal attempt in '89, and predicted his death 'to his face'. The two were friends; but there's no love lost between Wicks and Warby. Both go out of their way to backhand each other's approach. Warby, Wicks says, is living in the past. Wicks, Warby says, is a 'media whore' with a flashy website and a lot of computer programs, none of which will make up for lack of experience and a boat you have built, yourself, from scratch.

*

Ken Warby and Russ Wicks, though, agree on one thing. That is, 'it's all about building a better mouse trap,' as Warby puts it. They just have exceptionally different ways of doing it. 'American Challenge Inc. is using the latest computerised design, simulation and manufacturing processes,' says Wicks. 'The craft will utilise an augmented stability and control system and be manufactured of the best materials available.'

Advising in the design of Wicks's boat is an ex-director of

technical affairs at Boeing, a United Airlines pilot and a US Navy engineer. They use sophisticated design software on secure web networks, which can test for structural strength and aerodynamic efficiency.

When running across the water, on-board computers and sensors will monitor Wicks's progress, and help make the delicate adjustments required at 300 mph. Asked how he can place ultimate faith in a piece of machinery, Wicks says, 'My faith isn't and never has been solely with a piece of machinery; it is with the process. The people involved in this project have done many record attempts, and flight test programs of new aircraft. I'll be strapped into an ejection seat, which has proven reliable in conditions similar to ours. This is maybe more calculated than you think.' Asked when he thinks he might have a boat, he says, 'Those decisions have not been made yet. Once the engineers are satisfied with the validation of the design per our performance and safety goals and the manufacturing process is completed.'

The manufacturing process for *SoA II* happened in Ken's backyard, again – this time in Cincinnati. It took six years and cost around A$250,000. The rudder assembly on *SoA II* alone cost more than the last boat in total, although Warby says he'd rather not think about the cost. He still has no major sponsors. 'My name's not Thorpe,' he laments.

The boat is designed and based on the original *Spirit*. 'The first boat was a learning curve,' he says. 'This is the next generation.' *SoA II* has 50 per cent more power than the original. That had 6000 hp. *SoA II* has that plus an afterburner, should they need it, which delivers 9000 hp all up. It is partly constructed of wood.

Ken believes it can do well over 400 mph (643.6 km/h), which is what he'll be telling the world this October when the boat is shipped out to Australia for unveiling on the anniversary of the record. In 2004, they'll begin trials on Blowering Dam, assuming it's above its current capacity of one per cent.

All things going to plan, they'll have a new record towards the end of next year. Then, with the war of words being academic, it will be the job of the two other teams to chase it.

'You have to have a lot of faith in your ability and your designs. The old boat, when I first put pencil to paper, it was my dream. It came true because I had faith in it,' Ken says, in probably the second most romantic thing you'll ever hear him say. If nothing else, it's all about faith. It's just a matter of where it's placed. If the *American Challenge* crew sees the Warbys as a Dad's Army collective, then Russ Wicks must surely be Roger Ramjet. His website talks about 'elevating American patriotism' and showcasing 'our country's leadership in aerospace and high technology'. He compares his endeavours to those that put Neil Armstrong on the moon.

If you don't have computerised simulation, Wicks says, you are not in the game. Warby's reply: if you are going to rely on a computer rather than feel and intuition to tell you how to drive a boat at 600 km/h, you're in the wrong game.

The rules of this game are simple. The boat builds up pace over a five-kilometre stretch of water. It's then clocked through a 'flying kilometre'. Once top speed has been hit, it takes another five kilometres to slow down. The boat is then refuelled (at full throttle it uses about a gallon per second), the water surface is left to settle and the drivers have an hour to turn around and do it again. Easily said. The land speed record stands at 763 mph (1227.6 km/h), yet the water record is only a third of that. The problem is water is 800 times denser than air, and it moves. To travel through it quickly, drag must be minimised.

This is achieved by getting the boat up on the plane (hydroplane), leaving as little of it in contact with the water as possible. On *SoA II*, Ken says, this will be 'three areas about the size of a dinner plate'.

Even with this amount of contact, to double speed, thrust must increase by a factor of eight. This means the boat literally flies across the water, making the aerodynamics touch and go. Too much downward pressure with foils and weighting causes the water to push the boat back up. Too little and it takes off. Either way, air gets under, the boat gets airborne and the driver dies.

*

Ultimate truths make men philosophical, and David Warby is as quietly reflective as his father. 'When you've been around speedboating for a while, you realise that unfortunately people get hurt and killed,' he says. 'I've learned to accept it, but obviously come record day, you're going where no man has ever gone. Hopefully everything you've done in practice and theory, and all the knowledge you bring to the boat, well, that's the test.'

The guys that get killed, he says, aren't really into boat racing: 'They get other people to design their boats and then learn to drive them and try to sort the problems out from there.'

He's referring to Wicks, who, in appraising the Warbys' attempt next year, says, 'We believe that modern technology is required to minimise the risk while moving the barrier forward. Logically, you would expect the evolution of a proven design, even if developed in a backyard such as Warby's, to make at least a small gain. I don't know much about David or his abilities, though. My understanding is that a majority of his motor sport experience is racing model boats. To be honest, I'm not sure what to think of that, and it's not my call.'

Like his father, David is not afraid to return serve. And like the old man, he's confident. Both also trust what they know. 'If you have a background in boat racing, you've got a feel,' he says. 'You know how to sort a boat out on water. When a boat starts to react in certain ways, you can relate that back to a circuit racing boat. 'These guys put blind faith into boats that look good on paper, but they are way out. They're putting their lives on the line to prove their design, when the main design process should come from when you get in a boat and drive it.'

'Warby has been the record holder for a quarter of a century,' Wicks counters. 'I wish him the best, and respect his past accomplishments. Statistics, however, show that four out of five that have attempted the record have perished. I am not going to be the one to predict someone's demise, but Ken has done so with regard to all other challengers.'

When the sum of the risks are put to Ken Warby – about how his son's mortality will rely entirely on the boat he has built – he is as laconic as always. 'Dave has always been nuts over hydroplanes. It's always been a given that he'll go for the record,' he says. 'People say, "Why do you let him?" Well, my answer is, "How do you stop him?"'

'I'm sure that come record day any parent would have nerves in their stomach,' David says. 'It's the ultimate test in his design. Not only did he build the boat, but he built the driver.'

And in 2004, it will all go on the line, flying, at well over half the speed of sound.

Inside Sport, October 2003

WET WET WET

Liquid substances have had a lot to do with Australian sport. We look at some of the different applications. Carl Hammerschmidt studies the uneasy relationship between soul surfers and their commercial confrères, Peter Lalor analyses Boonie and beer, Leisa Scott goes sailing, Richard Yallop takes an acrobatic look at Alisa Camplin and snow, and Will Swanton goes the whole hog.

SOLD TO SOUL

Carl Hammerschmidt

Fight a war or surf. As choices go, it wasn't that simple. In 1970 Wayne Lynch was the golden-haired child of Australian surfing. For the preceding four years he'd been national junior champion. As a boy in his late-teens he was carving a new future for the sport. On the long, heavy boards of the time, no one had ever managed his power turns from the base of the wave to the lip, or put them together in such killer combinations.

When people watched the fisherman's son surf his home breaks around Lorne on Victoria's west coast, they felt like history was being made. In 1969 he starred in a film, *Evolution*, with Nat Young to document the future of surfing. The vibe around the guy was electric.

At the turn of the decade, Lynch was odds-on expected to win the world title. He was also expected to go to Vietnam. Lynch had heard the horror stories. He had friends who were killed over there. Like many, he thought the war was a con. He was also sick of endless competition surfing that didn't provide anywhere near enough money to live on.

In 1970 Lynch turned his back on the chance to officially be called the best surfer in the world and fell off the map. To avoid national service he went walkabout in the remote south-west of Australia; living rough in the bush, staying out of sight and off the radar, exploring, riding powerful swell pushed up by the Southern Ocean at spots that had never been ridden. No contests. No photographers. Not even any other surfers. He didn't re-emerge for five years.

*

It was only a couple of years ago, and, as choices go, there wasn't one to make. Pro surfer Craig 'Warto' Warton was at the World Championship Tour (WCT) event at Bells Beach when he was asked to go on a trip. He wasn't competing. Warto gets paid handsomely by Quiksilver – the biggest surf company in the world – not to compete. It works out well because Warto hates competitions.

Warto was at Bells doing promotional duties – such as signing magazines that carry photos of him flying through the air eight feet above a wave like few other surfers can. It's Warto's job to be photographed pushing the limits of what surfers can do. The easygoing bloke from Byron Bay represents a cutting edge of surfing that helps his employer sell product. All grommets want to shred like Warto.

Quiksilver's marketing manager asked Warto if he had a passport. He was told to be at the airport in a couple of days. Quiksilver wanted him on a two-week surf safari through the Mentawai Islands, an isolated archipelago in Sumatra, Indonesia, with perfect reef breaks. All Warto had to do was pack his bag and show up. Quiksilver would take care of the rest.

Within 24 hours of boarding the plane, Warto was on a 150 foot, purpose-designed charter boat surfing killer waves. There was a photographer on board. Warto just had to paddle out and shred. One of the boat's crew was a cook. At the end of a day's work, Warto remembers with joy and disbelief, he would paddle back in, sit on the deck, have a beer, and watch the waves roll in while someone made his dinner.

Despite the trimmings, Lynch, 52, and Warton, 26, represent the same thing to different generations of surfers. They both turned their back on competitive surfing. They both place surf exploration in remote places above a world ranking. They're both known for pushing the limits of what a surfer can do on a board. In a sport that considers itself a way of life before anything else, they both represent one of its most slippery yet important concepts. Even though Lynch and Warton would never refer to themselves as such, they are 'soul surfers'.

The difference in their circumstances is an indication of how far their sport has come in 30 years. Lynch is seen as a template for the concept. His reputation came from the time when the phrase was invented, a radical time of social change in the post-hippy, wild and woolly '70s when competition surfing for money was a new phenomenon.

'Pro surfing got its start in the early '70s, and there was a real split between surfing for money and because it was important for you spiritually,' says surf commentator and journalist Nick Carroll. 'There was this big debate about whether it was cool to be a competitive surfer or whether that wasn't true to the spirit of the sport.'

Lynch did what he did out of necessity, circumstance and 'because I had so many other things going on in my life', not because he thought it was good for him spiritually. Somehow, though, Lynch is held up as the soul man's soul man from a time when waves were supposed to be uncrowded and everything was pure.

Warton doesn't chase spiritual enlightenment either. In fact he was told by Quiksilver that if he pursued competition surfing, they wouldn't sponsor him. Warton's reputation as a soul surfer has been developed in an era when WCT competitions are a staple for nightly news reports like any tennis or golf grand slam. The sport's champions are supernova celebrities and the public face of companies like Quiksilver and Billabong, which are listed on the stock exchange and share in a 'surfing lifestyle' fashion and equipment market worth $20 billion a year worldwide.

Few other pastimes have come as far as fast in the last 35 years, both in terms of being a professional sport and a desirable lifestyle all over the world. However, along with that fast expansion there was also a whole world of growing pains, and those pains have always been centred on the contradiction between the constraints of professional competition, and the promises of a lifestyle based around nature, escape and freedom.

Surfing's core attraction has always been its major philosophical problem. That's why, since the late '60s, when money first started to flow into the sport, it has wrestled with the concept of its soul. And now it seems that as the sport gets bigger, richer and more powerful than ever, it needs that concept, and the surfers that represent it, more than ever.

One constant in surfing is that no one can tell you what soul surfing is. The closest thing to a definition you'll get is that it's the surfing that happens when people do it for their own reasons.

'Soul surfing is the indefinable addiction people have for catching waves,' says Jimmy O'Keefe, editor of *Australian Surfing Life*. 'It's a word used to describe the rush you get the first time you stand up and the feeling that you'll do it for the rest of your life.'

'It's just that biological urge to go surfing – screw everything else – and just doing it for the sake of surfing,' says Sean Doherty, editor of *Tracks* magazine. 'It's what 99.9 per cent of surfers do. It's just that, for want of a marketing term, it's had that soul surfing tag thrown on it.'

When that gets broken down even further, soul surfing becomes a term for all the surfing done outside competitions. It is also something that everyone is passionate about – and every surfer thinks exists. As a catch-all phrase, and something every surfer believes in, soul surfing is a very powerful marketing tool.

'One thing that has really crept up in the sport over the last seven or eight years is the marketing of the idea of soul in surfing,' says Carroll. 'I've found it a little bit offensive. It's ironic that the image of the soul surfer, or the soul of surfing, should be used as a marketing tool when really it should be the opposite.'

The rise of 'soul' in the marketing of surfing has been in conjunction with another phenomenon – the cult of the 'free surfer', or as Doherty puts it, 'the paid free surfer'.

'They're in the mags, in the videos, but never set foot on the tour,' says Doherty. 'The big companies all have guys that are on the books to generate photos, just go surfing and push the brands in ways other than contests.'

The free surfer epitomises the surfing lifestyle promise of free-wheeling individuality. They are portrayed as surfers in the traditional sense – outsiders who live by their own rhythms. They highlight the fact that every wave is different, and no two surfers will ride it the same. They also live the dream of being paid to traipse the world, surfing perfect waves.

The other major point is that free surfers are not part of the army of 44 surfers that march around the globe together from contest to contest, from heat to heat, all fighting over the same three winner's cheques. In short, free surfers help the industry overcome the problem of trying to use a guarantee of unique-ness to sell the same 100,000 pairs of board shorts.

'Not everyone aspires to be a professional surfer,' says Garry Wall, the national marketing manager for Quiksilver. 'Most people enjoy driving down the coast with their mates. [Soul surfing] is very much a part of our whole campaign of making people connect with our surfers and our product. Not every-thing is about being the best and winning the race.'

'The companies which make a lot of money out of surfing require people who make them look good,' says Carroll, 'and sometimes competitive surfers make the companies look com-petitive and gnarly and scary – or unpleasant somehow – because they want to compete and win.'

The sporting professional who is unattractive because they win is a strange concept, but it exists in surfing. If you are a race-car driver, it's cool to win a Grand Prix. If you are a footballer, it's cool to win a premiership. The difference comes with the fact that a surfer faces up to Mother Nature first, and other people second. When you place the science of winning against the weather, the ocean and physics, it becomes slightly intangible and in purists' eyes, something that can't be measured.

Carroll's brother Tom won the world title twice, in '83 and '84, at a time when competitive professional surfing was working hardest for acceptance by the public. He was also the first surfer to sign a sponsorship deal worth $1 million.

'Recently there has been a certain rejection of competitive surfing by the public,' he tells *IS*. 'As a professional surfer – especially one who got pushed a lot during the '80s – I have been sensitive to that, especially growing up in the '70s. Surfing is a vibrant competitive industry now, and companies have to pick up on all sorts of feelings to survive in that. The problem is that someone can quite easily call themselves "soul" and stand on this pedestal and look down on the world.

'Image is more important in the marketing of surfing than it has ever been. There are elements of hypocrisy going on at the moment. Imagine saying this is soulful and that isn't. It's lame beyond comprehension. If surfing somehow touches you in your heart – which it does and every surfer knows it – how can you say one surfer is OK and one isn't?'

The hit surf film of last summer was Jack McCoy's *Blue Horizons*. It's a big-budget project made by surfing's best cinematographer. The tag line is 'Two paths ... one journey'. It's a story about two surfers: two-time and current world champion from Hawaii, Andy Irons, and soul surfing's pin-up boy of the moment, the free-surfing Aussie David Rastovich. Both are Team Billabong surfers and by contrasting them, *Blue Horizons* is a parable of how modern surf marketing works.

'The average surfer would have come away from that film thinking, "Gee, that Andy Irons is a bit of a dickhead. He's just a heavy competitive guy out to get the bucks,"' notes Nick Carroll. 'Whereas Rasta is supposed to be cool as a cucumber and really in touch with the true meaning of surfing.'

With these two polarities, surfing's obligations are fulfilled – the need for it to be a grown-up professional sport, and the need for it to be free. The problem is, of course, that those who know Irons will tell you he is one of the greatest soul surfers because he lives and breathes the sport, and in the general scheme of things only spends five per cent of his time in the water competing. You also then have to ask how a guy who is not supposed to be competitive gets to be the highest paid free surfer in the world.

The consensus in the industry is that Rasta is on an annual salary with Billabong that approaches $500,000. It's been suggested it could be more. Certainly guys in the top half of the WCT earn much more than half a million a year, even if in all of the 12 events that make up the tour for a year, first, second and third places only earn US$30,000, US$16,000 and US$10,000 respectively.

In 2001–02 Taj Burrow was the only surfer to make the BRW 50 Richest Sportspeople list. He came in at 31 with an annual earn of $1.5 million, and would easily rank as Australia's highest paid surfer, but it's hard to be certain, because surf companies hate people knowing how much their surfers earn.

'They believe it will distance the stars from the average surfer,' says Jimmy O'Keefe. 'Surfers like to pretend they are not starstruck.'

Unlike soccer, where a player's market value is almost better known than his shirt number, surf companies go to great lengths to conceal sponsorship deals and few people in the industry are willing to speculate on the record.

'We pay purely what the athlete is worth in the market and what the athlete is worth to Quiksilver,' says Garry Wall. '[Signing surfers] is like a footy team: you can't have all ruckmen or wingmen, you have to have a balance – soul, aerial, tow-in, WCT ... it's a balancing act and it's a crowded market and getting harder and harder to find the right kids.'

Wall believes the market has dictated the rise of the free surfer, and that their numbers and pay packets will continue to grow. He notes that in the '80s surfing contests were held at beaches that would attract the biggest crowds but had the shittiest surf. At the time, all surfing aspiration was directed to the WCT format and eventually the public got bored with it.

With the advent of internet streaming and a more intense media coverage, the WCT realised that the better the surf, the more airtime it would get, so now the events are held at blue-riband spots like South Africa's Jeffreys Bay, Teahupoo in Tahiti, Tavarua in Fiji and Mundaka in Spain.

'The guys on the WCT are the most fortunate soul surfers ever,' says former world champion and now president of the Association of Surfing Professionals (ASP) Wayne 'Rabbit' Bartholomew. 'They have 12 commitments for the year, in the best surf locations – and that's all they do. If that ain't soul surfing, then what is?'

Despite the rise of the free surfer, there is still no doubt that the world's best surfers appear on the world tour – for the sheer fact that it is still the best paid gig in professional surfing, and there have been some massive increases in prize money over the last few years.

'About five years ago, when Kelly Slater dropped out of the tour for a couple of years, it lacked some credibility,' Doherty says, 'purely because he was the best surfer that ever lived. But with him back, 95 per cent of the world's best surfers are there now.'

Ross Clarke-Jones hasn't surfed in a WCT competition since 1992, but he is still one of the best known surfers in the world. Clarke-Jones is a pioneer of big-wave tow-in surfing, and one of the best. He is one of the world's most watched surfers purely for the shit-meets-pants nature of his discipline. The three or four truly standout days the elite tow-in guys manage each year get shown in all mainstream media, and that's why his sponsors pay him.

'I am a soul surfer because I surf for the love of it,' says Clarke-Jones. 'Fortunately I get paid for it and it is my job, career, business … but I ride big waves because I enjoy doing it – for personal reasons.'

In recent years big-wave surfing has been getting even more exposure for the six-figure bounties being offered for the biggest wave of the year and while Clarke-Jones agrees that it makes things more 'gladiatorial', as a surfer, it messes with his focus and ability to excel.

'That's when it starts to affect your soul,' says Clarke-Jones. 'It changes the reason you're doing it. All of a sudden you're trying to get the biggest wave for money. You're going for the wrong reasons. You have really got to go for that wave because you want to ride it. There's enough danger in it – you have to be sharp, and focused on the right reasons.'

*

In 1968 surfing in Australia went feral – for all the right reasons. Surfboards went from being nine-foot planks for cruising to six-foot jets for fast top-to-bottom carving. At the same time, surfing aligned itself with the counter-culture of the day and marked itself as a subversive activity.

Coming out of the hippy movement, it was a time when youth sub-culture was exploding worldwide, and it was an unprecedented period of expression. It was then that surfing, in the eyes of the media and the public, became a statement.

That statement was all about turning your back on the city and taking up country living. Commercialism was fake. Nature was real. The look was long hair, and the MO was endless searches for perfect waves in Kombi vans. Everything was tinged with an air of psychedelia.

This was where the idea of soul surfing started. It was also a time that produced the Big Three companies – Billabong, Quiksilver and Rip Curl – that would eventually go on to shape the sport worldwide into a multibillion-dollar industry.

'[Soul surfing] is an incredibly important part of our company,' says Doug Warbrick, co-founder of Rip Curl. 'We have a set of core ideologies, our company values and principles, by which we run our company. In them we talk of "The Search". That's what we call soul surfing. We believe it is the fundamental reason for the creation of Rip Curl.

'We've always been true believers in adventure surfing, travelling a little bit further to find that uncrowded wave … that's at the core of our existence. They're the reasons Brian [Singer] and I started the company. We were doing two or three fundamental things, trying to make enough to stay in the surfing lifestyle.'

To men like Warbrick, it's only logical that what he does has translated into commercial success because it's authentic, and surfers will never go past a product that is genuine and authentic.

Warbrick says that 'with respects to the harder-edge side of business', it hasn't been that difficult sticking to the soul-surfing credo. 'As well as our principles and values, we have another set of brand values. They are frequently discussed with all staff members of Rip Curl worldwide. They believe in those ethics and they use them in their daily work.

'We have an extraordinarily high level of surfers in the company. Those philosophies resonate with them and they use them in their daily work. That's why you see the expression of that stuff in our marketing. They are not necessarily contrived marketing plans. They are our true beliefs.'

*

Nostalgia is not authentic. However, 'old' is often confused for 'genuine'.

Like all youth lifestyles, popular music plays a big part in surfing. It provides almost the entire soundtrack to every surf film, and is a great cultural barometer. Right now, the forecast for the culture is 'old' as it embraces a campfire-style of folk music that harks back to an era when Neil Young was king and the sound of an acoustic guitar was a mark of 'honesty'.

This nostalgic yearning started five or six years ago with the emergence of surfer/singer Jack Johnson. Hawaiian Johnson was a sponsored surfer for Quiksilver, but his music career took off when he was spotted by Ben Harper. Then, when it was touted about that Johnson was a good mate of Kelly Slater's, and they often went on surf trips together, jamming on their guitars after sessions, surfing's imprimatur had been given to a style of hippy, organic folk rock last heard in the early '70s.

One of Billabong's high-priority surfers at the moment is Californian Donavon Frankenreiter. Frankenreiter is another tropical troubadour, whose debut album is currently selling truckloads. He's notable for his love of '70s single-fin boards and his caterpillar moustache. The 32-year-old has been a sponsored surfer since he was 13, though he's hardly set the world on fire. In fact, it's arguable whether anyone would have ever heard of him – in the world of surfing or pop music – had he not had the backing of good mate Johnson.

At the moment, however, as part of Team Billabong, Frankenreiter currently sits alongside world champion Andy Irons, long-time legend Mark Occhilupo and arguably the world's most exciting surfer, Taj Burrow.

'The soul pro surfer is now a cliché,' says Nick Carroll. 'He is pretty groovy and got a bit of facial hair. He's got to play a musical instrument. He's au fait with movies of the early '70s like *Morning of the Earth*, and he's got to ride old-school surf equipment to prove he's in touch with his roots. You can tell him in photos because he has got his eyes cast down and he is smiling faintly because he knows there are bigger things going on in the universe.'

'When people look back to the '70s it looks simple and romantic,' says Jimmy O'Keefe. 'But it was just the same fashion thing then that it is now.'

'I've never quite understood the cliché and what they are getting at,' says Wayne Lynch, who, for the last 30 years, has worked as one of Australia's best board shapers. 'It's always seemed to me to be a marketing exercise by magazines if anything.

'I guess what they are getting at is the lifestyle of surfing, and how people incorporate it into their life and not purely as a career and not purely as a sport. Most people don't care about the pro tour – but there is not a single surfer alive that doesn't get inspired by looking at some unbelievable-looking wave in some beautiful place. That's the dream.'

Dreams are spiritual and soulful, and there will always be an element of surfing that will be spiritual and soulful. The fact is, though, if you are a hardcore surf company, that spirit and that soul has to be a very real part of your bottom line.

Inside Sport, July 2004

FIFTY-TWO NOT OUT

Peter Lalor

All sports love a statistic but none more than the summer game. Numbers and averages are as important to cricket as bat and ball. Records stand like Himalayan peaks, pointed reminders to those in the foothills of the heights that others have climbed: Don Bradman's 99.94, Matthew Hayden's 380, Courtney Walsh's 519. Cricketers and cricket tragics know the significance of these numbers and the circumstances in which they were achieved. For many years, there was another figure that taunted Australian cricketers – Doug Walters' 44.

The score can be traced back to Australia's Caribbean tour of 1973. Ian Chappell's team had spent three months compiling a hard-fought two-nil series victory over the West Indies. Walters had had a fine summer, averaging 71 with the bat, knocking up two 100s and three 50s, and bagging 5 for 66 in one outing with the ball. The boy from Dungog was already a legend in Australian sport, as much for his love of ciggies, booze and horses as for his swashbuckling cricket. His mate Rod Marsh had also done well in the Tests, gloving 17 catches behind the stumps and averaging a healthy 49.5 with the bat.

The pair were looking forward to getting home, and while the flight wasn't particularly comfortable – players travelled economy in those days – at least the beer was free. Big drinkers both, they'd worked up a murderous thirst under the Caribbean sun. Walters remembers Marsh turning to him and asking: 'How many cans do you think we'll have before we get to Sydney?'

'That's where it all started,' Walters recalls. 'I said "25." He said, "It's a 30-hour flight – we'll have 35."' The pair set about testing this new method of measuring distance but encountered a serious problem.

'They ran out of beer,' Walters says. 'We had to count spirits and all sorts of things and I don't know what the final tally was.'

Still, a seed had been planted. Word passed around before the team left for the 1977 Ashes tour that the Walters-Marsh drinking experiment had escalated into a full-blown competition. Players, management and journalists were invited to join in. A quarter of a century later, memories are a little clouded by time and the passing of brain cells, but *The Weekend Australian Magazine* has interviewed many of the people who made the trip in an effort to sort fact from folklore.

Rules were drawn up, wagers were laid and the drinking began. Only alcohol consumed in-flight was counted, so anything sunk in the transit lounge was, effectively, a dead ball. Competitors scored one point for a beer, wine or mixed drink, although wine drinkers were looked upon with great suspicion by the egalitarian Australians. In fact, nobody remembers a wine drinker in the competition. The team was in a bullish mood, having beaten the Poms in the Centenary Test three months earlier, while the game itself was about to be shaken by the rise of World Series Cricket and would soon need a stiff drink of its own.

Leg spinner Kerry O'Keeffe, now an ABC commentator, incorporates the story into his public speaking routines. He says bets were taken on everyone except one team manager. 'You were allowed to back yourself, but he drank 24 hours a day and nobody accepted his wager on himself,' O'Keeffe recalls.

While he is shaky on some details, he does remember that the field was well spread even on the first leg. 'Kim Hughes was a runaway leader early. He'd had six spirits when most of us were on three cans of beer, but shall we say he didn't stay the course.' Walters, playing tortoise to the young hare, also recalls the baby-faced West Australian batsman stealing a break. 'I remember Kim being involved and he said "does it have to be beer?" and I said "you can drink whatever you like", and he drank rum and something – not rum and Coke, but rum and ginger or something like that. But he'd had quite a heap to Singapore and I don't think he had another drink for three weeks on that tour.'

Hughes, just 19 at the time, admits with good humour that he might have misjudged his run. 'I was a young bull in those days.

It was my first major tour away for the team and I didn't see Singapore because I got out of the gates early and got my total to 11 or 12 brandy and dries, and collapsed in a heap.

'You got a point for a full beer or the spirits in the little bottles. I was never a beer drinker so I started with a little suggestion of brandy and a fair bit of dry, and pretty quickly it was all brandy and no dry, and that was why I didn't see Singapore. But I was leading the pack by a substantial amount for a very short period of time.'

Hughes regained consciousness while approaching England to find he was not the only casualty. 'I suppose I shouldn't mention his name because it wasn't very flattering and he was an older bloke,' the future captain recalls. 'He was about 60 and he had his blazer on, but he was on the aisle seat and he was asleep and he had his false teeth hanging out with saliva dripping out from the teeth onto the emblem on his pocket. Mate, it wasn't a great sight.' It was a member of the management – the one they wouldn't let bet on himself.

Greg Chappell, Australia's straight-backed captain, tries to downplay the competition as 'a bit of fun that has probably been blown out of proportion over the years'. The health-conscious vegetarian admits he 'had a few' until Singapore but then decided, wisely, to sleep. Walters and Marsh kept drinking and drinking. And drinking.

This was another time, of course – long before the team had fitness advisers or dietary consultants, an epoch of hairy chests and walrus moustaches permanently wet with beer. Neither the players, airline staff nor the general public had heard the words 'responsible service of alcohol', and it is a measure of just how far in-flight service has slipped that no player can recall a problem with getting a drink. 'You wouldn't get that service on a plane now,' Walters laughs. 'Then, every time they walked past Marshy and I they dropped four cans on our thing [service tray]. They were probably the instigators more so than us.'

O'Keeffe waved the white flag at Bahrain, realising he could not keep up with Marsh or Walters. 'Doug dropped back in the pack, knowing he could go the journey,' O'Keeffe says. 'He just ground them down.' Walters confirms this tactic. 'I'm a sipper,' he says.

'I can sip all day and it doesn't have a great effect, but I can't put 'em down at a hundred miles an hour. I'm not a fast drinker.' He does, however, admit to being a 'reasonably' big drinker.

As the plane arrived in London, Walters raised his 44th can to his lips and drained it as though it were his fourth. From all accounts, he wasn't in bad shape – not if you consider he'd had 44 beers at high altitude and a couple of unofficial palate cleansers during the stopovers. 'He was all right – just,' says O'Keeffe. 'He was lighting cigarettes filter-first. I guess that's all right. You can do that sober.'

Marsh's score is a mystery. Dennis Lillee, who had injured his back in the Centenary Test and was not on that tour, recalls the wicket-keeper claiming he had gone can-for-can with Walters. Sadly for Marsh, no one recognises his efforts, and it was Walters – the boy burdened in 1965 with the mantle 'the next Don Bradman' – who claimed a title that has defined his years in cricket more than any particular innings or series. Even now he is asked more about the 44 cans than his famous 100 at Perth, a tonne notched up in a single session and crowned with a six off the last ball. 'If it's not the first question I'm asked, it's the second,' Walters says. Does it bother him? 'Not really. I enjoy life, mate. I think you're dead a long while – that's what I was told and I haven't seen any proof of that not being right.'

Of course, no in-flight drinking record is complete without a successful re-entry. All witnesses report that Walters and company were drunk, but did not disgrace themselves. 'We visited the bar when we arrived, I think,' says Walters. 'We had a press reception at the hotel when we arrived there.' They did, and memories of the Australians' performance vary widely. 'I've got to say that the press conference, with Fleet Street hovering, was pathetic,' says O'Keeffe. 'It was not the best press conference held, not with the inebriation that was around, but they didn't pick up on it too much.'

Veteran cricket writer Alan Shiell, who thinks he tallied 38 cans on the flight, recalls arriving in London. 'I know Marshy and Doug were pretty much the worse for wear at the press conference at the Waldorf late that morning. We had some big nights on that trip – you're talking about some exceptional characters and some exceptional drinkers in Marshy and Dougie.'

Hughes remembers arriving. 'I had sobered up and we were being introduced at the Waldorf and everyone was pretty excited, but we had to hide Walters and Marsh because they had just kept going. We could hear during the introductions "Hear hear, Chappell", and it was Marsh and Walters up the back, still having a quiet beer. We tried to keep them quiet, but they made the odd noise.'

And how did Walters perform on tour? '1977? It was my worst. Oh, no it wasn't – '72 was my worst. Well, I didn't have any real good tours of England anyway.'

Well, none that he remembers. In fact, Walters managed a half-century in each of the first two Tests but came away with an average of only 25, and the Australians flew home with tails between their legs having been thumped three-nil. Kim Hughes debuted in the final Test but made only one run.

*

Cricket is a slow game that rewards patience, and so it was that Rodney Marsh returned to Australia nurturing a grudge, but knowing that his time would come. He was six years waiting. The 'keeper has kept his silence on the 1983 flight to London, but his good mate Lillee has recorded it – twice – in his autobiographies. In 1984's *Over and Out*, Lillee says that 'second best was not good enough for Rodney', who announced to his teammates well before they left for the World Cup that he was going to beat 44.

Surprisingly, the fast bowler decided to sabotage the attempt. 'I didn't want him watching the World Cup series on television in the drying-out ward of some London hospital,' Lillee writes. Rather than try to convince Marsh of the benefits of moderation, Lillee used the wiles that made him a great bowler long after his pace had left him. He started egging on Marsh to drink before they left Perth to join the team in Sydney. They stopped off in

Melbourne for a few more at a Qantas cocktail party, then flew north and hit the town. Lillee sacrificed his own health to save his mate's and despite a roaring hangover he pushed Marsh to have three shaky schooners at the airport next morning. But it wasn't enough to stop the determined Sandgroper.

The Australian cricket team had taken on a more professional air by 1983 and a lot of planning went into the record attempt. Somebody worked out that it was a 24-hour flight with three legs – Sydney–Singapore, Singapore–Bahrain, Bahrain–London. Marsh would have to consume 15 cans a leg. Lillee didn't think Marsh had a hope, but the little wicketkeeper hopped into it, warning the hostess of his intentions the moment they sat down. 'You drink them, I'll bring them,' she reportedly replied.

Fast bowler Geoff Lawson was part of the team despite the fact he did not drink. 'I have a fairly clear recollection about it,' he says. 'The announcement was made before we got to the airport. I was the official scorer. I wrote down the brand and the size on the back of a sick bag.'

Lawson confirms Marsh had three at Sydney airport. 'He said that you warm up before you play, so you've got to warm up before one of these things, and he had a couple more in Singapore and they weren't counted either.' Lawson has another remarkable revelation: 'Marshy slept from Singapore to Bahrain – he slept the whole leg.'

Lillee contradicts this and says it was he who slept from Singapore to Bahrain, 'and to my horror I awoke to find Rodney draining the drops of can number 30'. The fast bowler says Graeme Wood was the official scorer and Marsh slept only during the stopover. Wood confirms he was the scorer, perhaps with help from Lawson, and says Marsh kept drinking throughout the flight except for two 20-minute naps. Lawson remembers that, to make the trip more comfortable, the pace-setters and the scorer moved from their seats. 'In '83 – I'm pretty sure it was '83 – we actually went downstairs in the plane. We got in the service lift and went down into the cargo hold. I can distinctly remember Rod drinking there. It was like a storeroom and we were surrounded by beer, and you just had to reach out and grab 'em from the shelf, basically. I remember because the roof of it was six foot tall and, with me being six foot four [198 centimetres], I couldn't quite stand up.'

By this stage, the whole plane was aware of what was happening courtesy of an announcement by the captain – a point confirmed by Lawson and Lillee, although everybody is keen to point out that this was 'a quiet drink' between mates. 'It wasn't a big deal,' says Lawson. 'I think if anything had got out of control, a lot of people would have disapproved, but it never did, you know. There was no rowdiness or anything. It was just a quiet drink and a chat, you know.'

Marsh's 43rd beer coincided with the plane banking on its approach to London. 'I swear to this day I could see beer about to spill over his bottom teeth onto the floor,' Lillee records. The 'keeper drained his 43rd and sipped painfully at his 44th, equalling the Walters record. Then he gurgled a surprising announcement: 'I can't make it.' This was a time for mates to stand together. Lillee remembers them giving Marsh a word of encouragement – 'Bullshit!' 'The challenge had by now assumed the significance of winning an Ashes series,' Lillee writes. 'There would be no capitulation. We tilted Rodney's head back and literally force-fed him.' And so the bar was raised, but not without some difficulties. Lillee says Marsh was 'history. Drunk as a monkey. Full as a fowl'. The fast bowler and Wood had to put him in team uniform and load him on to a luggage trolley to get him to customs. Wood says Marsh wisely gave the press conference a wide berth. Photographs taken at the airport appeared in the next day's papers with the headline, according to Lillee: 'Marsh attempts record and takes two of his mates with him'. The bowler felt cheated – he hadn't had a beer since Singapore. Marsh complained of terrible jetlag and did not front for training the next day.

Lawson says Marsh and Walters were big drinkers who never disgraced themselves. 'I've known Doug Walters and Rod Marsh a long time, and I've seen them at all hours of the day and night, and I've rarely seen them pissed, despite their reputations as drinkers. They just didn't get pissed – it was that simple. Apart from Rod being pissed after the 45th one, I don't recall ever seeing those guys pissed, and they drank a lot of beer. And it didn't affect their cricket, either.' Well, nobody is blaming the drink, but Australia were terrible in the World Cup, losing their first game to Zimbabwe, their second to the West Indies and fourth to India. They came home boasting one win, which was against Zimbabwe in the return match of the pool.

*

And so to the infamous twilight zone flight of 1989 and a record many say will never be beaten. The mystery arises from the fact that the holder of the title denies the attempt took place. The Australian team was led by the earnest Allan Border, known to his charges as Captain Grumpy, with the fanatical Bob Simpson at his right hand. Simmo, who introduced the modern obsession with fitness to the Australian team, was not the sort of fellow who would look kindly on beer drinking competitions. Nor could the team be especially confident about the tour. It had been beaten 3:1 at home by the West Indies over summer and lost the previous two Ashes series, earning itself a reputation as the 'worst team ever' to tour the old country.

Perhaps that's why they decided to get in early – to put a trophy on the shelf before a ball was bowled in anger.

Whatever the reason, it is claimed in certain circles that David Boon, the nuggetty Tasmanian opener with a similar physique to Rod Marsh, set out with the intention of breaking 45 cans. Boon refuses to confirm this. 'Never spoke about it, never will,' he tells *The Weekend Australian Magazine*. Maybe it was a mass hallucination, but some people on that flight recall a man who looked like Boon drinking a lot of beer.

Lawson says he was scoring, and in this case nobody begs to differ. He also remembers a different tone to the Boon assault. 'Nobody accompanied Boonie,' he says. 'We were all a bit more sensible. There weren't too many big drinkers in the team then. I think the culture of the '70s changed through the '80s.'

There were in fact three or four others involved, but more in a spirit of companionship than competition. Mark Taylor, a captain in the making, says he had 'a few beers with them along the way' but was not there at the end: 'I enjoy a beer, there's no doubt about that, but I don't think I can drink anywhere near that much.' Victorian fast bowler Merv Hughes is initially reluctant to talk. 'I won't mention any names,' he says eventually, confirming he was among the party of four or five who retired to the galley while the rest of the plane slept.

It is the Victorian batsman Dean Jones who speaks most candidly about the 1989 flight. It was Jones's first tour and his father had advised him to sit next to the opener to pick up hints on batting in England. 'Boonie had plenty of advice for me as we had just left Singapore and we had just finished our 22nd can of beer,' Jones writes for the Australian Paper website. He went upstairs and fell asleep, waking later to 'tumultuous' applause. Simpson thought somebody had won a card game until the plane's captain announced Boon had consumed 52 beers. 'Simpson went purple with anger and I mentioned to [selector Laurie] Sawle that maybe Boonie should be sent home and I would bat in his spot,' Jones recalls.

It's a record Boon has never claimed, but Lawson confirms the score and says with great regret that he wishes he had rescued the sick bags from the plane. 'They would have been worth a fortune,' he laments. 'You can imagine Tony Greig selling replicas of them summer after summer after summer.'

Lawson and Jones say Boon walked from the plane unaided. Mercifully, Boon was not asked a question at the press conference. Taylor recalls Simpson getting stuck into the team about the flight. 'When we got off the bus, Boonie was in quite a bit of trouble with Simmo, who was disappointed with him for drinking so much, and he called us into a team meeting and said, "Righto, a couple of things: David, I'm very disappointed with you and you're on probation, but also I don't want this story to leave this room. It's not to leave the Australian cricket team." And Merv Hughes at the back put his hand up and said, "Oh, Bob, I'm sorry mate, I've done radio interviews with …" and he named four or five stations he'd done interviews with, and said, "Mate, it's all over the world." Everyone started laughing and I think Merv got put on probation along with Boonie.'

Hughes confirms the incident, with variations. 'I told a radio station I worked for that we had already knocked up the first 50 of the tour,' he says. 'I got into more trouble than the protagonist. I was shitting myself that I would be sent home – it was my first tour and I was on my last chance the moment we reached the first hotel.'

Jones went to bed to sleep off his hangover but was called to the foyer by the concierge, who asked him to pick up his sleeping room-mate, Boon, who went on to average 55 on that tour. Australia reclaimed the Ashes and has not relinquished them since. Nor, despite many a bold attempt, has anybody managed to beat Boon's 52.

Over the years the odd non-cricketer has attempted to break the record. There have been unconfirmed reports that former Olympic swimmer Neil Brooks beat it. Nothing has been verified. On the recent Kangaroos tour several rugby league players attempted it but fell pathetically short; Sydney Rooster Mick Croker top-scored with 36 cans. The victorious English World Cup rugby squad is also rumoured to have had a crack, with hulking centre Mike Tindall coming close to 50 cans. 'You can rest assured David Boon's record is still standing,' Tindall's centre partner, Will Greenwood, said later. 'Tinds had a real go at it, but we wanted to leave the Aussies with at least one title to hang on to.'

The Weekend Australian Magazine, 20 December 2003

HELL AND HIGH WATER

Leisa Scott

It's not just the exhilaration of flying on waves at heart-pump-ing speed that draws Adrienne Cahalan to the sea, though she loves that. It's not the social whirl of international yacht racing that attracts one of its true stars, though she does like a party. It's not money, or ego, or fame. It's about defying fear: the awe-some, adrenalising thrill of being 'on the edge'.

To set a 110-foot (33-metre) racing catamaran in the path of the best winds and current, to hear the boat screaming under pres-sure as it accelerates to an astonishing 44 knots (82 km/h), to lis-ten for the noise to drop as a mighty hull rises out of the water and to know that right there, right now, the wrong move could mean 'kaput, she's over': that's where Cahalan wants to be.

'I've got that fear factor that I tend to thrive on,' admits Cahalan, a pocket dynamo at just 161 centimetres. 'It's not because you like to be scared, but it's an achievement to beat it.'

Talk about achievements. At the age of 39, Cahalan has com-peted in 13 Sydney-to-Hobart races, most notably on board *Nicorette* in 2000 when she navigated it to victory, becoming the first Australian woman to take line honours. She was part of the team that won Australia the prestigious Admiral's Cup in 2003, for the first time in 24 years.

A convert to multihull ocean sailing, she helped break five world speed records in 2002, four of them aboard the 110-foot catamaran *Maiden II*. In one mad dash, the crew broke the record – reaching speeds of 44 knots and averaging 29 knots after Cahalan picked the optimum route from Norfolk, Virginia, to a point 697 nautical miles (1289 kilometres) away, near Bermuda. That's a blistering pace; the fastest Sydney-to-Hobart race, over a comparable 630 nautical miles, was sailed in just under 44 hours.

Cahalan has sailed around the world – and the perilous Cape

Horn – in the Whitbread race. She's been nominated three times as World Yachtswoman of the Year, and last year was bestowed with the equivalent Australian title. International yachtspeople regard her as one of the top 10 navigators in the world. According to Ludde Ingvall, the skipper of *Nicorette*, 'For her to make top 10 comes against the problem of gender. It's like being the best guy on the planet and making number one position. She's unique.'

For all this, Cahalan remains a relative unknown in Australia, able to cruise her local streets of Collaroy, on Sydney's northern beaches, unrecognised. Yacht racing may be one of the most skilful and dangerous sports around, but its stars don't become celebrities. It's one thing for the cameras to follow professional tennis players or Olympic swimmers, but Cahalan's swimming pool is somewhat larger. It was never bigger than in 1998, when Cahalan faced one of her great disappointments in the Southern Ocean off Cape Horn. She was with a team of 12 women attempting to win the Jules Verne Trophy for the fastest circum-navigation of the world, then at 71 days. They'd spent 26 of the previous 43 days in the Southern Ocean, rarely seeing the sun, and were on target to break the record. The closest land was 2000 nautical miles (3700 kilometres) away; the water so cold it could freeze a person to death in minutes; the yacht was tearing along at 30 knots, the waves were barrelling mercilessly, and it was dark.

And then Cahalan heard a crack. Then a really big crack. Next, a crewmate yelled the two words no sailor wants to hear: 'Rig's gone!'

'I hit the mayday,' says Cahalan. 'It's the only time in my life I've had to put out a mayday.' The scene on deck was terrible: the mast was broken in three places and had crashed over the port side of the catamaran, trapping three sailors in the hull. They had no idea if water was coming in.

It took a few frantic minutes to establish that they weren't tak-ing water and that the sailors were safe. Cahalan cancelled the mayday and the women set about jury-rigging the boat and re-sewing the sails. Within 11 cold and bitter hours, they'd erected a shortened mast and were limping, devastated, on a 16-day journey to Chile.

Some might have called it quits after that, or at least stayed clear of the Southern Ocean. Not this blonde bombshell. Cahalan's big dream is to break the new record of 62 days to 'do a lap' of the planet. She was set to join a *Maiden II* campaign this year, but funding fell short. She really wants to round the Horn one more time. If Cahalan can do that and join an America's Cup team, she'll have met most of her outstanding goals.

*

It all began innocently enough when a 14-year-old Cahalan, the fourth of six kids from a Catholic family in Sydney's riverside Lane Cove, went to Papua New Guinea for a holiday. Friends had a Hobbie 16-foot catamaran, and they set out on an emerald sea from Port Moresby Harbour with a steady 15-knot wind. Then her sailing buddy mentioned sharks, and Cahalan decided not to foul up.

'And it was fast,' she recalls. 'I was out on the wire, the trapeze, and we were just zipping along on this beautiful day. Obviously, that kind of introduction to sailing was going to bite you forever, wasn't it?'

After that, she messed around on any boats she could get her hands on, finally buying a Laser, or sailing dinghy, at the age of 16 for about $1000. By the time the bright Cahalan got to Sydney University, the competition between sport and law studies was under way.

Sailing wasn't the only thing that occupied her time at university. Apart from Laser regattas, then 12-foot skiff racing and sailing on a family friend's yacht at weekends, she excelled in rowing and cross-country skiing. And partying. 'I like to go out,' she says, deadpan. 'That's what sailing's all about, it's the way the industry works … it's up to you to go out there and tell people you want to be a part of it. If that means there's a social aspect to it, all the better.'

As if to emphasise her point, the phone rings. It's a girlfriend from Hamble, the yachties' village near Southampton, England.

Last year Cahalan bought a home there which she uses as a springboard to the US and Europe six months a year. In a big year, her circuit can take her from Australia to the US, on to Mexico, the Caribbean, then back to Europe.

Much of her life is spent living out of suitcases, and her Collaroy digs reflect the impermanence of a jetsetter. Apart from a couple of sailing photos on the walls and some Christmas decorations waiting to be put away, her beachfront flat is light on for personal touches. There's a mattress in the living room for the many visitors she and her flatmate have to stay. A yacht mobile dangles from the can opener and a piano awaits a moment of her time. Cahalan's sister Damienne says that's all the creature comforts her big sister needs: 'She needs to wake up and see the sea. She needs that. She's addicted to the ocean.'

It's an addiction that drove her to join a Sydney-to-Hobart race at the age of 20. It was 1984, and the 150 yachts would be belted by strong to gale-force southerly winds on the run into Bass Strait. Only 46 boats – including the 36-foot *Mystic Seven*, with Cahalan and five others on board – would make it to Hobart in conditions that rivalled those of the 1998 race in which six sailors died. (Cahalan didn't have to face the 1998 storm: a broken rudder forced her ride, the Iain Murray-skippered *ABN Amro*, out of the race off Bateman's Bay.)

Despite the heaving seas of 1984, Cahalan has no memory of being scared. She recalls, almost fondly, the size of the waves, the distance the bow travelled as it dipped and rose, and the cute bloke with whom she shared a watch.

Still single, Cahalan says that as a 20-year-old she saw a future of marriage and children. She still does, but like so many women in their late thirties she's caught between a career that's reaching its pinnacle and the biological clock.

'I don't want to be sitting around in a yacht club in five or ten years with just a bunch of regatta shirts,' she says. 'But I don't think about it all day. Life goes on. Nothing I've done has been planned, until recently … You always see yourself as having endless sports time, really.'

The beginning of her professional racing career is indicative of her 'go with the flow' approach. She was at the NSW snow-fields, competing in a cross-country event, when a call came through from a representative of cosmetics company Ella Bache. They wanted to sponsor a female skipper to sail 18-foot skiffs, those magnificent light and fast racers often seen dancing across Sydney Harbour. Was she interested?

'And I said: "Ohhh, yes, that's me",' recalls Cahalan, who promptly packed her bag and hitched back to Sydney for a meeting the next day. Signed up and with two men on her team, it wasn't long before she was winning titles, the first woman to do so.

Her mother, Patricia, has no doubt what attracted her daughter to the 18-footers. 'The speed,' she says. 'And the challenge.' Widowed, and having lost two children – Paul, to a diving accident while sailing in the Pacific at age 23, and Maryanne at 39 to smoking-related cancer – Patricia admits to concern about Adrienne's daredevil life, but not worry. 'I think it would be very exciting to do those round-the-world races,' she says. 'I think she needs the stimulation of something like that.'

After six years of 18-footer competitions (including three world championships), finishing her double degree in law and arts (with Honours in philosophy), working as a maritime lawyer, a couple of Sydney-to-Hobarts (one as skipper) and time spent in Fremantle filming *Wind*, a movie about the US's 1987 recapture of the America's Cup, Cahalan's next step would throw her into the international arena in which she now thrives.

The Whitbread Round-the-World race was starting in 1993, and an all-girl team was being formed. The quadrennial race, since renamed the Volvo Ocean Race, is one of the most arduous on the yacht racing circuit; each of the then six legs was worth points, the winner being the yacht with the highest score over the entire distance. Cahalan flew to the US to throw her hat in the ring and, within months, she was setting off from Southampton on board the 60-foot monohull *Yamaha*, on a journey that ended nine months later.

It could have ended much sooner. After the first leg finished in Uruguay, Cahalan and a crewmate abandoned ship. They did not feel safe. The campaign was poorly financed, the skipper 'quite inexperienced' and her crew more so. Cahalan, who had taken a senior role as navigator and helmsman, loves speed but not unnecessary risk. (Real fear for Cahalan is sitting in a deserted train station at night.)

'There needed to be changes if we were going to get through the Southern Ocean,' she says. 'It's a dangerous place to go without things properly sorted.'

Brewer Heineken agreed and took over sponsorship of the boat, refinancing, renaming and reskippering it. It was an important lesson for Cahalan about the politics of yachting and the need to stand up and express concerns: 'You've got to be confrontational at the right time. You choose to be there. You have to sort it out.'

It was rugged; not just because of the high seas, the bitter cold, the appalling reconstituted food and the physical demands on the body, but the psychological effect as well. Damienne, a sports therapist who has specialised in working with professional yachties, thinks people forget that the entire time is spent racing. 'There's no down time,' she says. 'They set off, and for us on shore it all becomes very abstract. You forget that they're out there 24 hours a day in race mode, mentally and physically, and it never, ever lets up.'

One of the biggest hurdles for Cahalan, a sun worshipper who hates the cold, was leaving Auckland for the next leg back into the Southern Ocean. 'Psychologically, it's awful. You just want it over with.' But keeping her focused was that holy grail of ocean sailing: rounding the Horn. Known for its roaring forties and screaming sixties winds, Cape Horn digs deep toward Antarctica at a latitude of 56 degrees south. (The bottom of Tasmania is 13 degrees higher.) Pack ice is never far away, the current is incredible and the winds – unimpeded by any land – keep coming furiously from the west.

'We ended up about 60 south and getting back up wasn't so easy,' Cahalan says. 'I remember it was very, very rough.'

Still, they got there. As navigator, Cahalan had to count down the miles and give the official nod that they'd made it, a personal victory for any red-blooded ocean sailor. Cheering broke out and the cameras flashed as everyone held up a sign saying, 'We're here.' And she knew she'd have to try and return. Her days as a lawyer were numbered.

*

Cahalan is perched on a cushion at the navigation station of Andrew Short Marine, a Volvo Ocean 60 yacht she navigated in her 13th Sydney-to-Hobart last year, becoming the most capped female in the race's history. For three days, the bench seat, desk and computer console were her world – the place she worked, ate and slept.

Sometimes she'll help with a sail change, maybe work on the grinders, but the life of a navigator is spent largely below decks. In heaving seas, she'll trawl over the latest forecasts she accesses via the internet, study currents and consult weather models to calculate probabilities, weighing up where the boat should be and when, to get it home as quickly as possible. 'The difference between winning and losing can be a five-degree wind shift … you've got to try and predict it and position yourself.'

At her disposal are the high-tech tools that have revolutionised some elements of navigation. The multimillion-dollar yachts Cahalan sails are kitted out with internet access, radar and the now ubiquitous global positioning systems which pinpoint a yacht's position using satellites. But the science of forecasting remains inexact: 'It's got something to do with chaos theory and that butterfly that flaps its wings,' quips Cahalan. Her job is to try and wrestle that chaos into a plan. Some places are harder to forecast than others – the trade winds of the tropics are largely predictable, she says, while the conditions off Sydney Heads are some of the most changeable in the world.

Once the racing bug truly bit, Cahalan knew that if she wanted to make a career of it, she needed to specialise. Though her broad experience was getting bigger with every campaign, her size and weight – only 55 kilograms – were not. No matter how strong the determination, a small woman is no match for a big man on deck.

The answer was to specialise in navigation, where brains, not brawn, are the key. She'd always enjoyed it, and had squeezed in a meteorology course at TAFE while studying at university. 'I love charts, I could look at charts all day. And I love watching the clouds.'

Last year, Cahalan completed a Master of Science (Applied Meteorology) at Britain's Reading University, to help further her chances of making an America's Cup team. To Cahalan, the America's Cup is like a Wimbledon, the oldest and most prestigious event on the yachting calendar and one of the most expensive, with campaigns costing about $150 million. Competition to join the teams is fierce, and their composition will be decided this year as the lead-up races begin for the final showdown off Valencia, Spain, in June 2007. Cahalan is keen to be active on a yacht, but with her weather routing skills, a land-bound job of advising tactics is also a possibility.

Being a team player – a characteristic vital in an America's Cup campaign – is one of Cahalan's strengths, according to *Nicorette*'s Ludde Ingvall. Never dictatorial, she involves her skipper and senior crew in analysis of her findings. Some navigators are known as 'corner bangers': those who risk sailing to the edge of a course in the hope of picking up a winning wind. Cahalan will do that when there's nothing to lose, but is more reliant on probabilities, and sailors such as Ingvall respect that. 'I trust her,' he says. 'You have to live in an environment of tremendous trust on these boats. She's been able, against the normal odds of being a girl in a man's world, to develop that reputation and trust.'

And friendships; as she leaves the yacht and strolls up the finger of the Cruising Yacht Club on Sydney's Rushcutter's Bay, people stop Cahalan for a chat. She's running late, but she keeps talking. She beams one of her brilliant smiles and has a laugh – a big, open, happy laugh. Yachties, Cahalan says, have sunny personalities, and she's a walking advertisement.

Around the corner at Double Bay, the reception is the same. 'G'day Ado,' people call from a pleasure cruiser. Cahalan still catches up with old mates whenever she's in town. Vanessa

Dudley, the editor of *Australian Sailing*, says people just like to be around her. 'She's got this huge life force about her; people are drawn to her. If she's in town, everyone knows it.'

It's all part of her high-velocity lifestyle, says Damienne, recalling how she joined her sister on *Maiden II* off Antigua last year. 'It's the only pleasure cruise I've been on where I haven't moved from the spot I got on – I didn't have the guts. We were doing about 36 knots and it was a truly hair-raising ride. You're hit by the whole adrenalin and excitement and speed of it.'

Which is exactly how Cahalan likes it. Like a southerly buster, she's burst into international yacht racing with a power and persistence that demand notice. Letting go isn't an option. Just like the time she was high up the mast in the Southern Ocean, racing under spinnaker and the boat turned side-on and almost parallel to the waves.

'I just tightened my grip and held on for the ride.'

The Weekend Australian Magazine, 7 February 2004

SITTING PRETTY

Richard Yallop

There was always a devil in Ms Camplin, though she looked like a tiny, blonde angel. She kicked up a stink at seven when Melbourne's Viewbank Primary School refused to let her play in the boys' cricket team; was twice banned from the gym at Methodist Ladies' College; and made her sister Georgina die of embarrassment one day by doing a Gene Kelly impersonation on the bus to athletics training.

As a child, she won everything in athletics, which she dreamed would be her ticket to Olympic glory. She and Georgina, taking after their father, Geoff, who had been a good runner in

Launceston, would take the bus to the track in Doncaster, in Melbourne's eastern suburbs. Hyperactive Alisa, then 13, would normally spend the journey swinging on a rail in the bus. This particular day, seared into Georgina's memory, 'She sat on the floor of the bus with the umbrella up, performing "Singing in the Rain". I think she did it to embarrass me, because I was a lot more shy. The other passengers tried to look out the window and pretend she wasn't there. She was a hell-raiser, and very mischievous.'

Camplin's mother, Jenny, says her eldest daughter's behaviour was 'challenging'. 'There was a time when she was 11 that I nearly disowned her, and so did the gym teacher at school.' Camplin was one of only two people ever banned from the gym at elite MLC. Call her daredevil, adventurous, fearless; she had it in spades. The family used to have a property in the old Ballarat goldfields, and there were some deep mine shafts roundabout. Alisa was always the first one to abseil down the shaft into the blackness.

*

Fast forward to November 1999, and Camplin waits in the start-gate at the top of the aerial skiing jumpsite at Fortress Mountain, high in the Canadian Rockies. After a succession of childhood injuries stopped her from reaching the Olympics in athletics or gymnastics – she excelled at both – it's all or nothing now for Camplin in aerial skiing (the sport likened to somersaulting off the top of a four-storey building at 60 kilometres per hour). She'd already spent $100,000 of her own money over five years pursuing this dream. She'd scraped and saved: delivering pizzas, cleaning people's homes, coaching gymnastics, working at the ANZ Bank, all while studying full-time at university.

Camplin is about to make her 18th training jump of the day, to perfect a complicated twisting double somersault. Everyone else has finished training and gone in for the day, but not Camplin. She's tired, it is dangerously windy, but there is still work to be done. Camplin believes it's imperative to 'practise as you mean to compete', so she lines up for another shot at perfection. She focuses her thoughts and tips forward down the in-run, gathering speed. She flies into the air, twisting and flipping her body, in the three-and-a-half seconds she has before landing. Her timing is fractionally out, and she flips past her feet straight onto her back, smashing her head into the snow. The impact, from 13 metres in the air, is three times her body weight. The lights go out. She struggles with consciousness for several minutes, and remains concussed for six days.

She's no stranger to concussion, or injury. Soon after she took up the sport she found herself strapped beneath a helicopter ambulance flying over Eiger Mountain in Switzerland. She's broken both ankles; torn knee ligaments; separated her shoulder; ripped her Achilles tendon; broken her collarbone; dislocated her sternum; broken her hand, and countless ribs. For Camplin, physical pain is relative, and can be handled. After she was first introduced to aerial skiing at the ski show in Melbourne, when she was 19, her mother asked her if she'd thought about the prospective pain. 'Pain? What's pain?' said Camplin.

Having won an IBM scholarship to Swinburne University and gone on to work as an executive for the IT company, Camplin is clearly intelligent enough to know that flirting with a head injury is something altogether different. Most aerial skiers have had concussion once or twice; Camplin has been concussed nine times.

This time, at Fortress Mountain, she has reached a crossroads: does she stop now, to eliminate the unknown risks of brain damage, or does she pursue her dream all the way to the 2002 Winter Olympics regardless? She visits the Calgary neurologist who works with the prestigious Calgary Flames NHL Hockey team, who tells her that if she were a hockey player, he'd make her quit – unless she wants to risk the unknown, and potentially end up like Muhammad Ali at 60.

Shifting Alisa Camplin once she has set her mind on something has never been easy: she only relented from her primary school protests about not playing in the boys' cricket team when they let her captain the rounders team. Then there was the matter of her diving at MLC. Her father told her not to dive because of the danger of neck injuries, but she did anyway, winning the inter-school championship.

After consulting the Australian team doctor about her multiple concussions, Camplin weighed up her options. 'To have stopped then would have been mortifying,' she says. 'I was so close to fulfilling my dream, in my third and final sport. It took me two weeks to finally decide that if I didn't compete at Salt Lake City, I'd regret it for the rest of my life.'

So she continues, and wins Olympic gold, and the 2003 world championships, and sets three new world records, and takes out successive Overall World Cup Titles in 2003 and 2004. She now dominates aerial skiing as the world No. 1, and is to Australian female sport what Ian Thorpe is to male sport.

*

Camplin is sitting in the lounge at the Melbourne Hilton wearing jeans and a Collingwood jumper (her father barracked for Carlton, but no one was going to tell her who to support, even if it infuriated Dad). Ever businesslike, she has been using the waiting time in the hotel to sort out her business activity statements and travel receipts. The Alisa Camplin you see here is pretty much the one you see on the slopes – 157 centimetres of intense, organised, meticulous, disciplined professionalism. Before we met she had asked if she could look at the article before it went to print, to check the facts and photographs. She's a sparky, chatty soul ('The Camplins can all talk underwater,' says Georgina, one year younger than Alisa, 29), but does bristle at the suggestion she's a control freak.

'That can sometimes be a nasty word,' says the gold medal winner. 'I have a large amount of attention to detail. If you leave things open to chance, you're exposing yourself to error. Risk management, in sport, as much as in business, is integral to ensuring success.'

Perhaps if we'd all known before Salt Lake City in 2002 that Camplin had a mind like a steel trap, and had lived and breathed the Olympics since she was five, we wouldn't have been so surprised when she won the gold medal. The script was supposed to be that Victoria's Jacqui Cooper would win, but then Cooper was injured in training just before the winter Games. Camplin took her chance and became an instant, pocket-sized star – long, blonde hair, attractive, articulate – the perfect sporting package.

The success was no surprise to Camplin, or to other members of the Australian women's aerial ski team, who are now global leaders. For one spell last season, Australia – the first country to successfully convert gymnasts into aerial skiers – had the top three jumpers in the world: Camplin, Lydia Ierodiaconou and Elizabeth Gardner.

Camplin spent $250,000 of her own (or borrowed) money to get onto the winner's podium in Salt Lake City. Her campaign had been planned to the utmost detail. Two years before the Olympics she knew she was technically capable of performing two jumps, which if executed well and landed, would give her enough points to get on the podium. To perfect her preparation, and because her father had always stressed the importance of good coaching, she employed her own technical coach, American Todd Ossian, as well as sports psychologist Barbara Meyer from the University of Wisconsin.

'I invested everything, financially and emotionally, but it was worth it because I knew I was capable of getting a medal. I'd only ever known myself as an academic student, as a professional at IBM, and most importantly as an athlete. I wouldn't have given myself any credit for my entire life if I hadn't achieved what I thought was possible in sport.'

Ossian says: 'After a couple of days working with this girl I had no doubt she could win the Olympics. She has an incredible work ethic, combined with a determination to cross every t and dot every i. There aren't too many athletes who are that disciplined.' Meyer helped with nutrition, time management, mental preparation, visualisation and planning for every eventuality that might arise in Salt Lake City. So Camplin trained in fair weather and foul. In the lead-up to the Games, she sent separate pairs of skis and boots on different airlines in case one set was lost. She spent one day jumping in strange boots, to see how it felt, in case the worse came to the worst. She and Meyer even projected how she would handle any possible break-up with her long-time partner, Canadian aerial skier Steve Omischl (it didn't happen then, but has happened since). To focus better, she stayed at her own apartment at the foot of the mountain, rather than in the athletes' village, and she decided against marching with the other 27 team members at the opening ceremony.

Australian chef de mission Geoff Henke, who is also chairman of the Olympic Winter Institute, which runs the highly success-ful aerial program, recalls: 'Alisa wanted to march, but was wise enough to realise it might interrupt her focus. She is so method-ical, and logical. She's not a loner, and there was no standoffish-ness; she just thought it would help her to focus better. She gets on very well with the others, and everyone accepted her deci-sion because of her friendliness in other things. Every athlete is different, and you respect their opinion.'

On the day of Olympic competition, when Camplin won gold, the only thing that had not been pre-visualised was that Jenny and Georgina would be there to share the celebration. Before the Games it was decided the family wouldn't go because of the potential for distraction. But in the end mother and sister could not contain themselves, and Camplin did not see them until after her winning second jump. Yet still the driven Camplin could not rest. Two days after winning gold, she told Henke: 'Now I've got to prove to others that this is no fluke.'

*

When Geoff and Jennifer Camplin married in Hobart in 1970 they planned on having two boys; instead, they had three daughters, Alisa, Georgina, and Alexandrea. When all three girls showed talent and aptitude at sport, their parents gave them every opportunity. Geoff says: 'Alisa had a fire in her belly from day one, and we fed it at every occasion. She was gifted, like the other girls, but she understood that the glittering prizes went to the persistent, rather than those with natural talent.'

Alisa cannot remember a childhood without sport. 'Our

parents wanted to see that if we were committing ourselves to something, we were putting in a fair dinkum effort. When I was five I was winning every race I was running, and the expectation developed that I would win every time I stepped onto the track. When I was seven, I remember being furious with myself not winning, and vomiting after I crossed the line because I pushed myself so hard. I want things more than other people.'

At home, she was a tomboy, and a terror. 'I grew up in a street of boys, and ran against boys. My two sisters had dolls; I had Lego. I didn't wear dresses because they got in the way of kicking the footy. I developed into more of a lady over the years.'

Georgina says: 'Alisa was always much more of a risk-taker than I was. When she was about seven, and I was six, we used to climb out of the bathroom window and run away and play with the boys in the court. I just followed her around.'

From Viewbank, Alisa and her sisters moved on to MLC, as her parents, of moderate means, made the sacrifice to give their children some of the opportunities they themselves had not enjoyed. The Camplins separated in 2001. Geoff is a retired businessman and Jenny is an industrial relations manager.

Georgina recalls her sister in the early days at MLC: 'She was really active and loud and naughty. She was a shocker, and always in trouble. She hated ballet, so she took to gymnastics, because she liked the tumbling. She tried hockey, but she's not a team person. We played in the same team and ended up screaming at each other. She finds it frustrating when other people make a mistake and she has no control over it.'

Stress injuries forced Camplin out of athletics at 13, so then she turned to gymnastics. Cathy Oswald, former gymnastics head at MLC, remembers the day Camplin walked into the gym for the first time, curious to try out every piece of apparatus. First off, she saw the other students doing aerial cartwheels with no hands – a level-seven trick. 'She did it straight off,' says Oswald. 'She had this tiny little body with all this leg strength and amazing power from the athletics she'd done. She was one out of the box. She didn't know how to land, and she hurt her knee that first day, but it didn't stop her.'

Oswald, now commercial manager for the Sydney Swans AFL team, twice had to ban Camplin from the gym: 'She was naughty sometimes – but you need that bit of spunk, or chutzpah, and she had it. Other people think they can win; Alisa thinks she will win. Look at that first day in the gym. She'd never done the cartwheels, but she didn't think she could do it, she knew she could. She was going to be the best in the world at something.'

Then came another setback – back injuries meant Camplin had to give up a second sport. 'I knew I would never be an Olympic gymnast, but I dreamed of medalling in the Australian championships, and it tore me apart that I didn't achieve all I wanted to in the sport. When I came to aerial skiing, I had unfinished business. I'd felt the pain of not fulfilling my potential in both athletics and gymnastics.'

The moment of destiny arrived at the Melbourne ski show when she was 19, doing an IT course at Swinburne University and feeling pretty miserable about never having channelled her sporting talent into an Olympic team. By chance, she accompanied a friend to the show, and drifted along to the Mount Buller stand. Kirstie Marshall had already lifted the sport's profile, and Jacqui Cooper, on the stand, was coming up fast. There were plenty of role models for Camplin. Two days later she sent a fax to Olympic Winter Institute director Geoff Lipshut asking what she had to do to sign up. She was on her way to gold.

Winning in Salt Lake City brought its own challenges. Camplin says: 'When you're Olympic champion, you can't hide anymore. I'd never been watched so closely by media and other competitors. I was making myself sick with worry. I had a hiatus hernia from stress. It took me a long while to realise it didn't matter that I was in a fishbowl; I just went out and did my jump.'

She is attempting not to drive herself so hard in the lead-up to the Turin Olympics in 2006. She plans to compete less this international winter, focusing only on the 2005 World Championships and 2006 Olympics. With less training and fewer events on her plate, Camplin hopes to stay energised and hungry, while enjoying herself more.

She has no steady partner at the moment after splitting up with Omischl in March. Oswald, a good friend, says: 'If it came to a choice between what she wanted to do, and fellows, I think fellows would come second every time. Not because she's unfeeling, and she's gorgeous. She's only been out with a handful of men seriously, partly because she spends so much time away.'

Lipshut says: 'Alisa's better than anybody at controlling the controllables. She goes to bed thinking, "I can't make that mistake again", and it's hard to keep up that intensity after five years. She's at the top of her game now. I think she's had to let go of some of her intensity. She's a perfectionist, and her struggle is knowing how to deal with expectations.'

Camplin also faces an ongoing battle with the elements, and fear. She sees competition as a calculated risk, and wears knee braces and a back brace to cushion the impact. Whiplash is a constant occupational hazard. Each day she trains and competes, the physio has to put her pelvis back into alignment.

'You can't be soft in aerials,' insists Camplin. 'It hurts; it's an impact sport; you have to take the smashes, brush the snow off, and keep going. Unless the bone is sticking out of my knee, I'm not injured. Any amount of pain, I'll suck that up, and keep going. You get knocked and bruised and bumped every day. Every day I wake up really sore.

'Sure, I feel fear in bad weather, when the conditions are bad: fear of failing; breaking my neck; letting down my coaches, and my country. There are times I don't want to do my jumps, but I won't allow myself to put it off. I would loathe myself if I backed away because of fear. The only way to overcome fear is to face up to it. At the end of the day, all you have is your pride and self-respect.'

The Weekend Australian Magazine, 29 May 2004

THE WHOLE HOG

Will Swanton

The hooter sounded at Jeffrey's Bay. Nathan Hedge had beaten Kelly Slater. Finally, he knew he belonged.

After slogging away for seven years on the World Championship Tour (WCT) for a mediocre best ranking of 20th, the man they call 'The Hog' decided at the beginning of 2004 to start going hard. Even harder than before. He trained like there was no tomorrow. He attacked every heat as though his life depended on the result. He came good.

Hedge's victory over Slater, who was wearing his sleek and intimidating all-white wetsuit, in the quarter-finals of the Billabong Pro at J-Bay in South Africa last week paved the way for his second straight appearance in a WCT final.

But there was a greater significance.

Go back to April.

Hedge was soundly beaten by Slater at Bell's Beach but even worse than the loss was the awful feeling in his stomach of being completely overwhelmed by the six-times world champion. Hedge felt like he barely deserved to be in the water with the great man; that he needed to perform at a super-human level to be even remotely competitive. Hedge surfed horribly until the heat was dead and buried and only then, when all hope was lost, did he begin to loosen up ... and hold his own.

It made him think.

It made him think that maybe he was as good as these guys, surfing normally.

It made him think right.

Slater had given Hedge a whoopin' at Bells. 'That's two now,' said Slater in reference to the lopsided results of their only head-to-head meetings. The comment, delivered so matter-of-factly, was probably nothing more than a throwaway line from Slater, words he would never give a second thought, but they stayed with Hedge, motivated him, travelled with him to J-Bay.

Scowling and steely-eyed, Hedge won by almost three points. That's a good margin. Not quite a whoopin', but a very good margin. Hedge kneeled on his board and punched the air with a clenched right fist, howling in triumph as Slater paddled silently behind him in the uncustomary role of the vanquished. It's rare for Slater to look lost in the water, but he didn't appear to know where to go. Paddle in? Stay out? He had predicted earlier in the day that Hedge would be lucky to get past the fourth round. Wrong again, Kelly. When Hedge gets on a roll like this, adrenaline pumping, nostrils flared because there's a sniff, look out. There's no determination like it.

'The last few times he's beaten me, so it's good to get third time lucky,' said The Hog. 'Get a bit of revenge on him, you know. Last time at Bells we were in the water and he looked at me and said what he said … it hurts. So that's maybe what got me through today.' Hedge couldn't resist. 'That's two-one, mate,' he told Slater after the heat. Must have felt good. Slater looked around as though there had been some kind of mistake; as though he was waiting for the real heat to begin. 'The thing about Hedgy is his desire,' he said. 'He's really focused and really intense. He's got the right mind for it. If his surfing comes together and he gets the waves, he's hard to beat.'

Respect. Finally. Hedge kept his game face on. There was another score to settle. Three months earlier, Hedge had masterfully worked his way through the draw at the feared break of Teahupoo in Tahiti to reach his first WCT final. You need balls to surf Teahupoo. Courage. It's the kind of place that can give you the ride of a lifetime, or kill you. She's a little difficult to predict. Some day the organisers will be up for manslaughter when three surfers paddle out for a heat and only two come back. If you fall and you're lucky, you'll get scraped across the cheese-grater reef lurking beneath the surface and escape with cuts and bruising. If you fall and you're unlucky, you'll have your skull crushed. Teahupoo has killed, and will kill again. Sane people hold back, carefully picking and choosing their waves. Hedge charges. His gallant run to the decider included beating world No. 1 Andy Irons in a classic semi-final.

With one minute on the clock, Hedge needed nine points to win. He paddled furiously and got to his feet. He ducked into the barrel and held on for dear life. He emerged as though he was running through a brick wall, his face all grim and determined, the wind howling, the rain pelting down, an extreme environment if ever there was one. He sat on his board in the channel with a furious look on his face and slammed the water and gesticulated to the judging tower, daring them to deny him … again. Years ago, on the exact same reef, Hedge had been robbed blind when the judges underscored him on a final wave that should have given him a win over Irons. It was such a bad decision that a mild-mannered born-again Christian photographer named Sarge threw down his equipment and jumped off his boat in protest as boos and jeers filled the warm Tahitian air. Don't underestimate this as a statement from good old Sarge: he hadn't been in the water for years. This time, the judges gave Hedge what he deserved and he was through to the final against CJ Hobgood.

On the cusp of his first tour win, literally centimetres from emerging from another hissing, spitting tube that would surely have delivered him a 10; right at the last second, right when his nuggety little frame was about to shoot from the spitball – he was *right there*, you could actually see him coming out – he was knocked base over apex and his left shoulder was ripped from its socket. Silence. Disbelief. This wasn't in the script. Hobgood had snapped his board on his opening wave, and Hedge had just seemed destined to win. He was trying so bloody hard, he deserved to.

He didn't know how to give up. He tried to paddle back out. Then, writhing in pain on the back of the surf rescuers' jet ski, he begged the doctors to undislocate the dislocation; to put his shoulder back in so he could keep going. Three doctors tried, but Hedge's body was so swollen with adrenaline that they couldn't get it back in. He tried again to move his arm in a paddling motion, as if to say, 'Nah, I'm alright, look' but no good. He could barely move it an inch. He was forced to with-draw. It was painful to watch, let alone experience. Mick Fanning collected Hedge's runner-up trophy at the presentation cere-mony as the man himself lay numb on a hospital bed, doped up on morphine with his arm in a sling.

'He'll win some day,' said Fanning.

Maybe today.

Hedge parked himself on a wooden bench in the J-Bay com-petitors area, the best seats in the house, with music blaring from his earphones and his buddies all around. He glared at the waves. His game was still on. Even between heats, he smoul-ders. You remember times in the past when you'd wished him good luck and thought he was going to hug you in return. *Thanks maaate*, he'd say as if he'd known you all his life even though, really, he didn't know you from Adam. Brimming with confidence after beating Slater, because if you can beat Kelly Slater you can beat anyone, he psyched himself up and dis-posed of another former world champion in the semi-finals: Hawaii's Sunny Garcia. Another heat, another large scalp, this one weighing 100 kilograms and covered in tattoos. 'I've just backed myself and it's happened. I'm just feeling privileged to be in the same league as these boys. To be able to compete against them is an honour.' He psyched himself one more time but lost the final to Irons, who proved why he's numero uno by nailing a perfect ten-pointer.

It was something else, the 10: Irons took off on his two-metre canvas and locked into one tube, emerged, pig-dogged into a second tube, swept high on the face in a smooth and stylish arc, spray going everywhere, ducked into a third tube just for kicks and came out once more, whooping it up with his million dol-lar a year (plus bonuses) smile. Game over. No shame in that loss for Hedge, however, and his disappointment was short-lived. You can fluke one WCT final, but not two on the trot. Standing on the dais with a large Australian flag draped around his neck, thousands of people cheering for him, *go Hog!*, his blue competitors' singlet soaked in beer, one arm hugging his trophy and the other around Irons, it was official. The battler had arrived in the big time.

Current world ranking: four.

'Jeffrey's is a very special place,' he said. 'I'd like to thank God, my family at home, thanks for your support, I couldn't have done it without you. And lastly, Malcolm Brown my doctor, who looked after my shoulder after Tahiti. He said if I get up on stage I must do a handstand, so could you all make some room, please, because I'm going to do a handstand now.'

And he did.

'It's game on for the rest of the year,' he added. 'I've solidified myself as one of the top surfers not just making up the numbers like last year. I've never had to skip an event before like I did in Fiji because of my shoulder, but it really put the fire in my belly to come back. I've put a lot of hard work into my shoulder and it's paying off. It isn't 100 per cent yet, and the doctors have told me I'm still at a pretty high risk of damaging it again, but I'm doing the right things and it's all going to plan.'

Bloody hell. He thinks he can win the world title. He says it like he means it, too, not like other athletes who mouth the words without feeling it in their hearts. And it makes you wonder about the nature of self-belief. It makes you wonder how someone like Nathan Hedge can be struggling to re-qualify for the tour one year, and be gunning for the big prize the next. It makes you wonder how someone like Nathan Hedge can become so outrageously optimistic all of a sudden without any real right to be, while an infinitely more successful surfer like Layne Beachley is so inexplicably weighed down by self-doubt.

You remember back to May, at Teahupoo, when you were sitting on the shore with the women's world champion. In hindsight, Hedge was probably out there surfing at the same moment because with the sun out and the swell up, and a contest beginning the next day, you couldn't imagine him being anywhere else. Beachley: you remember being a bit overawed. Here you had a woman with unbridled success – the most successful surfer in history; the only person, man or woman, to have won six straight world titles. Not even Slater won his six in a row.

Here you had a woman with financial independence, so much so that she was able to knock back a huge contract offer from Billabong and hold out for something more. Here you had a woman beginning to transcend her sport, being voted the Australian Athlete of the Year. Here you had a woman with a happy home life, having shacked up with INXS guitarist Kirk Pengilly. Here you had a woman still blessed with her looks, her wits, her capabilities, a guaranteed place in Australian sporting folklore. Here you had a woman who was about to receive the sporting equivalent of an Oscar, a Laureus. Here you had a woman who had it all. And here you had a woman who was talking about insecurity.

Amazing, but true. Layne Beachley – *that* Layne Beachley – fights enormous amounts of self doubt, periods of low motivation, excruciating nights of over-analysis when 'the chatter in my head won't stop,' being torn between her domestic bliss and the necessarily nomadic existence of a board-rider, persistent feelings of vulnerability about staying No. 1, and a sense that no matter what she achieves, she can never achieve enough.

'I always go to extremes, and it's happening again,' she said, almost apologetically. 'All of a sudden I've reached this point in my career where I don't feel like I'm good enough. Yes, I know it's bizarre. I get a lot of accolades and nice phone calls and letters from people telling me that I've inspired them, but for some reason I never really let any of that sink in. I know I've achieved a lot and maybe even taken women's surfing to a different level, and yet now I don't feel like I'm anywhere near good enough. That's how your mind plays games with you. I have to learn to control those kinds of thoughts.' She pauses. 'You'd think I'd have learned by now.'

Another pause. 'People probably imagine that I think of myself as being unstoppable, unbeatable, superhuman. Believe me, I feel so human. The more you think, the less chance you have of winning, but I still can't help thinking too much. It keeps me up at night.'

What does?

'Everything. I think all the girls on the tour are thinking that this is the year they're going to get me. I know they are. From the first press conference of the year, Chelsea Georgeson went, "It's over for her." They've thought that every year, but I guess this year I'm a bit more sensitive to it. Maybe because I do feel a bit more vulnerable. It's funny how after all this time you can experience such a state of vulnerability. How can I have achieved so much and feel worthless for it? I don't really feel that worthless, I suppose … it's just that I feel like I could be doing more.'

Like what, exactly? Winning a seventh world title? An eighth? When is enough enough? Compare Beachley's tentative state of mind with Hedge's gun-slinging optimism. It makes no sense, really. He shouldn't be feeling so good. She shouldn't be feeling so bad. Perhaps that's the beauty of it all.

Nathan Hedge eats, sleeps, lives, breathes and dreams surfing. His blonde hair and freckles are testament to the amount of time he's spent in the sun and water over his 25 years on the planet. Whether he's at home at Narrabeen on Sydney's northern beaches, or on tour, he's always, always, among the very first surfers in the water; a walking, talking dawn patrol. He'd be even more tanned if his first waves of the day weren't so often caught in the dark. He's enthusiastic. He's fiercely patriotic. He's selfless. He's immensely popular among his peers. In his barren years, he would routinely follow early-round losses by sticking around the contest site to scream his support for the rest of the Australian contingent.

They haven't forgotten.

Now they're screaming for him.

The likes of Mark Occhilupo, Luke Egan, Joel Parkinson and Fanning are still aiming high themselves, of course, but they're taking a great deal of delight in Hedge's recent successes because they know how much it means to him, how hard he's worked for it, and for how long he's been hoping it might happen.

AAP, 24 July 2004

SEX, DRUGS 'N' FOOTBALL

The 2004 seasons for both the Australian Rugby League and the Australian Football League saw more of the dark side of football culture exposed than ever before. The off-field behaviour of some players from the Canterbury Bulldogs and St Kilda has overshadowed their continuing success on the field. Whether or not criminal charges of rape and sexual assault eventuate against players from both codes, the events themselves made nearly every football follower feel sick. Football is part of the larger Australian way of life, not as we sometimes like to think outside or above it. Unhappily many of our role models are just like many of us. This section explores the events in NSW and Victoria as news, comment and impact on football followers.

UP YOURS, CAZALY

Philippa Hawker

When I saw the TV ad for AFL Women's Week, my first reaction was uncharitable. What's the point? Women – plenty of women – are involved with footy all season, all year. Why this special commemorative event? It sounded as dodgy as Secretaries' Day to me. At least it wasn't Beatification of James Hird Week, I thought: and then remembered, no, we already had that, at Easter.

The TV advertisement features women – some well-known, some anonymous – who are, in various ways, part of the game: women who follow it, work in it, play it. It looked to have been a cruel irony, at this point in the season, that, in the last segment, the exuberant supporters who leap to their feet and applaud are wearing Tiger colours, but that's the glorious uncertainty of football, or at least the glorious certainty of barracking for Richmond. And then, as Friday night's game showed, it turned out to have been prophetic.

The words the women speak are not their own: they come from a verse of 'Up There, Cazaly'. They conclude just before the song's pay-off – the crescendo, the roar, the bombast and assertiveness of lines such as 'in there and fight' and 'show 'em your might' and 'you're out there to win'. The women of footy are given more seemly, restrained emotions than this. The words 'for love of the game' are superimposed over the image of yellow and black floggers, waving optimistically.

It's easy to be suspicious and churlish towards an AFL campaign, to perceive the smell of niche-marketing and the whiff of condescension: no doubt it's well-intentioned, certainly it's invoking 'love of the game' as something women have and can make something of. And there's a forum that's part of Women's Week, with speakers from different fields. It will provide information on playing the game and how to pursue a career in it: it's not just a case of PR and drumming up business at the turn-stiles next weekend.

But there are plenty of reasons to feel dubious about the way women are portrayed in football, even as more and more of them work for clubs, take decision-making roles in the game, write and broadcast about it. They might be admired for their commitment, idealised as supportive wives, mothers, partners and family members – even celebrated as Brownlow Blondes – but there are times when they're treated as threats to the very fabric of the game. In a 1994 AFL report, single mothers were blamed for the decline in junior participation in the '80s: anxious about the danger of contact sports, they supposedly ushered their kids into basketball, soccer and making paper planes.

In the debate following allegations of sexual assault levelled against footballers, it was amazing to see how often women were portrayed as the aggressors. Predatory figures, stalking and harassing helpless players. Temptresses, leading boys astray. The other kind of football sirens.

So perhaps we should be grateful for the kind of attention we get during Women's Week and the Mother's Day round. All you need is love. Me, I like football. Very nice, very admirable, and nothing much to do with intensity, excess, absurdity and ambivalence, the things that football seems to me to be about. And hate. Let's not forget hate.

If I made a brief TV spot about footy, it wouldn't be as warm and fuzzy as the Women's Week production. There's so much about football that sends me to extremes of despair, rage and frustration. It's not about abuse hurled directly at players, coaches or other supporters. It's about strong emotions. What I love, after all, is reflected in what I hate. (And there's a parallel universe, junior footy, where I applaud the opposition's scream-ers and the umpire is a pillar of virtue.)

My imaginary football promotional exercise would be a litany of hate. It would begin with the unsayable, the ultimate heresy. I hate James Hird. Head prefect, ornament to the game, defender of free speech. He who must be admired. It would be un-Australian not to.

I hate the carry-on about captains, when all they really have to do is know the difference between heads and tails. When they pay eight points for a 'captain's goal', then the phrase might actually mean something.

I hate the cargo cult of coaches, the way they are thought to move in mysterious ways, their every utterance is raked over for deeper meanings and Machiavellian mind-games. I have seen the best minds of my generation totally sucked in by Kevin Sheedy ...

I hate the way that grounds change their names as often as David Beckham changes hairstyles.

I hate the way two-thirds of the crowd at the Grand Final probably doesn't barrack for either team.

I hate Akermanis's pissy little post-match handstand.

I hate the idea that there's a need for a home strip and away strips, for jumpers with a contemporary, stylish, twenty-first-century leisurewear feel, although there's a part of me that can't help appreciating the way West Coast jumpers get more and more grotesque-looking each year.

I hate the pre-season, the Commonwealth Games of footy. Even when your team wins, it's meaningless.

I hate 'international rules', that perverse invention that tries to mess up one of the best things about the game – the fact that no one else plays it. We can't beat another country at footy – what a glorious relief.

I thought I hated Channel Seven. And then Channel Nine came along and raised the bar. All the jostling egos in a confined space, Dennis Cometti with his suave patter, as if he's auditioning for a role in *The Producers*; Dermott with his wise-after-the-event, I-told-you-so tone and his infuriating 'yup'; Garry Lyon as Itchy Brother, the ingratiating suck-up sidekick. And Eddie doing his double act: the Commentator with his Evil Twin, the President.

Dr Eddie and Mr McGuire. Can you tell the difference between E1 and E2?

I hate the fact that one of the best features of the game will soon become folklore, that the appearance of kick-to-kick after the game at Telstra Dome is about as likely as the return of tram conductors. And I can believe that the AFL think they can call it a Dome. It's not a dome, it's a large grey building with a sliding roof. It would make more sense to call it Tracy Island. Maybe then I could come to terms with the TV coverage, if I thought of Dermott as Jeff Tracy, Eddie as Grandma, Garry Lyon as Scott, and Dennis Cometti as Brains. (Or Dennis as Virgil, with Bruce McAvaney in a special guest appearance as Brains? Shane Crawford as Alan, Christi Malthouse moonlighting as Lady Penelope? Kevin Sheedy as Parker? Could Andrew Demetriou be the Hood? Am I getting carried away here?)

And I hate myself – for getting so worked up about all this, for getting optimistic so early in the season, for all the energy and anxiety and righteous anger that gets siphoned off into football, into something that is, after all, only a game.

I hate myself for the time when a friend asked me, what's Franco's first name, and I said, quick as a flash, Josh. And he said, slightly puzzled, but still trusting me, Generalissimo Josh Franco?

Ah, I said. No, that would be Francisco, and I went scarlet with embarrassment, and didn't even admit that I'd been thinking of Josh Francou, and vowed not to read the sports pages first of all the next day but go straight to the world news. After I'd checked the teams.

The Sunday Age, 2 May 2004

SAINTS 2004: A GAME, A JUMPER, A SONG

Stephanie Holt

One Sunday afternoon in March, in a paddock ringed by back-yards, deep in Melbourne's suburbs, a traffic jam is developing. Sun glints off bonnets and windscreens as engines idle. Lydia, my daughter, is part of a mob wandering lazily through it all, just one more kid in a St Kilda guernsey covered in signatures, one more kid wearing a brand new badge for a new favourite player. 'Thanks Mum,' she tells me, holding my hand, swinging my arm with hers, 'That was one of the best days ever.'

We almost hadn't made it. Not after the Saturday night we'd had. Not when the last splutter of energy from the night before had been spent in a dash to the milk bar for the morning papers. (*There's tomorrow's front cover*, I'd declared to a bemused husband-and-father watching the replay in the early hours of the morning, as Stephen Milne perched in a mid-air bear hug halfway up Fraser Gehrig moments after the siren.)

But the poster for the Saints Family Day had been magnetted to the fridge for a month now, and we'd been looking forward to it in a lazy, pre-season sort of way long before we had a victory to celebrate. We'd been promised a 'Carnevale', and a few of the players had been setting the tone, grinning out into the kitchen tricked up in ruffles and Carmen Miranda flourishes. Lydia had been hooked by an invitation to *enter the draw for a chance to present one of the Saints with their official 2004 guernsey*. Nice touch, I'd thought, getting the fans involved. Even though my streetwise 11-year-old insists she never wins anything, and her name would be one of thousands from equally excited and deserving fans, the prospect of this moment in the spotlight beckoned.

And what a day it was. The sun shone on uncharacteristically lush Moorabbin grass. Jokes about mud and sprinkler systems rippled around the crowd. No one seemed to be bothering to collect the entrance money from non-members – I guess they figured non-members wouldn't be non-members for long.

For the past couple of months, as we've done at this time of the year for as long as we can remember, St Kilda fans had been scrutinising footy fixtures, checking the latest news from the team, deliberating earnestly and declaring – as we always do – *This might be our year* ... Now we're coming to terms with wishes that might come true. Four wins in a row and a pre-season pre-miership. Anything seems possible. But first, like participants in the original *carnevale*, the ritualised medieval mayhem before Lent began, we're about to enter a period of privation. As eager as we are, the home-and-away games are still two long weeks away.

Out on the ground, kids swarm around players, proffering textas and autograph books, or wander about in search of com-petitions, rides, food, some kick-to-kick. 'If you can't find us, we'll be in the alcohol tent,' a mother calls to her rapidly van-ishing children. I look up from the sport pages spread across the grass and catch her eye, exchange smiles. Behind its no-nonsense 'alcohol' sign, we've spotted a roped off area of plas-tic chairs and tables, an oasis of calm on the edge of this chaos.

This is a day for the kids, who love these players innocently and without reservation but perhaps sense the complex pas-sions the jumper stirs in their elders. And it's bringing out the kid in each of us. 'Hey, look at these ...' says one Dad, nudging me, grinning, as our respective children home in on the coach. He's clutching a couple of dog-eared footy cards of a young Grant Thomas, but only gets a slight cock of the eyebrow from the coach when he holds them out for signing.

Under the old outer scoreboard, there's a huge crowd around the dunking chair, and the players are taking shifts getting dropped into a pool of water. It's hard to tell which is the bigger attraction – the slapstick fun of it all, the chance to see the play-ers acting like kids themselves, or the sight of our personal favourites in board shorts and bare chests. (*There's Nick Riewoldt, Mum*, says Lydia, with an eye-roll worthy of Benny Hill. And I admit, I look, and then have to look away.)

I hover at the back, waiting for the kid who's burrowed in for a few more photos and autographs, and find myself tracking round the fence, along the terraces, counting the steps till I'm staring at the spot we'd stood at for so many long ago Saturday afternoons, long wintry days when every match was a struggle, the smallest triumph a cause for celebration. Where we'd stood defiantly, resolutely, week in week out, in comradeship with people whose familiar voices buoyed us and whose names we never knew. The last season I'd spent there I'd been pregnant with Lydia; by the time I started taking a red, white and black-swaddled toddler to Saints games, the cruise down the Nepean had given way to the trek out to Waverley. But there, where the SnoDeli sign used to be. About there, a few rows down, maybe around to the wing a little, just past that railing. *Our* spot. It all comes rushing back.

When the day's MC comforts a lost child – 'It's OK. We're all family here' – as glib as his comment is, it feels just right. Like some shambolic extended family, footy fans tell the same jokes, use the same nicknames, treasure the same mementoes, let slip the same secrets, pass on the same latest news. Like family, we rally at times of greatest joy and greatest need. Gather here, where Allan Jeans urged a crowd to action at a Save Our Saints rally, his voice breaking, when one much-loved Victorian team had already gone down fighting and a few more were on the ropes, and I introduced a wide-eyed little girl to a couple of teenage rookies and promised her Joel Smith and Aussie Jones would be champions by the time she was grown up; here, where we celebrated after 1996's Ansett Cup win; here, where we watched training before the 1997 Grand Final, nervous and dis-believing, overcome by familiar figures lingering nearby (Carl Ditterich, standing quietly behind the crowd, the first tall, blonde Saint I fell for); here, where we offered each other com-fort afterwards. Like family, we hold close the same memories and make our way back to the same home, and let ourselves believe in a fragile ideal of refuge and generosity and common cause.

Of course, the highlight of the day is still ahead – the symbolic presentation of the players' guernseys, and first there's the important business of drawing the presenters' names. The kids spread out in front of the stage, a cross-legged carpet of red, white and black, as one by one names are read from slips of paper. There are awkward pauses, names read and reread, stumbles over pronunciation. Squeals follow each name, and the excitement is infectious, even though each of us watching must be hoping for some other name to be called. And then, as the names are coming faster, moving things along, it's *Lydia Holt, from St Kilda*. This takes a moment to sink in. Then she's turning around, searching the crowd behind, and I'm pointing and yelling and willing her to stand up.

Lydia returns a little while later from the huddle beside the stage to report that jumpers will be handed out in the order names were called. It hadn't taken her long to work out she was too late to give Nick Riewoldt his number 12 and too early to give Robert Harvey his number 35; she'll be handing out number 28. 'I don't mind,' she reassures me, 'They're all Saints.'

In a football dreamtime of grainy black-and-white newsreels, tinted cigarette cards and elegant magazine caricatures, it must have meant something very different to be presented with a guernsey at the start of the season. Guernseys that would be washed and repaired carefully, game by game, ending the season battle-scarred and bloodied. Now – with players pampered and cossetted, provided with everything they need, their guernseys instant memorabilia to be sold to the highest bidder – this act has become ritualised. A symbolic start to the season, it's also, if we choose to see it, a reminder of an abstraction greater than any one player, any one team, and almost impossible to describe. *Do it for the jumper*, we say, in a call to higher gods, higher purposes.

Before long, Lydia is waiting patiently in the guernsey-presenting queue as rules are read out and friends and parents are shooed away. There are a couple of late withdrawals and a few fans are called up from the emergency list. There's a bit of movement off the interchange bench, too, as seasoned warriors step aside to give the youngsters a taste of the action. Like Justin

Koszitsche bequeathed Stewie Loewe's number, some solemnly take on another's identity. *My name's not really Peter,* four-year-old Brittany confides to Lydia, *Peter's my Dad ...*

Then, one by one, they climb on stage. As Aaron Hamill stoops to shake the hand of a boy about a third his height, we soak up the moment. Then the players start relaxing, the crowd warms up, and before long handshakes give way to hugs and kisses. When the MC calls 'Danielle' to the stage to present number 10, and quickly corrects himself, Stephen Baker goes ahead and gives Daniel a kiss anyway, to the cheers of the crowd. Lydia, concentrating on doing everything right, takes the stage right on cue, hands over a jumper as Leigh Montagna is introduced, turns and heads off stage. It doesn't stop until Stephen Milne accepts number 44 and sweeps a grandmotherly type off her feet. This is our day, and we feel ready for anything. In cheerful cacophony, we rouse ourselves for the club song.

'He asked me if I'd like a kiss,' says Lydia, when I pump her for details, afterwards, and though she'd been too nervous to answer, she is delighted by the brief, gallant brush on the cheek she received. 'He's really *really* nice,' she tells me.

We head off to buy a Leigh Montagna badge. Lydia's beaming fit to burst.

*

Less than two days later, we wake to the news that Stephen Milne and Leigh Montagna have been accused of sexual assault. Less than two days: just long enough for Lydia to tell and retell the story of her wonderful day; to fill her Dad in with all the details, to ring her uncle and her grandmother and recount her special role; to come home from school to report that one of the teachers had been in the crowd, had recognised her up on stage. 'You'll be lucky if you're still doing that together when she's fifteen,' Mum says to me, proud to share Lydia's moment, after I'd finally wrested the phone away from a chattering granddaughter. When I was somewhere around Lydia's age, growing painfully out of childhood, our relationship had moved toward an antagonism that had taken years to repair.

I'd been watching the TV over Tuesday's breakfast when Rod Butterss, St Kilda's president, had come on the screen, tense and pale, reading a prepared statement. 'There's some news you need to know about,' I'd told Lydia, fetching her from her room, giving her the gist of it, as calmly as I could, leaving the players' names till last, brushing over the detail that whatever happened had happened the night after Family Day. She didn't believe it was true. I searched for ways to not believe, too, and found myself hoping that the media had overstated things, that the club had overreacted.

The news was everywhere. For weeks, salacious and distressing details of New South Wales' Bulldogs 'sex scandal' – the jaunty phrase the media throws about almost gleefully – had been filtering down to Victoria. Now we had our own; the template was ready. After years of rumours, stories passed from fan to fan, passing outwards from inside sources at countless footy clubs with who knew how many distortions and elaborations along the way, the front pages were primed, ready and waiting. And we'd played into their hands. St Kilda, which for over a century had made failure and self-destruction an art form, had moved into its mannerist phase, coaxing absurdly glorious hopes, only to dash them, devastatingly. Everything we thought we knew was collapsing, barely recognisable, under an excess of drama.

In the days that follow, we go from shock and denial to anger, and from anger we each, slowly and in our own way, start trying to make sense of it. A few days after the story breaks, Lydia suggests it as a discussion topic at school. They regularly discuss current affairs, big issues. They've debated wars, explored injustices. But this is something, Lydia is quietly told, best talked about at home.

The media hubbub goes on, all sound and fury, signifying nothing. Talkback fills with opinions, rumours, truisms, soul-searching; *The Footy Show* trots out a panel of women before returning to business as usual. On autopilot, I'd gone to the chemist that Tuesday and collected the photos put in for developing, amid great excitement, the day before. Time and again in the days that follow I get them out, leaf through them, hands shaking, voice shaking, to show people, as if there's some comfort in these desperate recitations: 'That's us at the Wizard Cup final', 'That's Lydia with Grant Thomas' … There's the team with the pre-season cup, Lydia with Brett Voss, now holding up a football jumper, now small and blurry on a distant stage.

A couple of days in I get a four-word email from my best friend – *How are you feeling?* – and for days afterwards distress, confusion and recriminations pour through the phone lines, my computer to hers, moments of clarity, attempts at analysis. *What have I got my daughter into?* I say, and calming words come back, gentle and insistent.

I cling to the smallest of mercies. The club announces that memberships are rising, but we've had ours for months. Fans declare their allegiance, some with a struggle, others defiantly, and I'm glad my jumper is so obviously a relic of earlier times, an old knitted thing, complete with floppy white collar.

Like most mothers, I imagine, I'd anticipated, pleasure tinged with nervousness, a time when I'd be talking to my daughter about boys, hearing about crushes and kisses, answering tentative questions about sex. Instead, I'm trying to explain rape to her. I can't get an image of two blonde heads, a girl and her mother in a car outside a police station, cameras crowding around them, out of my mind.

When Lydia dresses for the first game of the season, badges for her three favourite players are pinned to her guernsey. We head off to the ground, and as carefully as a club official wording a statement to the press, I tell her *I have no doubt something happened that was very, very distressing for those girls, and that those players have done things they should feel very, very ashamed of.* I don't tell her how much courage it takes to report a sexual assault, how hard it is to prove. I don't tell her how fraught the idea of consent can be, nor that most sexual assault involves people known to each other, family even, friends, partners. I don't tell her I think Leigh Montagna has an angel's face, that he is just a boy, so young.

Investigations continue; neither the police nor the club can say how long they'll last, much less what they'll reveal. Speculation and rumour fill the void.

'Are you sure you want to wear that?' I ask, pointing to Lydia's newest badge. Montagna's not even playing.

She flicks the tail of her scarf over it, and I squeeze her hand, as we walk towards the station.

*

There's so much to forget over a summer. How narrow the seats are at Telstra Dome, how tightly packed the rows. How long the queues are at the food stalls, how slow the service. Behind us in the line at the hot dog stand a mobile phone rings: 'Yeah, I'm still in the queue … yeah, I know … I know … I *know* …' The girl behind me has a grumble to no one in particular as she pockets her phone: 'We'll still be here when the game starts!'

The noise bounces around, off concrete and steel, tumbling around the stadium. Kids wander past in packs, shrieking at each other, bouncing their footies, darting around to keep control of them. There's a mother with three boys strung out behind her hand-in-hand. Conversations float by, talk of the season to come, of the summer just passed, the fans are catching up, nervy, keeping it light.

Lydia and I head for our agreed spot, find the rest of our mob, then struggle along, balancing chips and hot dogs, stepping self-consciously over feet, bags and debris, weaving past knees, to a couple of empty seats. We're ready for action but short on match practice, and I'd forgotten all this – not the fact of it, but the feeling. How close the crowd is, how unrelenting their noise. How strong my own voice is, escaping from deep in the belly as the final chords of the national anthem die down.

We're sitting next to a grey-haired man in a crisp short-sleeved shirt and pressed trousers, a sharp crease running up each leg. Behind him and stretched out beside are a couple of sons and assorted grandkids. I can't tell who he barracks for, or whether the family's come along in solidarity with each other or to enjoy a bit of family rivalry, so as the game gets underway I make a note to be on my best behaviour.

It's a messy start. Two weeks has proven a long time in football, and the fans are on edge. We seem unsure how to react, desperate to lose ourselves, prove ourselves, test ourselves. Every summer, we look forward to the day when we'll be back at the footy. To a time when speculation and hope will give way to action and results. To barracking, with its catharsis and exhilaration. We hunger for that weekly fix of passion and forgetting, of shutting out the world, immersing ourselves in the moment. Today we're struggling.

Out on the field, our boys are fumbling, hesitant. A few minutes into the game, Aussie Jones takes a kick out of trouble from a team-mate and worries himself into the middle of three Geelong players. The man next to me slaps a rolled up *Record* against a neatly trousered leg so violently that I jump.

The first time Stephen Milne comes into the play, the crowd is subdued. When he takes a set shot at goal, a little while later, he's kicking into a jeering Geelong cheer squad. The Saints struggle on.

We're on the watch for any signs of hope, of a lift, when there's a fine St Kilda dodge on the opposite wing, and the girls in the row behind start cheering. 'We don't want fancy,' spits out my neighbour, 'we want hard work.' He's perfected the morose chuckle and the ironic cheer. 'It's going to be a long night for St Kilda fans,' he declares, as yet another stray kick ends up in the wrong hands.

Then, slowly, the game starts turning. Late in the second quarter, when we've got the ball front of the centre but no one to kick to, Milne emerges from a tangle of players just outside the 50-metre arc. Someone's yelling 'to Milney, to Milney!', and I realise it's me. Slowly, the game turns, catches us up in its excitement, carries us along in its momentum, takes us back to what we know and love.

By the time the final siren sounds, the Saints are winning convincingly, and Milne has kicked four goals. He pumps the air, and is swept up in his team-mates' arms. The players regroup and, like Andre Agassi, pace out the centre square, stopping at each corner to acknowledge the fans in each quadrant of the ground. The TV cameras track their progress, and follow the final, exhausted shuffle toward the dressing rooms. The cameras have found the shot they want: there's Milne, picked out through the throng, projected larger than life onto the big screens. There's tomorrow's front page, I think, turning away.

The Geelong ranks have already thinned – it's a long trip back down the highway, as we've been reminding them for a while – and now we spill out too. 'When the Saints Go Marching In' echoes again and again through the stadium; each time the strains of the big finale linger and then the sound system goes silent, for just a little too long, before cranking up again. These are familiar cues, and welcome. We sing along in rasping voices, made hoarse over the past couple of hours, falling into a role rehearsed over many seasons, honed win by win: how convincingly, how easily, we play the victorious fans.

Just for tonight, we need it to be about this: a game, a jumper, a song. About heading home on a train full of exhausted bodies, all in their colours, and coming out into the cool night air of Windsor station, up the ramp into Chapel Street, with people spilling out from the pub on the corner, and hanging around the backpacker hostel over the road, and milling outside the pizza shop a few steps further on, and hearing a voice, wired for Saturday night, call out 'Hey … How'd they do?' as we walk past.

'Saints,' I call over my shoulder, 'Doubled 'em.' There's a rumble of *Great!* and *OK!* and Lydia has stopped to tell someone the final scores.

I head after a girl dancing down the footpath ahead, disappearing into the Melbourne night waving a red, white and black flag. Lydia runs up behind and takes my hand. Footy's back, and we're in for a year like no other.

An extract from *One Week at a Time: Sex, Footy and the Flag*,
Coulomb Communications, 2005

AFTER COFFS: ABOUT THAT NIGHT …

Christine Jackman

Almost six months on, things are pretty much back to normal in Coffs Harbour, the NSW coastal town where sea-changers come to stay and backpackers come to play. The *Coffs Coast Advocate* is again full of stories about water restrictions, the city council is poised to debate its flying fox management plan and, while holidaymakers don't pack the beaches like they do in summer, there are enough cool-climate activities – from whalewatching to skydiving – to keep vital tourism dollars flowing.

For many locals, however, winter in a region where the unemployment rate runs at roughly double the national average must seem interminable. For them, the Big Banana, a 3.3-metre ferrous concrete behemoth proudly touted on its website as 'indeed Australia's most famous icon', and the Clog Barn – 'all the colour and charm of Holland … and Coffs Harbour's largest range of collectable spoons' – have long since lost their novelty.

By now, memories of summer, with its welcome influx of new faces and new experiences, have begun to fade. But not completely. And not for everybody, particularly the women at the centre of two incidents that have forever changed them, their town and broad Australian attitudes to two great national pastimes – sport and sex.

One woman is now rarely seen outside the home she shares on a quiet, leafy street with her parents and infant son. And while the other woman has proven less shy – in March, 'Kate' (not her real name) appeared on *60 Minutes* to detail an alleged sexual assault early last year involving three members of the Bulldogs rugby league team – she says she no longer feels safe in a town she once considered a friendly haven. 'I'm a bit paranoid, worked up, like someone's always looking over my shoulder,' says the single mother.

Kate says she's tried to educate her girls – she has three

daughters and five kids in all – to take care of themselves and that, no matter their age, they're always at risk. 'What am I supposed to say to my 16-year-old when she says, "Mum, how come they weren't charged? Was it because they were footballers? And why were they allowed to come back?"'

The question hangs like a smudge over Coffs Harbour and the Canterbury Bulldogs. Since the events of that hot February night this year – and despite an intensive two-month investigation by 11 police officers and a furious trial by media – many Australians still feel they are no closer to answering it.

*

The first fingers of dawn stretched across the horizon above the Pacific Ocean shortly after 6 a.m. on Sunday, 22 February. According to Bureau of Meteorology records, the sun rose at Coffs Harbour at 6.32 a.m. and it was already warm.

That was not unusual, for summer dies hard in Coffs. The night before the events that would transfix a nation, it was hot and sweaty inside the Plantation Hotel, a squat building that hugs the Pacific Highway as it slices through Coffs Harbour. 'Milkshake', hip-hop artist Kelis's anthem to in-your-face female sexuality, was booming across the bars and dance floors with its hypnotic, thumping chorus – 'lala-la-la-la, warm it up, lala-la-la-la, the boys are waiting'.

And, indeed, the boys were in town, had been all week. The Canterbury Bulldogs – one of the star teams of the National Rugby League – had been preparing for a trial match against the Canberra Raiders, which they went on to win comfortably that Saturday afternoon.

Post-match, the players dutifully attended an official function at the Coffs Ex-Services Club. But with those obligations fulfilled shortly before midnight, it was just a quick dash across the highway to join the milling crowds at the Planto, the town's most popular nightspot after a multimillion-dollar refurbishment a year earlier. Inside, amid the pub's gold-flecked banana trees, crowded pool tables and throbbing speakers, at least one local girl was eager to party with the pin-up boys. In a town where it's almost as hard to find a man as it is to find a job, an influx of fit, well-paid young sports stars demands attention.

But eight hours after the post-match hijinks at the Planto, that same young woman would be found sobbing, wet and dishevelled in a car park at the Novotel Pacific Bay Resort a few kilometres down the highway. As guests filed into Charlie's Restaurant for their breakfast coffee and croissants, she would tell hotel staff that she had been gang-raped by up to eight Bulldogs players by the hotel pool.

To attempt to explain what happened in those pre-dawn hours is to sift through the quagmire of rumour and speculation that remains after a two-month police investigation that raised at least as many questions as it answered. If there was a rape – and, indeed, Detective Chief Inspector Jason Breton described the incident at Coffs Harbour as 'a very vicious sexual assault' – why was no individual held accountable? Had the investigation been mishandled? And, if so, where was the outrage from the media commentators who had campaigned so vociferously on behalf of the anonymous woman?

And if there was no rape, why were innocent men pilloried, their careers jeopardised, their game smeared? Had an increasingly elitist commentariat allowed its own bias to obscure its analysis of an exceedingly complex case?

As almost always, in cases of intimate betrayal, the answers remain in the shadows, in the void of sexual congress that lies between the black of 'no' and the white of 'yes'.

*

This much we know, from witness statements and other evidence. This was not the first time the young woman had returned with members of the Bulldogs to the Novotel Pacific Bay Resort, proudly billed the 'Home of the Wallabies' after Australia's rugby squad adopted the picturesque haven as its training base in 2000.

In a statement given to police, the woman said she had also visited the resort three nights before the Bulldogs Canberra match, and had had consensual sex with four players, a claim verified by the men involved. Sources close to the team dispute whether it was 'group sex' or sex with four individual players at separate times during that night – an indication of the delicate complexities of the debate about group sex, subtleties which were largely lost in ensuing media outrage.

The Bulldogs also denied media reports that players were drunk or badly behaved after their win on Saturday. An independent inquiry into allegations of brawling and sexual harassment, ordered by National Rugby League boss David Gallop and conducted by former chief of detectives Ken Bowditch, later vindicated the team. In addition, Plantation Hotel licensee Harry Barry sent his own letter to then Bulldogs CEO Steve Mortimer commending his players' conduct. 'I did not see, nor did anyone complain to me or a member of my staff, about the behaviour of the Bulldogs while at the hotel,' Barry wrote. 'Indeed, staff, regular customers and the Bulldogs had a most enjoyable night.'

One player more than most, perhaps. Recognising the young woman from the pre-match bacchanalia of Wednesday night, this player – a younger member of the squad – flirted with her in the bar before disappearing to have sex with her in a room at the backpackers' hostel that forms part of the sprawling Planto complex. (Although the woman lives with her parents and her 18-month-old son just a few minutes' drive from the pub, her friend Kylie Hubbard lives more than 30 kilometres out of town and the women apparently often used the hostel as a base when they planned a big night out together.)

What happened next, after the woman returned from her assignation in the hostel bedroom, is more contentious. Several players told police she pestered them as they played poker machines clustered in a quiet corner of the hotel, away from the main dance floor and bar. Sources close to those players say she harassed high-profile forward Willie Mason particularly insistently. Lawyers for the Bulldogs complain that a surveillance tape from the Plantation Hotel's security cameras which would have proved or disproved these potentially damning claims was taken by police, who assured them they would be able to make a copy but later reneged on that arrangement. 'We have received instruction [the woman] was jumping over the backs of the players and pressing the payout buttons [on the poker machines] without their permission,' Bulldogs solicitor John Carmody said, when asked what he believed the tape would show. 'We also have information she picked up a player's glass and began licking it with her tongue.'

A doorman at the hotel later told police he had been slapped in the chest by the woman after he refused to intervene on her behalf when a player barred her from sharing his cab back to the Pacific Bay Resort. The player – understood to be Mason – allegedly swore vehemently at the woman as he told her to leave him alone. 'It's pretty ironic and unfair that people have assumed Willie had something to do with this when he was probably the most verbose in rejecting her,' says a senior source in Bulldogs management. 'And that he could even have been fined for using bad language in public to reject her. He was nowhere near the Wednesday night stuff, either.'

Says another, a veteran of the game: 'She was after a trophy [star player] – and she didn't get it. This sort of thing is an elevated form of autograph hunting. A very physical form.'

Flick through any women's magazine, scan any pop music show, and a contradictory image of modern woman emerges: on the one hand, a sultry huntress prowling the night; on the other, a princess pining for her knight. Even dance-floor divas like Kelis recognise that balancing these two forces can be tricky: 'You must maintain your charm, same time maintain your halo / … Then next his eyes are squint, then he's picked up your scent / Lala-la-la-la, warm it up, lala-la-la-la, the boys are waiting.'

Dr Michael Flood, a gender studies specialist and Australia Institute research fellow who is serving on an NRL-appointed panel researching sexual attitudes among footballers, says young women are given mixed messages about what it means to be empowered.

'On the one hand, there's a trend that's gone on, encouraging sexual assertiveness,' says Flood. 'Young women are given permission to flirt, to pick men up, to dress more provocatively.

That's new, that's only 20 or so years old. But there are other parts of the culture that suggest that's unsafe. We encourage women to be like that but we punish them. Our society gives young women contradictory messages: be sexy, reveal your body. But then we punish them as sluts.'

*

Despite the disinterest – and, in some cases, outright hostility – displayed by some of the Bulldogs towards her, the woman eventually shared a cab back to the Pacific Bay Resort about 5.30 a.m., accompanied by the player with whom she had had sex earlier in the night.

She later told police she wanted to go to the resort only to return a wallet to her friend Kylie Hubbard, who had gone back there with a player. But her credibility was thrown into doubt when police later established she had not taken the missing wallet to Pacific Bay; it was left all night at the Planto.

It is here that the timeline – and the evidence of two key independent witnesses – becomes critical. One witness, a maintenance worker at the Pacific Bay Resort, told police he ran into the woman and man shortly after he started work about 5.50 a.m., when she asked him for directions to a semi-private beach adjoining the resort.

About 25 minutes later, he encountered the couple again. By then, they were near the resort's Charlesworth Pool, talking to two young men he had just seen put two other girls into a cab. The girls were 'very young, say 16 to 18', the worker recalled. 'I thought it was a bit late for them to be out at that time.' If nothing else, this evidence suggests at least two other Bulldogs players that night openly flouted the club's unwritten code outlawing women being brought back to the hotel.

A second witness, a pool technician, spotted the couple 'actually in the act of sex' in the pool about that time. The man told police it was about 6.30 a.m. and broad daylight when he arrived to take water samples from the Charlesworth Pool, one of three pools at the resort. 'There was a girl in the water with her back towards me and there was a fellow sitting on the edge of the pool taking his weight on his hands and I presumed they were having oral sex,' the man said in his statement to police. He added he deliberately shut the gate loudly to warn them he was there.

'When that happened the girl sort of rose up out of the water and pivoted around beside the bloke and just sat there alongside him ... I wasn't really interested in what they were doing; to me it was just a couple of people having an early morning romp. The girl was just sitting there and I just minded my own business.'

Some time after 6.30 a.m., the maintenance worker also entered the pool area to empty bins. He saw the young woman 'swimming in the pool breaststroke, virtually in the one spot. She looked like she was enjoying everything. There was nothing unusual about her.' The young man with whom she had arrived was nowhere in sight. But the pair he had seen farewelling two younger women in a cab were lying by the pool on banana lounges.

At least one golfer is believed to have been on the course that hugs the pool – a putting green sits just five metres from its perimeter fence – at that time. By 7 a.m., the golf shop and snack bar that overlooks the area had opened; by 7.15 a.m., when the pool technician returned to do more work on the Charlesworth Pool, it was deserted.

The young woman originally told police the assault happened some time between 6 a.m. and 7 a.m., although she later broadened that window to between 5.30 a.m. and 7.30 a.m. If the independent witnesses are to be believed, and physical evidence of time, weather and locale taken into account, there seems almost no opportunity left in that period for six to eight young men to assault a woman undetected in a pool area overlooked by two large hotel blocks.

Nevertheless, at 8.30 a.m., an ambulance was called to the resort. An hour or so later, Bulldogs CEO Steve Mortimer walked out of his hotel room and immediately spotted football manager Garry Hughes speaking to a player who was gesticulating wildly. Mortimer's first thought was: 'Oh God, not again.'

*

Five months later, Kate wakes with a start in the dead of night. A face comes to her often like this, leering from the shadows, mocking her. She knows exactly when the nightmares returned. It was the week after that game on 21 February. The day she heard on the radio that a young woman had told police that members of the Bulldogs at Pacific Bay had sexually assaulted her. Almost exactly a year before, Kate had told police the same thing, alleging she had returned to the resort with a Bulldogs player she'd met at a nightclub, only to be assaulted by one of his team-mates.

These days, the 43-year-old divorced mother of five lives as a virtual recluse, her one foray in the past year to a club with friends lasting just minutes before she fled in the throes of an anxiety attack. But at least the nightmares – always the same, always featuring that second player taunting her, pretending to be the man who she had accompanied back to the resort – had subsided by Christmas.

Then she heard the boys were back in town. 'It's taken me until now to go through counselling, and to have good friends standing by me, and me yelling and screaming at them, to make myself stronger,' Kate says. 'Which I thought I was … until I heard what had happened to this young girl. And now it's gone backwards again.'

The police never pressed charges against the Bulldogs over Kate's case, telling her the question of whether she had con- sented to having sex with the second player would come down in court to a matter of her word against theirs. But in hindsight, she was sounding a warning that something stale and poison- ous lurked in league's dank corners.

*

Steve 'Turvey' Mortimer – the nickname comes from the Turvey Park Club, where Mortimer spent his early years before being signed by Canterbury – is widely acknowledged as one of rugby league's greatest ever players. He says that when he was installed as Bulldogs CEO in 2002 – following a salary cap crisis that saw the ladder leaders stripped of their points and their chance to win that year's premiership – it was clear that the club was struggling to come to grips with the obligations of the professional era.

It had been known, proudly, as the family club. For three decades, the Canterbury Bulldogs had grown strong under a dynasty welded together by former club patriarch Peter Moore. It was Moore who discovered three stylish young footballers playing in Wagga Wagga and brought them to Sydney. When the Mortimer brothers – Steve, Chris and Peter – met up with Moore's own nephews – Garry, Graeme and Mark Hughes – there was an irresistible alchemy. But by the time Kate made her complaint, the 'family' club was looking decidedly dysfunctional, with its two most powerful factions – represented by the Hughes and Mortimer brothers – increasingly at odds over the future of the business.

Mortimer is an avowed Christian – 'I don't hide from it' – but if there's a born-again fervour to any of his rhetoric, it is when he speaks of his business ethics and mentors, 'tremendous men, people I respect and admire, who' – and no one at the family club would miss the significance of the next four words – 'came from outside Canterbury'.

Shocked by the money and time players of the modern era had on their hands, Mortimer says he was determined to introduce further education and training at the proudly working-class club, to help prepare them for life after football. He also wanted to get them involved in charity work. 'It's good for the heart,' Mortimer says. 'The boys needed to be more community-oriented. They're up there on a pedestal and my belief was if you can do some good, it will come back to you tenfold. It gives them a sense of community and keeps their feet planted on the ground.'

Personally, he was appalled at the behaviour which led to Kate's complaint in early 2003. 'I said we can't afford this kind of stuff,' Mortimer says, pounding his fist to emphasise each word of his subsequent edict. 'So the rule is: NO ONE – BRINGS

– ANY – LADIES – BACK – TO THE HOTEL. It's like your home. If you're single and you live at home with your parents, you wouldn't bring a girl back home because it's disrespect to your parents. If you want to go out and have some fun, go and do it at her place.'

He insists that the players' committee agreed, supporting fines for players who disobeyed the new rule, and that the football department manager, Garry Hughes, understood. (Hughes would later pay with his job for the events of 22 February. He has since lodged a complaint with the NSW Industrial Relations Commission, claiming his sacking was 'unfair, harsh or unconscionable' and, with his case pending, will not comment.)

Supporters of Hughes say he had difficulty dealing with Mortimer, who was an 'inexperienced' CEO at best; at worst, he failed to communicate his plans adequately to his own staff and was downright contemptuous of the football department.

'Turvey was probably our greatest ever player,' says one, 'and he probably thought he could handle things. But the ego wasn't matched by results. The board knew they had a problem [with him] but they didn't act.'

By the pre-season rounds of 2004, the tensions had reached boiling point. Players had returned from the off-season on 5 January but the program of education, training and charity work which Mortimer insists he had delegated to Hughes to implement was never launched. 'It just never happened,' says Mortimer. 'I was trying to sign [sponsors] up and by mid-February I said, "What the hell is happening here?" And was told, "It'll happen, it'll happen." And then Coffs Harbour happened.'

*

Seated in his office at Fox Studios, the extensive complex adjacent to the Sydney Cricket Ground and Aussie Stadium which is home to an array of movie production houses, talent managers and casting agencies, NRL boss David Gallop sips a takeaway coffee and ponders the entertainment business that is rugby league.

Tall, thin and bespectacled, Gallop seems more like an urbane headmaster of an elite boys' boarding school than the over-worked and often besieged chief executive of the working man's competition. He is, in fact, a lawyer by trade, which may explain why he chooses his words carefully. 'I've got no knowledge of group sex being commonplace in the game,' he says. 'I've never been exposed to it. But I've never been a player, I've never been a manager of a team, I've never been with a club. I just wasn't aware it was something that happened often.'

For two days after news of the Coffs Harbour incident broke, Gallop waited by his phone for Steve Mortimer to explain whether it did, indeed, happen often. Or at all. But Mortimer didn't call – a decision Gallop now nominates as 'one of the disappointing aspects of how the Bulldogs handled things'.

The family club had bunkered down, adopting the steely 'us against the world' mentality which had served it so well on the football field. But with traditional alliances within the club already fractured, it was only a matter of time before the facade would collapse.

On 18 March, club chairman George Peponis announced Mortimer's nemesis Garry Hughes had been sacked, ostensibly for failing to ensure players dressed appropriately for their police interviews. Four days later, Peponis informed Mortimer that he, too, had to go, having lost the confidence of the board. Mortimer looked his former team-mate in the eyes and said simply: 'I've been wronged.'

Gallop has since concluded that the Bulldogs executives were simply incapable of grasping one of the most sensitive and explosive issues any modern-day board might be asked to handle: sexual misbehaviour by high-profile employees.

'Without sounding overcritical of their game plan, I just don't think they knew how to handle it,' Gallop says. 'It took a while for it to sink in with them that, irrespective of what their view of what happened was, it was a huge story that a woman had made that allegation, that it's a huge issue not only in rugby league but in the community. Allegations of gang rape are always going to be big news.'

But even he had failed to grasp just how big. While the NRL had taken legal advice not to take action while the police investigation was under way, and had subsequently decided to limit its own commentary on the incident, the media were under no such constraint. And it appeared some members of the police were actively encouraging the hysteria.

Two days after police were called to the Pacific Bay Resort, Sydney broadcaster Ray Hadley went to air shortly after 9 a.m., as parents were dropping their children at preschool and pensioners were finishing their breakfast, to read a graphic incident report from Coffs Harbour. 'Initial information to police was that the victim ... was taken to the lower pool area by about six to eight of the players,' Hadley read. 'She has then disclosed to a cleaner that at least six of them sexually assaulted her, without consent, by anal, oral and vaginal penetration.'

In the public furore that followed, it was rarely made clear to listeners or readers that an incident report is not a police statement of what they believe to have happened but rather a crime victim's description of an alleged incident. That report may change – as this one did – as time passes and the victim recalls or clarifies details. And ultimately, the police or Department of Public Prosecutions may decide there is not enough evidence to substantiate those claims – as also happened in this case. Exactly how Hadley got hold of what should have been a confidential police document remains unclear. (Hadley refused a request from *The Weekend Australian Magazine* for an interview.)

Certainly, if there is one thing that unites the otherwise estranged Bulldogs factions it is that the taskforce formed to investigate the gang rape claims, led by Detective Chief Inspector Jason Breton, had put considerable pressure on the club by constantly engaging with the media.

Mortimer insists the Coffs Harbour police who responded initially to the complaint were 'great'. But he says the constructive relationship he had sought to establish with police fell apart after his first contact with Breton. 'It came down [to Sydney] and that frigging ...' – it is the only time the earnest Mortimer swears during our conversations and he recoils visibly as the word spills out – 'um, yeah, all of a sudden he [Breton] phoned me and he talks through you, at you. And it just threw petrol on the fire.'

But the next betrayal – the one that Gallop believes exacerbated the issue 'from a huge problem to a massive problem' – did not originate with police. It came, allegedly, from within the family club itself.

*

'Some of the boys love a bun.' In a newspaper report titled 'Players reveal their side of the story', those seven words, attributed to an unnamed Bulldogs player, were buried in the last paragraph, as if the article's author could barely believe someone from the besieged club would be stupid enough to utter them. A 'bun-chick', readers were duly informed, was a girl who engaged willingly in group sex with footballers.

So sensational was the anonymous player's claim that 'gang banging is nothing new for our club, or the rugby league', Gallop immediately rang the reporter and his editors to grill them about the veracity of their source. Assured in no uncertain terms that a current player had given the interview, Gallop fronted a media scrum at the front of NRL headquarters and expressed his horror at such language, let alone the behaviour it described. 'That led to a lot of animosity between the club and us,' Gallop says. 'But it seemed to me to denote a disregard for women, even in a consensual situation. That's my view. Certainly, if it's the subject of expressions like gang bang, consensual or not, it seems to me … almost inarguable that appropriate regard and respect for that woman hasn't been operating in their heads.'

But if the NRL boss could see the distinction – that players who indulge in consensual group sex may be guilty of wanton obnoxiousness, but not of any criminal offence – it was lost on many in the media. From the moment that phrase 'some of the boys love a bun' was uttered, the focus of many reports switched subtly but significantly from whether six men were guilty of what Detective Chief Inspector Breton had called 'a very vicious sexual assault' to whether an entire sporting code was guilty of sexual behaviour which some in the media found offensive.

The fact that the young woman at the centre of the allegations had told police she participated willingly in group sex during that week was rarely discussed. Nor was the possibility countenanced that what had actually distressed her in those crowded hours around dawn on 22 February, when the opportunity for a violent, public gang rape seemed limited – was the rudeness, the callousness, the ignorant dismissiveness of men who had previously been quite happy to indulge themselves with her.

Instead, many journalists began building their own case against the Bulldogs without regard for the facts. A *Four Corners* · report on sexual violence in sport depicted the Charlesworth Pool in the dead of night. A *Sydney Morning Herald* feature described it as 'a place bathed in darkness, despite the lights that turn the water a seductive blue-green, a place where the roar of the ocean, only 100 metres away, drowns out most noise'. Except the pool wasn't in darkness and the ocean doesn't drown out the noise. As two independent witnesses told police, it was broad daylight when the woman was seen frolicking in the pool; one also told police that 'that morning, it was very calm, no wind, very quiet. If anyone made any noise, you can hear it from the Bayside Towers.' Indeed, any visitor to the pool would note that a thick ridge of scrub muffles the sound of waves breaking.

Disturbingly, a *Bulletin* feature told readers 'the public doesn't need to know the truth of events at a Coffs Harbour swimming pool to be appalled'. Regardless of what the Bulldogs had or hadn't confessed to, and of the right to be considered innocent until proven guilty, 'the public [had] begun to realise that such sexual antics go beyond matters of taste and morality, that they are part of something darker'. The nature of that sinister thing was implied in the next paragraph of the *Bulletin* story: 'Rape isn't about promiscuity or a moment of weakness. Rape is a crime. When the Bulldogs dawdled into the police station masquerading as beach bums, they unwittingly dared the public to explore football's underbelly of warped masculinity.'

Several commentators argued that this was specifically a rugby league problem. At best, it was an odd generalisation to make, given the avalanche of revelations that the Bulldogs case triggered. At worst, it was a biased and unsustainable slur.

Within two weeks of the Coffs story breaking, Brisbane woman Jacinta Dahms spoke on *60 Minutes* and ABC Radio about being assaulted by up to 20 rugby union players in the mid-1980s. In March, St Kilda players Stephen Milne and Leigh Montagna were accused of raping two women (the charges were later dropped), becoming the latest in a string of AFL players who have been accused of sexual assault since the late 1990s. And an almost identical crisis had rocked Premier League soccer in Britain last October, after a group of premiership players were accused of forcing a 17-year-old girl to have group sex in a £400-a-night London hotel room.

Ironically, many of the same commentators who would defend a woman's right not to have her past sexual history brought up in a court of law did exactly that in the court of public opinion in order to convict the Canterbury Bulldogs – and rugby league. Why?

'Class prejudice is alive and well in Australia,' says Professor Catharine Lumby, appointed by the NRL as a specialist adviser on gender relations at the height of the crisis. Lumby accuses an 'increasingly middle-class media' of being particularly laden with this bias: 'I think it's interesting that there were a lot of people talking in the media who were dreadfully careful about not stereotyping women, but were doing just that to men, saying this is about rugby league players.

'A barrister once said to me that men who play rugby league are animals who should not be put near women. I find that fantastically offensive. There are some great men playing football and some real animals running law firms.'

NSW Rape Crisis Centre manager Karen Willis says the witch-hunt against league players was fairly typical of what occurs when the community is shocked by claims of a particularly repellent crime: 'I'm not surprised that people are wanting to narrow it down. Because then [they can say] "my family and I are safe because we don't go to football in Canterbury". There's always been myths about rape; that we can spot one in the crowd, that all rapists are ugly, drunk and working-class, or black men, or they're from Lebanon,' says Willis, who was invited by Lumby to contribute to the NRL-commissioned research project into footballers' sexual attitudes and behaviour.

'It's always, "That's not our men; our men don't do it." Well, that's so far from the truth … It's not just about groups of foot-ballers. The common matter with gang rape is groups of young males. It's not that footballers are better or worse than others, or surfers or bikers. It's just groups of young men.'

That said, Willis, Lumby and Flood agree it is possible to iden-tify certain groups whose characteristics – a culture of secrecy, of 'us against the world', bonding and hypermasculinity – increase the likelihood of their members engaging in gang rape. Lumby lists college fraternities, the military and some surfing commu-nities as subcultures wherein gang rape has been documented as an insidious bonding or initiation ritual.

But all of those predisposing characteristics can be found in football also, where 'what goes on tour stays on tour'. Says Willis: 'In football, you've got alcohol, you've got money, you've got reverence, you've got group bonding and you've got secrecy. Male bonding is such an important, revered thing, above all else. And any time you develop a secrecy code, whether it's in the military or football, you're going to get some at the edges of that who are going to misuse that process.'

But, adds Lumby, that criminal minority is far outweighed by the majority of players. And, while condemning the former, she says we rarely acknowledge the latter for dealing, largely suc-cessfully, with myriad pressures: 'It's easy to overlook that these are very young men, often from the country, who are bought, sold and treated as commodities based on their bodies, and thrust under the media microscope.

'How many young men in that situation would suddenly act as a community role model? You find any 17-year-old man, put him in the limelight, give him lots of money and call him a celebrity, and he's bound to come up against some tough ethical dilemmas on the way.'

*

By mid-year, the fallout from Coffs Harbour – the town's name seems condemned to remain as grim shorthand for the grubbiest scandal ever to rend rugby league – continues to spread like a stain.

The financial toll is easiest to assess: more than $1.2 million in revenue lost after nervous corporate sponsors walked away from the Bulldogs; a $150,000 fine imposed by the National Rugby League, with a further $350,000 hanging over the club, should any of its players misbehave again before the end of the 2006 season; and a security bill of up to $250,000 for the season after the NRL demanded the Bulldogs do more to control aggressive fans at its matches.

The human wreckage is more difficult to measure. At the family club, the bonds shared by a band of brothers seem forever broken. Last month, Bulldogs captain and sentimental favourite Steve Price cited the scandal as a contributing factor in his decision to defect to the New Zealand Warriors next season. The wrongful dismissal suit brought by Garry Hughes threatens to bring further bitterness to the fore; 'he's absolutely determined to clear his name and his family's name,' a mate says.

Steve Mortimer still seems shell-shocked, although he insists he bears no malice towards the girl who triggered the crisis which ultimately cost him his job, and that of his brother Peter, who resigned as a director at the club in protest at the way Mortimer's dismissal was handled. 'Look, I didn't slag her,' Steve says wearily. 'I felt sorry for her. She's a human being. It may sound corny, but I prayed that she'd be OK and that commonsense would prevail ... Experience is a wonderful thing. I'm sure a lot of players will learn from this slip-up. And I'm sure she has, too.'

But ask what he has learnt and Mortimer pulls off one of those sidesteps for which he was famous in his playing days. He refers instead to the 'great comfort' he draws from news that his successor, Malcolm Noad, is implementing a comprehensive education, training and work experience program for players.

A week or so after Noad's appointment was made public on 1 April, Mortimer phoned the Bulldogs extension that used to be his own and left a message wishing him well. The indefatigably affable Noad returned the call, and invited the club legend to a match. 'Mate, there's too much pain in my heart,' Mortimer told him. He wasn't sure he was ready to confront the spectacle of a game he once loved, now changed utterly. Almost six months on, he still hasn't been back. 'One day,' he says, staring out at a grey twilight. 'But not yet.'

And in Coffs Harbour, on so many sleepless nights, Kate worries whether she did enough. 'Thinking of it all now, maybe I should have gone a lot further, done more speaking out,' she wonders aloud. 'But back then I was probably thinking to myself that maybe I deserved it, because I went back with some-body to a hotel … Maybe the other girl thinks that way, that maybe because she consented once, people will think: "What's she playing at?"'

Kate has never met the young woman at the centre of this year's scandal, although the odds are that their daily lives have overlapped at some unremarkable stage. But she doesn't need a degree in gender studies to challenge the fundamental inde-cency about the gossip that gets swapped across bars and in cabs, the slurs that suggest there's always women like that in towns like this. 'It's not the point, whether she's known around town or not. Nobody deserves to be treated like that; nobody deserves to be violated,' Kate says. 'I knew it was for that night only, I knew he was leaving. Boys will be boys. But boys can be decent … And after we went back [to the hotel], there was noth-ing decent.'

Back in Sydney, David Gallop will sit down this weekend, as he does every weekend through winter, and watch dozens of young men perform like gods on the field. And he will wonder again how some of them managed to fall to Earth so heavily.

'It was a perilous position that those young men put them-selves in,' Gallop concedes. 'But I'd hope we'll look back in a few years and say it was a time when the game drew a line in the sand about attitudes towards women.'

Asked what he believes happened in Coffs Harbour that night, he sighs and puts down his now-empty coffee cup. 'I fully accept that nothing criminal happened. But I think there were some victims, definitely. Garry Hughes and Steve Mortimer, I definitely feel sorry for them. It's not easy, that balance between leadership and being solid with your players ...

'And the girl. I feel desperately sorry for her because whatever happened greatly distressed her. She will, if ever, take a long time to recover from it.'

It takes a moment to realise why these three simple sentences sound so foreign. And then it dawns. Apart from Steve Mortimer's prayers, no one who has spoken about life 'after Coffs', either on or off the record, has voiced any concern at all about a woman in Coffs Harbour who cannot sleep and another who will not speak.

The Weekend Australian Magazine, 7 August 2004

MENTALITY OF THE PACK TOO MUCH FOR ONE ROOKIE

Claire Halliday

Wanna be a footy hero? James Murphy did. And he got the chance he dreamed of. Picked as a rookie by an AFL club, he started training with the big boys. Two weeks later he quit, deciding professional football wasn't the kind of environment that turned young men into role models.

Murphy, 21, says that instead of a true esprit de corps, there was a pack mentality, with a hardline code of secrecy surrounding bad behaviour, especially sexual infidelities. The all-for-fun spirit of the field didn't extend to the locker room, where a schoolyard pecking order pervaded.

'I felt like an outsider at the club,' he said. 'It's pretty much everyone for themselves … The talk was about keeping things silent … by doing that you had power over other people.'

In his first week of training with the Melbourne-based club, Murphy said the topic of sexual infidelity was raised repeatedly – not as something to be avoided, but in warnings to team members who had spilt the beans about well-known players' extra-marital flings. 'The concern wasn't that the players had cheated on their wives or girlfriends on the end-of-season trip. It was all about who had been talking … and how (straying) players got into trouble with their partners,' said Murphy. 'The lesson was that, in order to be a strong team, everyone had to stick together. A strong team covered up for each other.'

Deception and loose morals didn't sit well with Murphy's upbringing. He grew up in Fiji, and had a country-boy sensibility. Since the introduction of the national AFL draft in 1986, many players come from country football clubs – and country boys have long had a history of not adjusting well to the bawdy AFL brotherhood. 'It's all changing now though,' said AFL talent manager Kevin Sheehan. 'The TAC cup that started back in 1993 in Victoria has allowed the kids to stay at home and still play at a higher level.'

While young players were once largely left to their own devices, Sheehan said the introduction of welfare officers attached to each AFL club in the past decade had meant a smoother transition. 'The club normally put them into a foster home-type environment with a family – people who are known to the club who volunteer to help out – and then they might go into a flat with a couple of mates in their second year here,' said Sheehan. 'In the first year training is so hard, and it's really vital that they sleep well and eat well. It's a bit of a weaning-in type process. You don't just throw them in a flat with a few boys.'

Sheehan described the welfare management program as protecting a club's investment. 'Clubs have got very few new draft choices every year – on average about four or five new players coming into your club – and they are the assets of the club and they have to be developed. You don't want to let that asset run wild or go off on the wrong track. Welfare officers become, for want of a better term, father-figures,' he said.

Sheehan also declared the days of players partying all night as long gone. It was a change, he said, that evolved naturally with the heightened professionalism of the national competition. 'Given that our game has a huge endurance component – they run half a marathon every game – they need to be athletes, not just footballers and you just couldn't survive training 11 months a year if you were out clubbing,' he said.

Sheehan's assurances were echoed by former Sydney Swans player Harry McAsey. Now a publican in Sydney, and vice-president of the Sydney Swans Former Players Association, Mr McAsey's career spanned the 1980s, when, he says, partying was as important as playing. That had changed, 'in the last five years particularly', Mr McAsey said. 'There's more individual tutoring per player. They give the guys more advice for life outside of footy.'

Asked to comment on recent scandals, Mr McAsey called sex-related crimes 'absolutely outrageous', but considered media highlighting of 'everything players do' unfair. 'I think many of these things happen in normal life,' Mr McAsey said, referring to infidelity, rather than pack rape. 'People have affairs. It's not just found in AFL ranks or team ranks. It could happen in your office,' he said.

Sex industry professionals had mixed opinions about footballers' behaviour. Maxine Fensom, owner of Maxine's Naughty Lunches in Richmond, felt it had toned down in recent years. 'We had Hawthorn Football Club here for one of our shows and they must have only spent about $50 on drinks between them. They were all drinking orange juice,' she said.

On the other hand, the owner of a Melbourne-based stripping agency described most AFL footballers as 'pigs'. The owner, who refused to be named, said boys-will-be-boys behaviour still ruled.

Two years ago, an end-of-season party for a leading Melbourne-based AFL club ended with several players offering one veteran stripper cash for sexual favours. 'They all wanted to have a go. It was tag-team,' the agency owner said. When the deal was struck, one of the players offered an extra $50 to urinate on her, while another player offered $50 if she would let him defecate on her. 'They were disgusting. It's like a pack mentality and they think they can get away with anything,' the owner said.

Self-described 'quiet guy' Simon O'Keefe, 20 – de-listed last November after being selected for the draft by Essendon at the end of 2001 – said he did not fit into the tight-knit world of club life. He described his short time in AFL ranks as bad, more because of being controlled by the hierarchy than because of moral corruption.

'There wasn't any wild behaviour – it was quite strict – but they really controlled what you did and you were expected to hang around with each other all the time. It didn't work for me,' O'Keefe said. O'Keefe's former coach with the regional Murray Bushrangers team, Xavier Tanner, said the move to pro football could work for some and not for others.

Only 11 years old, the club has 61 draftees. 'I think interstate clubs need to do their homework a bit better and find out who these boys are and what their needs are before they just take them away from everything they know,' Tanner said. 'I think that the AFL is putting a fair bit of pressure on clubs to offer better welfare for players and their families.'

The Sunday Age, 7 March 2004

BEHIND THE TOUCHLINE

Melissa Campbell

Footballers' sex lives have dominated the headlines this year. Gang rape allegations rocked both rugby league and AFL clubs, resulting in police investigations. More recently, St George Illawarra player Mark Gasnier hit the headlines for the wrong reason when he was found to have left an obscene voicemail message on a woman's mobile phone after a night out with team-mates.

These recent scandals have given us plenty to consider about the culture of intimate, and at times sexual, group bonding that goes on inside football clubs. Strange, then, that football culture has so little to say publicly about sexual orientation – except perhaps for Paul (Fatty) Vautin donning a dress to take the mickey on *The Footy Show*. And spare a thought for those footballers who are gay.

Nearly 10 years ago, rugby league front-rower Ian Roberts outed himself to widespread public support. He remains the only professional footballer to have done so – in any code. While the proportion of gay men playing elite football in Australia probably isn't as high as in the general community, it would be naive to think there are none.

The absence of real discussion about homosexuality in football is made odder by the almost absurd eroticism in the game itself – sweaty men grappling with each other in tackles, scrums and marks. Soccer players, especially, exchange jubilant hugs and kisses when they kick goals. Then there's the locker room, complete with steamy cliches of all-male group showers, massage tables and whippings with wet towels.

At the same time, it's ridiculous to suggest that any of this means footballers or football culture are gay. It does a disservice to homosexual players to suggest they have ulterior motives for being involved in the game, when they probably just want to play some footy.

So, how do we describe the way footballers relate to each other, on and off the field? Rather than talking about 'homosexuality' or 'homoeroticism', the most apt concept is 'homosociality', says Professor Elspeth Probyn, head of the University of Sydney's gender studies department. Homosociality is a way of describing 'the circuits that happen around same-sex groups congregating in gendered places and doing gendered things', Probyn explains.

Women have their own homosocial rituals, from girls' nights out to knitting circles. But the male bonding that goes on in football teams is part of another tradition, says Probyn, who points to the armed forces and private schools. Within these institutions, men define their masculinity by being ritually initiated into a group. 'While football culture isn't quite so regimented, it does have a kind of residual tendency towards intensely physical bonding,' she says.

Homosocial rituals often involve dominance and subservience, and are sometimes highly sexualised. As the recent revelations of group sex have shown, a woman's body can provide the means for men to create intimacy between themselves. At the time of the sexual assault allegations involving Canterbury Bulldogs players at a Coffs Harbour resort in February, Dr Michael Flood, an expert in gender and sexuality issues, pointed out that rugby league at the elite level is a man's world. Flood, who works at The Australia Institute in Canberra, has conducted interviews with young men that revealed group sex can be an extension of teamwork.

The Bulldogs' response to the allegations showed just how tight their bonding was. While the club made the requisite contrite media statements and assisted police with their investigation, there was widespread criticism of the apparent cavalier attitude of players who showed up at a police station for questioning wearing shorts and thongs.

The defensive 'bunker' mentality of Bulldogs officials was also criticised by the press. The club refused to release the names of the players allegedly involved and conducted a 'truth meeting' before going to police. No charges were laid against any player. 'One of the great things about the Canterbury football team is that they really bunker down under pressure,' said the Bulldogs' chief executive, Malcolm Noad, on ABC's *Four Corners*. Asked if he disapproved of that culture extending off the field, Noad replied: 'In some instances, that's not a bad thing.'

Flood has also pointed out that male homosocial rituals go beyond group sex. Men gather to watch pornographic movies on football team buses, players have sometimes watched home videos of each other and celebrities having sex. In all-male environments, the absence of women enables behaviour such as communal nudity and penis-grabbing.

But homosexuality threatens to unravel the homosocial group. When being a man is defined by physical contact with other men, the possibility that this contact is also sexual throws men's gender identity into question. Probyn says while she would separate the two behaviours, most people don't. Instead, they're more likely to think: 'He's a poof; maybe I am, too.'

This anxiety sometimes spills onto the field. Ray Biffin, a VFL player for Melbourne in the 1970s, once unsettled his opponent, St Kilda's Trevor Barker, by kissing him on the lips and fondling his buttocks. 'It stunned Trevor,' Biffin recalled in 1996. 'The crowd just chanted that I was homosexual all day and it put Trevor off his game. I finished up kicking six or seven goals and we won the game.' There was a certain playfulness to Biffin's actions: Barker was good-looking and had a reputation as a ladies' man. His team-mates even dubbed him Alvin Purple after the raunchy Australian movie character, because he'd once locked himself out of a motel room in his underwear.

Biffin's antics tap into the Aussie male tradition of 'taking the piss'. Indeed, he and Barker later were able to joke about the incident. But nobody was laughing in 2001, when rugby league winger John Hopoate notoriously stuck his fingers up the backsides of rival players from the North Queensland Cowboys. Hopoate claimed it was merely a tactic to make his opponents drop the ball, saying: 'I'm a great believer in what happens on the field should stay there.' But the National Rugby League judiciary found Hopoate guilty of 'conduct contrary to the true spirit of the game', and suspended him for 12 matches.

Catharine Lumby is director of the department of media and communications at the University of Sydney. Working with gender and culture researchers from across the university, Lumby is conducting a six-month research project for the NRL called 'Playing by the Rules'. Through methods including focus groups with players, coaches and administrators, she and her colleagues are examining attitudes and behaviours surrounding gender and sexuality.

Lumby argues that sport is one of the few arenas where men are able to express themselves, physically and emotionally. 'You see men hugging and weeping and screaming and touching, but it's in a rule-bound context. They can only do it in really ritualised ways.'

And Hopoate's behaviour was way outside the rules. At the time, NRL judiciary commissioner Jim Hall said that during his 45-year involvement in rugby league, he'd 'never come across a more disgusting allegation'. Cowboys captain Paul Bowman, one of Hopoate's victims, testified: 'I know it's a tough game, but there's no room for that,' adding that if Hopoate 'was a man, he wouldn't do that'.

It's interesting that the homosexual connotations of Hopoate's behaviour should be seen so emphatically to strip him of his manhood, while his victims' manhood was only enhanced by their feelings of violation. But like other homosocial cultures, football culture thinks about penetrating the body as something that's only done to women and gay men. Hopoate's real offence was to call his victims' manhood into question; the NRL judiciary restored it.

In a way, the entire Hopoate incident was a perverse parody of the female sexual assault scenario. As Lumby puts it, 'the rules are there to ensure nobody thinks they're gay'. But the rise of the sensitive, well-groomed 'metrosexual' has made the rules harder to implement. Sporting culture doesn't seem to know how to categorise players who reveal aspects of themselves other than the gruff heroes they're expected to be on the field. And in the absence of wider definitions of manhood, the culture defines them as 'gay' by default.

Take swimmer Ian Thorpe, whose designer wardrobe and penchant for pearl jewellery raised eyebrows. Younger men in general are chafing at the 'straitjacket' of traditional masculinity, says Lumby; and they're also not convinced that masculinity is incompatible with femininity – or homosexuality.

Nonetheless, you can still find plenty of defensiveness in football. And it usually manifests as knee-jerk panic over perceived homosexuality, and fervent media speculation about individual players. Just ask AFL player and Hawthorn captain Shane Crawford.

Like Thorpe, Crawford's sexuality has become public property. He's articulate, he knows the importance of skincare, and he's taken acting, singing and dancing classes in the hope of pursuing a career in musical theatre. Perhaps most damning of all, in the eyes of some, he took his mother to the Brownlow Medal presentation ceremony. 'Even family have actually doubted me at times because of what people have said,' Crawford said last year. 'Early on, I found it ridiculous. I know that I'm not gay, but I do have friends that are gay. I respect them probably even more for saying they are rather than hiding the fact.'

He's grown angry at the continued gossip. 'You hoped it was true, so you could snigger,' he wrote in his recent book, *Shane Crawford: Exposed*. 'I hope you hate yourself. I'm not gay.' After this revelation, Crawford was featured in a Melbourne gay weekly newspaper, *MCV*, under the tongue-in-cheek headline 'If you can't be gay, be Shane Crawford'.

Crawford is one of AFL's renaissance men: articulate on a range of topics, and savvy enough to negotiate a media-saturated industry. A regular panellist on the AFL *Footy Show*, Crawford even played off the gay speculation in his role in the program's spoof soap opera, *Bulger MD*. A storyline early this year introduced the character of Dr Pink, played by the Richmond Tigers' Nathan Brown, as a love interest for Crawford's Dr Hank Bulger.

It would be stretching the bounds of credibility to think of the Dr Pink storyline as a breakthrough in gay acceptance. Instead, there's more than a dash of the old-fashioned piss-take involved, with a bit of self-reassurance thrown in. By acting out taboos surrounding gender and sexuality, footballers can pre-empt criticism and cement their status as happy-go-lucky straight guys. It's not so far away from Fatty Vautin and his dresses after all.

'It's like that Seinfeld joke: "Not that there's anything wrong with that,"' says Lumby. 'Even men who aren't homophobic still have to make jokes about "I'm not gay."' These kind of anxieties arise in any environment where you might find straight men bonding together, she adds. 'It's to relieve the tension to do with intimacy.'

Curiously, however, Brown featured in only two episodes of Bulger MD before quitting. The question was, wrote *The Age*'s Geoff McClure, 'Did Brownie jump or was he pushed?' According to the Tigers' football manager, Greg Hutchison, Brown decided 'off his own bat' not to proceed. 'He did a couple of pilots but, in the end, he came to his own conclusion that it would be best if he didn't go ahead with it.'

Greg Miller, the Tigers' director of football, questioned whether the media exposure would be 'portraying the right image' for younger players. Last year Crawford faced similar criticism from officials at Hawthorn, who argued he lacked the 'commitment' to the club that a team captain ought to show.

The Tigers officials were trying to redefine a 'real' footballer as someone whose interests lay solely on the field, and whose loyalty lay with his club and team-mates. But instead, they came across as reactionary and anti-gay. 'You could call me old-fashioned, but that's how I see it,' Miller said at the time. This year, the *Footy Show* host and Collingwood Football Club president, Eddie McGuire, said he was prepared to believe the Dr Pink incident wasn't homophobic, 'although it appeared at the time that it was'.

And there's the rub, so to speak. While there's little overt homophobia in AFL, or in other codes, there seems to be a pervasive discomfort surrounding the topic, and a willingness to avoid discussing it outside pantomimish role-play. According to one rumour, an AFL player was planning to out himself in the late 1990s, but was dissuaded by his club. This can only be detrimental to closeted gay players who quietly observe the way their peers portray homosexuality, and the almost panicky way their clubs clamp down on behaviour that could be construed as gay.

If masculinity is still ultimately defined as 'not homosexuality', it goes a long way towards explaining why so few players are willing to come out and say they're gay. Liz Guiffre, assistant editor of the Sydney-based queer magazine *Bent*, has listened to many stories of coming out, and is familiar with the pitfalls. She thinks football culture isn't necessarily keeping players in the closet – it's 'seldom easy' for anyone.

'Announcing homosexuality depends on the honesty of the individual and, of course, their personal strength,' says Guiffre. 'Half the battle is accepting yourself first.' Clubs also need to fulfil their part of the bargain, says Guiffre, and create a culture of gay acceptance. 'If the people [that players] respect – senior players, officials, etc. – stood up and said "This attitude is or is not acceptable", it may make a difference,' she says.

It's a vicious circle. Until a player declares his homosexuality, the leagues are unlikely to deal with the issue; but the lack of official recognition acts as a disincentive for players to come out of the closet in the first place. 'People need to be educated before this becomes an issue,' wrote four-time premiership player and coach Rodney Eade in *The Age*. 'Let's not wait until an unsavoury situation arises where a player is abused, ridiculed or vilified because of his sexual preference.'

So, what does the future hold? Eddie McGuire told the gay monthly *Q Magazine* that he'd be happy for the first openly gay AFL player to come from his club. 'Whereas once upon a time this would become a major issue, now it would be, "Oh yeah? Good. Next,"' he said. 'Good on him. Let's hope so,' says Lumby.

Guiffre is less optimistic. 'It's difficult to say that sexuality will ever be a non-issue anywhere,' she says. 'In my experience talking to people personally and professionally, and in particular where there's an extremely strong boys-will-be-boys mentality, as there is in league especially, things like alcohol abuse and infidelity may be more accepted [than homosexuality].'

Sure, there's a long way to go, says Lumby, but football is no more homophobic 'than your average law firm'. Footballers may even have better opportunities than most to work through what it means to be a contemporary Australian man, she adds, because its culture grants them a space to express themselves.

Shane Crawford has said that while it'll be hard for any gay footballers to declare their sexuality, he'll certainly lend them his support. 'It's gonna happen and I look forward to the day that someone stands up and says, "That's me."'

The Sydney Morning Herald, 3 July 2004

WHY FOOTBALL NEEDS WOMEN

Caroline Wilson

Suddenly it seemed as if there were only two types of females in football. One was bright and blonde and young and pretty. Not unlike Beverley O'Connor, the Melbourne Football Club vice-president who last week launched the AFL's million-dollar advertising campaign dedicated to women.

The other one was dark and damaged. You couldn't see her features because they were hidden, blacked out at her request by the television producers helping to expose her shameful secret. We have seen a lot of her type in recent months.

The game has finally acknowledged her existence and is making all the right noises about trying to help her. But if it had a choice it would have preferred she had stayed away from the Mother's Day round of matches and the first official week the game has dedicated to women.

In fact she gatecrashed Women's Week on day one, her blacked-out face and dreadful stories featuring on an ABC *Four Corners* report that left most fans sickened by what was alleged.

And the week off-field has not been unlike most others that have punctuated the 2004 AFL season. The past five days have witnessed more sexual assault allegations involving AFL footballers, more illegal drug allegations involving Carlton and drink-driving dramas at West Coast and at Hawthorn.

'It's too early to say whether it has the potential to damage the game,' said AFL chief executive Andrew Demetriou, who appeared on *Four Corners* on Monday night and has vowed to fight the anti-women culture that he now believes exists at too many levels of football.

'We've seen allegations again this week of sexual assault, the alcohol abuse and the drugs, but we've also seen the game at its absolute best and that has created a sensational back-up to what else has gone on.

'It's been suggested to me we put on Women's Week in response to some of the allegations but I can assure you it was always there. We began planning it midway through last season. We wanted to say thank you not only to mothers but all women, whether they be partners, employees or spectators.'

The truth is that life is never black and white and that women of all types represent the remarkable percentage of females who follow the code and therefore make it unique. Even O'Connor, the woman chosen to launch the ad campaign, has faced minor cultural battles. Last September she was advised not to attend a club function held to farewell the Demons' old MCG dressing rooms.

On Wednesday, more than 800 women attended the AFL first women's forum where Demetriou said there was no reason why a woman could not become an AFL commissioner. When it was pointed out that league chiefs have been saying that for seven years, he said: 'I tend to deliver on my promises.'

O'Connor is not the only club director who has been forced to battle what was an exclusively male culture. Essendon's trailblazing director Beverly Knight (who is married) was for years unofficially barred from the Bombers' dressing room inner-sanctum and once asked by a club official if she was 'a dyke'.

Carlton's first woman board member Lauraine Diggins was pilloried for asking why her father's name (Brighton) did not appear on the locker bearing his old number. An official scoffed that Diggins should have known that only 100-gamers get their names on Carlton lockers and therefore had no credibility.

Three club officials – none of them from Collingwood – were horrified when the Magpies latest director Sally Capp posed for a photograph in March holding a football.

And while *The Footy Show* highlighted that 80 per cent of staff at both Essendon and the Bulldogs were women, no one pointed out that the positions they held were almost all at the bottom end of the club hierarchy.

Having undergone some criticism for not appearing on an SBS TV forum focusing upon sexual assault in February this year – a program aired before the St Kilda rape allegations – Demetriou has since attacked the issue with a gusto comparable to Ross Oakley's campaign to eradicate racial and religious vilification.

While the *Four Corners* program lost points among the football industry for including former Carlton president John Elliott in the debate, the discredited businessman's view of Demetriou's call for women who had been abused by footballers to contact the AFL was fascinating for its lack of understanding.

Elliott criticised Demetriou, saying his stand would dredge up issues people had forgotten – presumably he was not referring to the victims. 'I don't apologise for doing that,' said Demetriou. 'It's for others to judge but I don't think it's a competition about who handles the issue better. I simply said in response to a question that if there were women who believed they had been assaulted by a footballer we would refer them (the victims) to the appropriate body.'

That the allegations against Michael O'Loughlin were finally aired in Women's Week was savagely ironic given the effort that went into protecting and boosting the image of the star Sydney Swan. For almost four years the club and O'Loughlin's management succeeded in keeping the player's name out of the public arena despite the allegations against him and the fact he had contributed a substantial portion of the $200,000 paid in an out-of-court settlement to the alleged victim.

The Swans insisted that O'Loughlin was never interviewed by Adelaide police while Port Adelaide's Peter Burgoyne and former Brisbane Lion Adam Heuskes were. They said the money he paid had been specified as no admission of guilt.

But there was another crucial issue. Sydney, desperate for a new focus as Tony Lockett's career was ending, saw O'Loughlin as its next media star. After he had flown to Adelaide with his manager in 2001 to meet Burgoyne and Heuskes and sort out who would bear what cost for the alleged sexual assault, a significant amount of time and effort was placed into the promotion of the two-time All-Australian.

But the early record of the victim's interview revealed on *Four Corners* last Monday night was disturbing in light of O'Loughlin and Sydney's protests of innocence in the alleged assault that took place in August 2000 outside an Adelaide nightclub. Suddenly the player's public statement that he had paid the alleged victim money to protect his family appeared more than hollow.

Demetriou's twin daughters Francesca and Alexandra are yet to reach their first birthday, but he did not hesitate when asked what reforms he would wish for his girls when they are old enough to buy an adult ticket. 'One is I would like to think we could get to a point in time where they could go to a game and not have to listen to disgusting language.

'I would also like to see them following football in an environment where women are making an outstanding contribution at senior level at both the clubs and the AFL.

'I would hope they would witness the benefits of our stand at the moment against on-field violence and recreational drugs and that these issues of sexual assault being raised at the moment, along with sexual harassment and discrimination in the workplace, are less of a problem for society as well as the game.'

In launching its theme rounds last year, the AFL focused upon only one group of women – mothers. The Mother's Day round failed to attract anticipated attendances in Melbourne, not surprising given the games involved – Melbourne–Port Adelaide at the MCG and the Bulldogs–Fremantle at Telstra Dome. Both matches attracted little more than 12,000 spectators and the decision to fixture the Demons on Mother's Day again would indicate that the league was not interested in wooing football fans away from their family lunches to the MCG.

Ben Buckley, the AFL executive who will devise the 2005 fixture, and the league's brand manager Tom Noble, who has been the driving force behind Women's Week and the theme rounds, both hinted the competition would consider a new Mother's Day policy next year.

'The question is: Do you play any games on Mother's Day?' Noble said. 'Do you give mothers a chance to be with their families without the distraction of football? Or would they want that? Or do you devise the fixture around the day so that families can do both?'

Buckley added that the league might also consider a Mother's Day blockbuster. Either way, the 5 p.m. start for tomorrow's clash between Hawthorn and Geelong will provide an interesting test for the AFL and Foxtel, which pushed for the late start in a bid to win over subscribers.

But Noble said there was a wider purpose to Women's Week than simply improving Mother's Day attendances and TV ratings. 'Women have never really been acknowledged by the sport for the role that they have played in it. Almost 50 per cent of our brand is women and it's not a bad thing to acknowledge that and embrace that and present it to people.'

When Demetriou said that the new expanded Women's Week had been devised in part as a way of saying thank you to the game's substantial female support, his gratitude was based on hard facts as well as emotion. Not only is the Australian football code unique in boasting women as making up 50 per cent of its supporters in Victoria and 45 per cent Australia-wide, but for the first time the game has also recognised the true financial value of volunteers in the industry.

In 2003, an AFL-funded research found that 56,500 Australian football volunteers contributed 5.1 million working hours worth $73 million in labour effort. Clearly those 56,500 included a significant number of women – and a significant number of those believe women who are assaulted by footballers have only themselves to blame.

And while Demetriou agreed that the series of scandals and alleged crimes against women had the potential to damage the code, there has been no short-term evidence of it.

Last weekend, more people watched football on TV than ever before, Telstra Dome welcomed the second biggest crowd in the stadium's short history, and *The Footy Show* continues to attract Melbourne audiences of more than 600,000. For all of this, football needs more women in O'Connor's image, and no more shaded by darkness with even darker stories. The AFL's work is just beginning.

The Age, 8 May 2004

PROFESSIONAL FOUL

Neil Jameson

Early this year when simultaneous sexual assault scandals overwhelmed both the NRL and AFL, more than one ex-player was heard to remark: 'You know, these blokes wouldn't be getting into this sort of trouble if they had proper jobs.'

A million words were written and uttered on the saga, but none came close to the aforementioned insight to skewering what's gone wrong. A decade on since our major football codes went fully professional, the revolution has made players financially comfortable but at one hell of a cost to what was good and admirable about those sports in the first place. The fallout from a situation of too-much-money-and-too-much-time-on-their-hands has been catastrophic: an ugly trend riding on a tide of booze and narcissism. And that's just the skinny edge of the wedge.

Now, those disenchanted with the major codes are pondering whether the plunge on professionalism is producing a generation of poorly mentored, socially stunted athletes trapped in a world of fart jokes, binge drinking and electronic games where the male instinct to remain forever-14 is indulged on a daily basis. Not so much heroes, as overpaid pests on the run from accountability. A harsh generalisation perhaps, but, by mid-2004, you could have been excused for thinking the NRL and AFL had been taken hostage by a bunch of delinquents.

For Warren Ryan, rugby league's pre-eminent coach of the semi-professional era and now an ABC Radio commentator, our footy codes are facing a crisis in which players have failed to recognise that all the wealth and privilege carries a measure of accountability.

'Players have too much time and too little responsibility,' he tells *Inside Sport*. 'It doesn't help that they have grown up in a society which has an almost total non-acceptance of responsibility.'

His words echo the sentiments of so many older hands concerned by footy's sudden lurch into chaos.

The trickle of horrors started pre-season and soon became a flood: February – allegations of sexual assault are levelled against two Melbourne Storm players; a gang rape investigation involving six Bulldogs players on a pre-season trip to Coffs Harbour is launched; March – St Kilda officials offer up the names of two players under police investigation for sexual assault; SBS's *Insight* program airs allegations of a woman raped by five footballers including a prominent AFL player; nine players from two AFL clubs are accused of raping two women at an Adelaide nightclub; two AFL footballers are investigated for the rape of a backpacker; a separate sexual assault complaint is made against two Melbourne Storm players. April – a former Hawthorn player and a club official are questioned by police over rape allegations made by a Los Angeles woman in Hawaii in October 1998. May – ABC TV's *Four Corners* details accounts of a series of sexual offences, including an alleged rape, during a Brisbane Lions end-of-season trip to London in 1999; drunken NSW State of Origin players are busted breaking curfew after Mark Gasnier left an unsolicited and sexually explicit message on a woman's mobile phone. June – an AFL call for women to report any alleged incidents of sexual abuse leads to the reopening of a rape investigation involving Carlton players in 1999; media reports identify Willie Mason as the NRL player fined $25,000 by his club for testing positive to cocaine … and so on.

We're not talking about misdemeanours here. Whether tested in court or not, the sheer volume and consistency of the claims pointed to a culture of serious, possibly criminal, behaviour flourishing unchecked within some of our proudest sporting institutions. As a sub-section of society, professional footballers had become a public hazard.

While the AFL and the NRL were in full damage-control mode, rugby union's slate remained relatively clean. But, at the elite level, the game was in revolt over a high-rotation international program that had imposed an enormous toll on players and devalued the concept of Test rugby. In its own way, rugby too had overdosed on professionalism. Soccer's woes were entirely different but equally dire. This year, the entire complement of professional national league players had joined the dole queue while waiting for the kick-off to a new league in 2005.

From where the player stands, the money exacts its own price: training regimens that would kill your average superhero, crippling on-field expectations and a level of public exposure that denies any semblance of a normal existence. Little wonder that in the winter of 2004 the term 'player burnout' became a cliché across AFL and both rugby codes. Rugby league international Jamie Lyon packed his swag and left Parramatta and a $400,000-a-year contract to head back to Wee Waa and normality. Until his team-mates talked him out of it, St George and NSW centre Mark Gasnier almost followed Lyon into early retirement. In May, Hawthorn's Nathan Thompson made the brave decision to go public about his long-running battle with clinical depression.

In the current climate, empathy and understanding are in short supply. Fans and the media, grown cynical on a diet of fat salaries and transient loyalties, are now far less forgiving. Witness the abhorrent vitriol directed at Richmond this season with coach Danny Frawley, infamously spat on by a fan, copping the brunt of it. Instead of compliant sports reporters, editors are throwing their police-rounds people into the fray. Media outlets that once turned a blind eye to off-field indiscretions, now no longer think twice about carving up a wayward footballer or team.

Total strangers to accountability and contrition, a few players have blamed the media. NRL reporters turning up at Bulldogs training at the height of the Coffs Harbour rape investigation didn't miss the message when one player tried to drill the media ruck with a venomously aimed kick. The negative publicity has driven players toward a siege mentality. Bonded by their shared 'oppression', the exclusivity of their calling and the rising tide of public criticism, their first instinct has been to turn inwards and wall themselves off even more from normality, in so doing creating a dangerous standoff between performer and society. Players have lost touch with the people best equipped to keep them grounded. Warren Ryan describes a situation that cocoons players from reality, a world in which a player reports for a recovery session on Mondays then goes to lunch with his team-mates where they pat each other's tummies and avoid critical analysis.

'They're living in an unreal world,' he says, 'fed a steady diet of bullshit by the media and denied the well-rounded wisdom that you find in other walks of life. They don't realise that it is a pretty fragile existence to base your entire life on what you achieve on the football field.'

For a clue to where this is heading, take a look at Australia's role model *du jour*, the United States. Twenty or thirty years ago rock'n'roll was easily the most substance-addled, sex-crazed, scandalised life form on the planet. In the past ten years it's been well and truly eclipsed by pro sports.

*

So, how did it come to this?

Back in the late '70s and early '80s, long before we started worrying about the impact of a Free Trade Agreement with the United States, the influence of American sport was introduced to Australian locker-rooms. To improve their teams' competitive chances, coaches like Hawthorn's Alan Joyce, rugby league's Jack Gibson and future Wallabies mentor Bob Dwyer were eyeing the way US college football prepared the individual player. The difference between the two markets was time: American trainers had almost unlimited access to their charges and could tailor programs to the individual. The Australians were mere part-timers – blokes who had workaday jobs and turned up for a couple of hours two or three evenings a week. Dwyer relates how he performed a cut-and-paste job on a US college training manual, re-editing it for Randwick Rugby Club. Bit by bit, the emerging generation of coaches, including Tim Sheens in rugby league and Essendon's Kevin Sheedy, began feeding components of the US programs into their preparations. They turned up at multi-sport coaching conferences and exchanged ideas.

Bit by bit, players discovered demands on their time were eating into their non-football life. Something had to give. Players needed employers sympathetic to their playing and training demands. They trained more, worked less. The shift to full-time professionalism was under way. The travel demands that came with the creation of national leagues merely accelerated the process. North of the Murray, the rivers of gold that flowed from the Super League war guaranteed nobody would have to report for work on Monday again.

But let's stop right there.

What was so *wrong* with the old ways? Playing a code exclusive to its birthplace, was there any real need for AFL footballers to become bigger, stronger, faster? Unlike soccer, there were no external rivals to compete against, no benchmark to beat. Australian Rules and rugby league, as played here, were the best the world had to offer. And, according to attendances, the fans weren't unhappy with what their part-time heroes were dishing up. Flick back through the yearbooks of that time and compare them with today's images and you'll be shocked just how slightly built and normal looking the players were back then. But we all thought they were bloody fantastic and nobody complained about the quality of the product.

Has all that muscle and greater strength been worth it? Increased speed and bulk mean players hit harder. Bodily components that can't be protected are breaking with greater frequency. More muscle mass and improved strength have placed unparalleled stress on tendon, ligament and bone with club doctors reporting a range of injuries rarely recorded a decade ago. Rugby league's Andrew Johns, with an injury list that reads like an anatomy lesson, understands the trade-off.

'We're playing at kilograms above what would have been normal bodyweight,' he tells *IS*. 'All that extra muscle gives you strength but it places incredible stress on the parts of the body that you can't strengthen.'

He suspects some injuries – like the anterior cruciate ligament he snapped in March – are by-products of that extra power. It's a sad commentary on full-time professionalism that all the agonising work in the gym may have, indirectly, cost league its best player for an entire season and probably shortened his career.

*

For personalities with an elevated passion for their sport, full-time professionalism permitted the time to improve skill levels, expand tactical possibilities and tap their full potential. Players with the competitive zeal of a Jason Akermanis or an Andrew Johns have thrived in a full-time era that has allowed them to explore the outer limits of their talent and imagination. Compared to the previous era, says Johns, this generation has been spoiled.

'We've been lucky,' he concedes. 'The Super League war came along at the right time and so did the rise in the property market. It's meant that we've had the time and security to concentrate on our football.'

That total focus has helped elevate rugby league's skills base and establish a new benchmark for how the game is played. It can be argued that without full-time professionalism, fans would never have been afforded a glimpse of what was possible.

Off the field, professionalism didn't make football instantly dysfunctional. The ingredients were already there. League and Australian Rules have long had their gallery of rogues, thugs and social misfits who got away with blue murder simply because they were stars. But the vast majority of rostered players led quiet lives, grounded by the imperative that they had to report for workaday jobs where they rubbed shoulders with ordinary people, including older blokes who fulfilled the role of mentors – knocking the rough edges off young dickheads in the time-honoured way that helps boys become men.

Compare that simple formula with today's reality within a pro football club: the pressure to perform is all-consuming; anything else runs a distant second. Competition is cutthroat, egos ping off each other like colliding neutrons. The ratio of young blokes to grey heads is about 30:1 – hardly an environment for healthy mentoring. There is no job to return to on Monday for a nourishing dose of reality and a break from the pressure. As Warren Ryan has observed: 'It's a great leveller to front up at work and, instead of someone pissing in your pocket, have one of your older colleagues tell you that you actually went like a busted the day before.'

Denied that time-honoured form of counselling, smarter players seek it elsewhere. According to the AFL Players' Association, last year 270 players sought assistance from the union's counselling service, a number of them requiring psychological support. In what could be interpreted as an admission that their sports are producing a maladjusted generation, in the wake of the sexual assault crisis of 2004, both the AFL and the NRL turned to outside expert help to counsel players on their attitudes to women.

The problem has not gone unnoticed by prominent commentators in the fields of masculinity and family studies. Dr Peter West, author of *What Is the Matter with Boys?*, has pointed out that it is useless spending money re-educating footballers only to have those young men thrown on the scrapheap once their physical prowess is of no value to the game. That observation goes to the heart of the semi-professional versus full-time professional debate: if players had vocations as well as sporting careers, their transition into football retirement would not be such an issue and they would be much better equipped to play meaningful roles in society.

In a recent article Dr West cited the 'boofhead role model', taking direct aim at how television, in particular, has projected footballers. He referred to the footy season delivering 'endless examples of how not to be a man'.

'We don't want [young men] to retreat into the harmful patterns of … stereotyped, mindless masculinity with binge drinking and viewing women as little more than sex objects; in brief, the way some rugby league footballers have behaved,' he cautions.

Talking to *IS* in his role as head of the research group on men and families at the University of Western Sydney, Dr West says football still has so much to offer. 'Australian life would be unimaginable without football,' he says. 'Today, it projects the best and worst of masculinity. At its best, it is still one of the most acceptable ways that boys can be around adults and learn from positive role models. But, we can do without the boofhead mentality and players who are obviously up themselves.'

*

Grog has always been the lubricant for fun times and miscreant behaviour by footballers. Rugby league and Australian Rules legends were created not just on the field but at the bar. The culture isn't exclusive to winter sports. When limited-overs cricket was included on the 1998 Commonwealth Games program, a hockey gold medallist was overheard expressing her dismay to a leading cricketer at how his team-mates could spend so much time on the booze and still view themselves as professional athletes. As with the football codes, the game and the grog were inextricably entwined. A few seasons after famously telling a Channel Nine reporter that his ambition in life was to never have a job, Australia rugby league skipper Brad Fittler was found in broad daylight drunk outside a Sydney police station, unable to tell an officer where he lived. The incident was hardly remarkable as it came amid an excess of alcohol-fuelled reports of players exchanging punches at weddings, brawling in nightspots and tangling with taxi drivers.

In the semi-professional days, that taste for booze was tempered by the fact that the player had to get out of bed early the next morning and show up for work. There was an in-built incentive to knock off drinking at a reasonable hour. Also, 10 p.m. was the closing time for most watering holes. Importantly, the drink of choice and tradition was beer – not bourbon, rum, tequila shooters or any other form of rocket fuel. Compare that with today: there are pubs and clubs that never close. Nightclubs actively encourage the patronage of pro footballers. With no clock to punch the next morning, footballers will stay out filling up to the gills on beer before they switch to spirits. Money is not a problem. It was getting close to dawn when the Bulldogs knocked off drinking at the Plantation Bar in Coffs Harbour and headed back to their accommodation where the alleged crime took place. It was at least their second big night out that week. When you consider those events, you can't help revisiting the observation about what might and might not have occurred had the players been engaged in worthwhile work outside of football.

*

narcissism *noun* **1.** extreme admiration for one's own attributes; egoism; self love. **2.** *Psychology* sexual excitement through admiration of oneself. **3.** *Psychology* erotic gratification derived from admiration of one's own physical or mental attributes, a normal condition at the infantile level of personality development. – *The Macquarie Dictionary*

Full-time footballers stand out in a crowd. You can pick them in the nightclubs: gym-sculpted torsos, bulging biceps and fashionable clobber. Tough male models with muscles. With that sort of profile, meeting the opposite sex doesn't require small talk, etiquette or social graces – you simply drain your glass and walk out with the nearest groupie. If it's a bonding night, half a dozen of your team-mates might follow. After that fateful night in Coffs, bystanders at the Plantation Hotel alleged that five Bulldogs had groped girls on the dance floor and scuffled with other patrons before being ejected.

For a decade now, all of us – media, fans, player agents, club officials, sponsors – have been stroking player egos and lining their pockets, making the more impressionable among them believe the sun rises out of their arses on a daily basis. In 2002, when the Wayne Carey scandal broke over North Melbourne with revelations that the club captain and best player of his generation had been conducting an affair with the wife of his vice-captain, we should have all paid better attention to the words of Carey's betrayed spouse. Turning on her husband's long-time manager and player agent, she cried: 'You're to blame for this. You're to blame, the club's to blame; we're all at fault. We never said no to him. We let him think he could get away with everything.'

The pity about full-time professional football is that it has cast too many of its players outside of society. The question now is how do we bring them back?

Inside Sport, September 2004

MEMORABILIA IS MADE OF THIS

Sports memorabilia is big business, and with the opportunity to make money from instantly collectible antique memories comes the opportunity to lose serious amounts of money. Or make some. Jesse Fink essays traps for young players, Bernard Whimpress surveys some genuine articles, and Tony Wilson has an idea for Tony Greig.

THE STING IN MEMORABILIA

Jesse Fink

Victor Yoog, the managing director of Legends Genuine Memorabilia, has turned on the full show for *Inside Sport*'s visit to LGM's showroom at a nondescript industrial estate in Sydney's inner west. First, the photographer and I are taken into a room that could be described as a den of memorabilia: wall-to-wall framed, signed photographs of every Australian sporting hero and world-beating team imaginable, including an enormous commemorative Olympic flag entitled 'Inspiration' adorned with 55 Olympic medallists' signatures.

Then, leaving our equipment in the boardroom, we are taken on a meet-and-greet tour of the building, being introduced to each employee and seeing the various stages of LGM's production line of limited-edition products. It's an impressive performance, and Yoog is the consummate salesman: confident, courteous, devoted to his product. The photographer whispers in my ear that Yoog bears a likeness to Roy Slaven, John Doyle's alter ego. The comparison is apt. Apart from the slight physical resemblance, Yoog, like Slaven, never loses eye contact when he speaks; he makes you feel relaxed, like you're good mates. It's no wonder he's such a success.

'Before we begin the interview, though,' he asks me as we return to the boardroom, 'I just want to know what made you think of doing this story.'

I'm surprised he even felt the need to ask. Love it or loathe it, it's hard to ignore the Australian sports memorabilia industry. One recent media report claimed sales of 'genuine' memorabilia, both 'one-offs' and licensed 'limited-edition' items, such as those manufactured by LGM, Elite Sports Properties and sundry other companies, clocks in at $40 million a year; a sizeable percentage of which, 15 to 22 per cent in LGM's case, flows on to the sports organisations and athletes who license their images and names to the products. (ESP and Channel Nine would not disclose their licensing fees to *IS*.) Which means there is some serious money to be – and being – made. David Fouvy, general manager of Cricket Australia's commercial operations, confirmed to *IS* that CA's 2002–03 licensing revenue from sales of branded clothing and CA-authorised memorabilia was up 40 per cent to $2 million, an all-time record, of which the players retained 'roughly' 25 per cent of total revenue.

And befitting such a growth industry, every need of the estimated 40,000 to 80,000 collectors in Australia is catered for. There's a dedicated magazine, *The Sporting Collector*, put out by LGM; the trading paper *Collectormania* lists every fete and fair around the country; and auction houses such as Charles Leski Auctions and Ludgrove's, which recently sold the world-record Bradman 1948 baggy green for $425,000 (though some reports suggest the figure was significantly lower), are doing a roaring trade in memorabilia.

Big business, then, by any measure. And one of the industry's biggest hitters is LGM. Started in 1993 by Yoog and Peter Higham, two direct marketing businessmen, and recently merged with Michael Fahey's Sports Memorabilia Australia, which specialises in one-off or 'game-used' memorabilia, it turned over just under $7 million for 2002–03 and has over 20,000 registered collectors on its mailing list. The merger, says Yoog, adopting sales-pitch patter, 'brings about the complete collectable service – whether you're wishing to buy a limited-edition piece, a one-off item, you want a valuation, you're wanting to disperse or dispatch with your collection – we're the complete one-stop shop'.

'In the first few years of the business we had to determine what it was we were really selling, and it was more than just a framed-up photograph with a signature. We were selling emotion, success, achievement … [for] the mums and dads of the street, who make up the greater part of our collector network, the signature is the authentic link to their sporting icon. Most people never get that opportunity to spend that five, ten minutes or half an hour with their hero.'

Barely an Australian sporting achievement goes by without TV viewers or newspaper readers being assailed to buy a limited-edition, signed photograph of that special moment.

Channel Seven is in on the act with its 7 Sport Store on its i7 website, while Channel Nine regularly interrupts its cricket telecasts with memorabilia infomercials. The network's commercially geared website, ninemsn, carries a '*Wide World of Sports* Shop' in which new memorabilia, including LGM and ESP items among many other companies' merchandise, is uploaded on a regular basis. Though curiously, when *IS* met Nine's vice-president of sports and marketing, Tony Greig, at his memorabilia-lined office at Kerry Packer's Publishing & Broadcasting Limited (PBL) headquarters in Sydney, he claimed the industry was experiencing a lull: 'To be perfectly honest, I think there's been a little bit of a flattening out in the memorabilia business. There's only so much space on walls around Australia.' Greig puts it down to 'a refreshing rationalisation' in the size of limited-edition releases and a tightening up of profit margins due to players 'getting far more selective … they are signing exclusive contracts with people like LGM'.

But take a look at LGM's lavishly produced website and there seems to be a special commemorative item released every time an Australian sportsperson blows his or her nose. The stuff is not cheap. Licensing, production, marketing and athletes' royalties account for much of the final price tag, though Victor Yoog says 'after ten years we have got a fairly good handle on what the market will bear' and LGM products offer 'extremely good value' compared to retail prices.

However, Glen McGoldrick, general manager of Ludgrove's which deals in one-off pieces, says the term memorabilia is misused: 'I would call it collectables rather than memorabilia, because of the very definition of the term. It's more, effectively, a production piece.' Memorabilia, by his definition, is 'something of a historical nature ... that would be the key differentiation'.

By 'historical nature' read one-offs. These were originally used for other purposes, ideally in the field of play for which the owner was renowned. Stored away in a cardboard box in the garage or chest in the attic over decades, they have intrinsic collectable and investment value. Auctioneer Charles Leski of Charles Leski Auctions, Melbourne, sold the famed Shirley Strickland collection as one lot in April 2001 for $400,000 plus commission ($60,000), but he has little time for the limited-edition side of the industry.

'We get offered a huge range of material ... every day there are probably three or four consignments coming in our door,' he says. 'And it's from all sorts of sources: the local framer buying photos and packaging them up himself; every man and his dog getting an artist to do an image of Lionel Rose or Kostya Tzsyu or Don Bradman and calling it a limited edition and selling them off; and there's the baggygreen.com phenomenon; there's Legends. There's no shortage of people pumping stuff out.

'What's happened in the US is what's in danger of happening here. The mass-marketed product takes such a huge chunk of the available capital out of the marketplace at inflated prices; it makes people unhappy when they come to sell it because they have got to keep it a long time to even recoup their money, let alone make a profit. And so they buy a few things, they fill the walls, they think they've got an "investment" and then they lose their jobs or the marriage breaks down or they lose interest in Gary Ablett's 1300th goal [sic] and they decide they want to sell it. And suddenly they find everybody wants to sell the same thing and there's no market for it.'

The US experience with sports memorabilia is a cautionary tale for Australian collectors. On 13 October 1999, agents of the FBI and the IRS raided over 60 businesses and private residences in 15 states in a major crime investigation into memorabilia fraud called Operation Bullpen.

The items seized, including thousands of forged autographs on sporting equipment, were valued at over US$10 million.

Operation Bullpen, based in San Diego, California, claims it was responsible for busting a crime network of memorabilia 'forgers, authenticators, wholesalers and retailers' which was reckoned to have been responsible for the sale and creation of bogus memorabilia worth over US$100 million. The sophisticated fraudsters even had a healthy sideline in fake 'authenticity certificates' and 'forensic authentication'.

The FBI puts potential losses in the sports memorabilia industry in the US at a staggering half billion dollars a year, a huge slice of the multibillion-a-year worldwide sales. Others put the figure for forgeries' market share higher. So pervasive is forgery in the US industry, in a story for cable network ESPN reporter Bob Lay said: 'You have a far better chance of buying a forgery than the real thing.' One Operation Bullpen official even put the figure for the whole US industry as high as 90 per cent. Victor Yoog, though, feels the figures are 'outlandish'. 'If it's more than 10 to 15 per cent I'd be highly surprised,' he says. However, Victorian police officer Damien Oehme, whose authentication company A-TAG has tagged over 32,000 items and which counts ESP and Oscar Swarv's Memorabilia Online (which provides items to i7) among its main clients, believes a 'massive memorabilia fraud market' exists in the US.

It's true that steps have been taken, since the success of Operation Bullpen, to clean up the US sports memorabilia industry. These have included authentication company WeTrak inserting microchips into memorabilia; Professional Sports Authenticator (PSA), a sports card authentication company, setting up an offshoot, PSA/DNA, to authenticate autographs using a process of DNA identification similar to A-TAG's use of synthetic DNA on memorabilia items; and sports management company Upper Deck, which handles Tiger Woods, using holograms and an innovation called PenCam to record every aspect of the actual signing, which is then presented to the buyer in CD-ROM form. At the athlete level, too, some athletes have developed two versions of their signatures to combat profiteering: one scrawled for professional autograph hunters, the other properly executed for real fans. Some athletes also make a point of personalising signatures, wherein they write autographs mentioning the name of the individual concerned – thus reducing the 'saleability' of the autograph.

However, while there is no evidence other than anecdotal of widespread forgery in the Australian sports memorabilia market, Michael McCabe of memorabilia retailer Superstars & Legends (S&L) claimed in a media report that the counterfeit collectables trade in Australia was worth an estimated $12 million a year.

Damien Oehme confirms the extent of the problem: 'A lot of the stuff is very suspect – Australian as well as US … there's fraudulent memorabilia here, no doubt about it.' Oehme told *IS* of two incidents in which he encountered forgeries in 'reputable retail outlets', both involving seemingly legit AFL-related memorabilia. 'Now if there's two that have come out of a reputable dealer who said he had no idea, that he thought they were genuine, how many others are out there?' he says.

Even sporting legends can get stung. Boxing great Jeff Fenech, a friend of former world heavyweight champ Mike Tyson, called A-TAG to his home in Sydney after buying bogus Tyson memorabilia from the US. 'When it arrived, he said the stuff looked nothing like Tyson's signature,' Oehme says.

But LGM's Victor Yoog believes the problem of forgery in Australia has been overstated. 'It irks me a little bit,' he says. 'I think it's a storm in a teacup. There are incidences of fraud and forgeries and fakes, but it really is insignificant in the total scheme of things. The majority of concerns out there, it would seem to me, are legitimate but I'm absolutely confident that it isn't as bad as pictured.'

Although LGM goes to great lengths to ensure the authenticity of its products by getting PricewaterhouseCoopers representatives to attend signings and countersign items, Oehme sees flaws in its system, flaws he claims A-TAG's 'eight-step authentication process', which involves laser foil and synthetic DNA application, do away with completely.

'The key to this [issue] is every item of memorabilia has to be marked with something; certificates of authentication are OK, but if you separate the certificate from the item, then you've got nothing … to [forge] a certificate of authentication is so simple,' he says. 'LGM have their system where they send out a representative to witness the signatures, but there's a number of issues with that.

'Their items aren't marked in any way, so a very good desktop publisher could reproduce that item. And I know that a representative from PwC countersigns or similar the athlete's signature. If a person was going to fraudulently copy the player's signature, what's stopping them copying the authenticator's signature as well? The other thing is, in 20 years' time, if you try to find the authenticator from PwC, he might go, "Yeah, that looks like my signature", but can he tell whether it is his or not?'

As for holograms, Oehme claims they're 'too easy to copy': 'We know a firm that could reproduce any kind of hologram in a couple of days.'

And what of Upper Deck's PenCam? ESP's division manager Matt Davies is not sold on it: 'People take photos of Michael Jordan signing something, but there's no way of saying that the product that they've got is the one that Michael Jordan was signing at time of photo … the A-TAG product is the only one that I know of that ties it back into each other.'

Oehme says he has approached LGM a couple of times to implement A-TAG technology, but that LGM has knocked him back, saying it's happy with the system already in place: 'It's beyond us a little bit … we thought [LGM would] jump at the opportunity.' But Davies, who extols A-TAG's technology 'as the best in the marketplace in the world', sees nothing wrong with LGM's 'four-step' process. 'I think it's good, I think it's sound. It's got a lot of credibility to it, LGM are a very credible company … if consumers are buying LGM products in the marketplace I don't think they have any concerns about them being forged.'

Memorabilia Online's Oscar Swarv agrees: 'It's above reproach … it is its own system.' But he acknowledges there are concerns about authentication across the industry: 'When you buy an item, isn't it sad that not only are you looking for authentication, but then you're looking for authentication of the authentication.'

Another area of concern for memorabilia producers, and buyers, is the growing problem of 'charity consultants' flogging bogus items on to unsuspecting fundraisers such as schools and sports clubs. At the time of writing there was an ongoing police investigation into memorabilia fraud relating to three boxing-related items that were sold at a Perth charity auction in 2002. The investigation is liaising with the FBI in San Diego and the New Jersey Police Department.

The investigation came about when an unidentified person bought a piece of memorabilia at the auction and then went to a S&L branch in the suburb of Cannington to have it authenticated and valued. He was horrified when S&L staff questioned its authenticity. It was later determined that two other suspect items were also sold at the same auction. What gave them away as fakes was the quality of the images (they were printed on computer printer, not normal paper) and spelling mistakes on the certificates of authenticity, which were glued on the back of the memorabilia. The authenticators' signatures also appeared to have been written in computer-generated 'autopen'. It was then that the police were called in.

The three items in question were all boxing-related memorabilia: a signed Tyson glove and poster; a framed poster entitled 'Champions Forever' featuring the signatures of George Foreman, Joe Frazier, Muhammad Ali, Ken Norton and Larry Holmes, which sold for less than $1000; and an Ali and Elvis poster signed by Ali.

'Once you've done the conversion to US dollars – and you're talking about five world champion boxers, they don't do nothing for nothing – it appears unlikely that [these signatures] are the real deal,' says Detective Sergeant Darren Seivwright of Morley Detectives' Office, Perth.

'These [athlete signings] are quite often organised. People from S&L actually went over to Chicago and went to an Ali and Frazier signing day. They've gotta pay the airfare to get across, then they pay US$300 just to get into the line. You can take four or five pieces at a time, that's no problem, but you also have to buy the gear, like $80 Ali Everlast shorts. So you start eating up all your costs, and that's just for Ali; and then you spend US$150 to get into the Frazier line. Once you've added up all those costs, to be able to buy a piece like that for under $1000 doesn't appear logical.'

Interestingly, two 'Champions Forever' items appeared at Charles Leski Auctions on 1 March and 22 May this year, though Leski himself was unaware of authenticity doubts over 'Champions Forever' items nor of the WA police investigation when *IS* contacted him.

Though the two items did not sell on the night of 22 May, the reserves for both items were low. Explains Leski: 'Our estimates on boxing memorabilia are low by comparison with apparent retail prices ... there seems to be a substantial stock, there are photographs of these guys signing, and despite the fact that they appear to sell to several thousand dollars in the retail shops, our estimates are based on what we've achieved for these items in the past when we've been able to sell them unreserved.'

Leski says that he makes on-the-spot appraisals of a large range of memorabilia before it's accepted for auction and, if requested, provides safeguards such as issuing a certificate, although much of the memorabilia he auctions already comes with authenticity guarantees, for what they're worth.

'We don't guarantee anything. We offer through our auctions the option for people to buy anything on extension, which means they have an agreed period during which they can submit an item to an agreed authority and they can get their own certificate if they have good reason to be doubtful. If it comes back with a bad certificate or a bad opinion, their money is refunded in full as well as the cost of getting that opinion. If it comes back with a good opinion, then they pay for that certification and the deal stands. We don't say we get it right every time, but we do our best to make that judgement.'

The best way to prevent getting sold a fake, it appears, is to buy from a reputable dealer, auction house or retailer either in situ or online – or simply don't take your chances with American memorabilia, especially on the web.

Says Leski: 'I try to discourage people buying that [American] stuff. I don't understand why Australians think they need sports heroes on their walls. And we tend to estimate it pretty low anyway. So the people who come in here know how we feel about it.'

LGM's Michael Fahey shares Leski's ambivalence about American-sourced product. 'I steer clear of US products,' he says, 'for this very problem … you've got no way of knowing where it's come from; it makes [authenticating] very difficult.'

Says Detective Sergeant Seivwright: 'Just because someone has a company name doesn't mean they have company premises … it's impossible for people to check bona fides if you're buying something over the internet. Either the goods aren't being delivered at all or the things they've ordered aren't to the specifications of what the purchaser thought. The only advice you can give people is beware when you're buying something: if it seems unreasonably low in price, then there's a very good chance it's a forgery.'

So, to the $750-plus-postage-and-handling question: is memorabilia a good investment? The sometimes extraordinary prices fetched for game-used items at auction has certainly convinced some that, like real estate, you simply can't go wrong putting your money in memorabilia. But talk to Victor Yoog and Peter Higham, and they get all coy about mentioning the I-word.

'That's an interesting question you pose,' says Yoog, carefully measuring his response. 'And it's something that we've always been very guarded about, communicating the investment angle. We've never, ever pushed the fact that if you buy a limited-edition product that it will appreciate in value. Ultimately the market will determine what will go up in value … if you look at any of our marketing literature we never push the fact if you buy a widget, you'll make X amount of dollars.'

The *Wide World of Sports* Shop, by contrast, informs visitors that its range has been 'chosen to appeal to collectors' and that 'limited-edition items ensure that, over time, your investment in great sporting moments has the best chance to appreciate in value'. Tony Greig, as any seasoned cricket watcher will know, also is given to occasionally muttering the magic words 'sure to go up in value' when memorabilia infomercials are flashed on the screen during drinks breaks or when bowlers are walking back to their marks.

'There are obviously products that have gone up in value,' says Greig when asked about the investment potential of the products he promotes. 'If someone dies who's signed a bat, it's a limited-edition bat, you're not going to get his signature again, one would suggest that a collector, a serious collector – I'm not talking about someone who just wants "that moment" because that's a fancy moment, you know – but a serious collector would say to you, "Well, you can't get them any more." And therefore I don't think that it's unreasonable to assume that there are products that will go up in value.' As for LGM's insistence that it doesn't push the 'investment' angle in its brochures, Greig says, 'Peter Higham's a brilliant writer. If you look at his brochures, if he doesn't use the word "investment" or if he doesn't allude to the fact this is good value, then, I mean [laughs], are you calling me an idiot? … it's a selling brochure.'

ESP's Matt Davies also is not shy of extolling the investment value of memorabilia: 'There are some products that we put out there to create a moment … they may not appreciate in value over time, but they hold a very special moment in time close to that person's heart. There are other products out there, and that's what we try and do … put quality product into the marketplace that will appreciate in value.'

But Charles Leski believes sports memorabilia manufacturers using the word 'investment' in their marketing are taking a risk: 'If they are I think the [customer buying the item] would have an action against them.'

And despite LGM's claim that it doesn't promote its items as investments, there is an implicit suggestion with phrases such as 'sought-after', 'collectable', 'exceptionally rare', 'cellar it', 'highly prized amongst collectors', all used in LGM's brochures, of worth, of value, of investment.

But Yoog dismisses this outright, suggesting instead that the expressions used in LGM's marketing sell something else: 'It's a high desirability … whether that translates into dollars is a totally different issue, I think. It's fair to say that the serious collector who is slowly amassing a collection knows at the very least if he or she buys quality collectables that they won't depreciate in value. At worst, they'll hold their value.' So they're fairly discerning on what they'll buy, from what company, what particular sporting identity if they're building a collection … I think there's a fairly well understood knowledge that they won't lose their money.'

However, asked if he can guarantee that customers won't lose money on their purchases, he says, 'Absolutely not. It comes down to one's judgement, and buying prudently, I guess.'

Glen McGoldrick from Ludgrove's believes the capital-appreciating potential of limited-edition memorabilia has not yet been proven; though according to anecdotal evidence supplied by LGM, ESP, Memorabilia Online, Tony Greig and others interviewed for this story, there are limited-edition items that have appreciated markedly in value since their release, Tony Lockett's 1300th goal memorabilia being a case in point. 'Only time will tell,' McGoldrick says of limited-edition memorabilia's investment value. 'To date, you don't have a secondary market for those items coming back on to the market, so if you look at LGM's site, where they have a Trading Forum, they do say that these items have appreciated … we're not far away from these items coming back on to the market, in which case it'll be proven each way whether they do have a resale value.'

Says Leski, bluntly: '[People] need to understand that they're buying pleasure, not just an investment.'

*

It's a reflection of modern-day sports that the childhood rite-of-passage of sidling up to your favourite sports star after a game for his or her autograph has become a distressing and infuriating experience for many.

In the US, some athletes who previously happily signed shirts, balls, hats, magazines, whatever was thrust in front of them, are now refusing to sign, instead retailing their autographs through memorabilia companies. LGM's Michael Fahey believes it won't happen in Australia, but thinks it is up to the sporting organisations that are profiting from licensed memorabilia to make sure it doesn't.

'The sporting bodies have to be quite heavy-handed with the people that are profiteering,' he says. 'It would be a sad day if you went up to Steve Waugh and he said, "I only sign for Upper Deck or Legends or whoever." That's not the way it should be.' Adds Victor Yoog: 'A fan will walk up at a game and go, "Will you sign six photos?" The sporting identity is quite in touch with why they're signing six photos. Tomorrow, those six photos might end up in a frame on eBay, being sold.'

But it is drawing a long bow to suggest that a few autograph sharks have the potential to spoil the innocence of a pursuit that has already been turned into a multimillion-dollar industry.

The innocence went a long time ago.

Inside Sport, September 2003

FUNKY BLUE, ODD BALLS AND A PIECE OF PITCH

Bernard Whimpress

When Colin Miller removed his cap to reveal Denis Rodman-style dazzling 'Federation Blue' hair in opening the bowling on the second morning of the Sydney Test match, 3 January 2001, the West Indian tailend batsman and captain, Courtney Walsh, convulsed with laughter. I'll have some of that [hair], I thought.

The not-quite rape of the locks took a month or so to secure. It was not for a personal collection, it must be understood, but an acquisition I was keen to make as curator of the Adelaide Oval

Museum. A gentle enquiry through my employer, the South Australian Cricket Association, to the Australian Cricket Board yielded nowt but the time came soon enough. Later the same month at the second Allan Border Medal award for the Australian Cricketer of the Year in Melbourne, my CEO and his wife came to be seated at the same table as Miller and his girl-friend. It is not relevant that Miller actually won the award: what is relevant was that the CEO's wife recalled that the hair was wanted and reminded her husband to ask for it. 'That's easy', said Miller's girlfriend, who produced a pair of scissors from her bag. Snip. And the locks were gathered in tissue paper in a handbag and on their way to a new home.

This was, of course, only the beginning of a story. I then had to preserve my new exhibit. At Artlab the receptionist sounded a little unnerved when questioned by someone seeking advice on preserving body parts. 'It's OK', I said, 'my name's not Hannibal Lecter!' The conservationist recommended placing the hair in a vacuum seal. Done. The museum had a relic.

Museums contain hordes of relics. However, as the American biologist Stephen Jay Gould pointed out in an article, 'Baseball's Reliquary: The Oddly Possible Hybrid of Shrine and University', in the March 2002 edition of *Natural History*, not long before his death, the primary responsibilities of museums are: '… the role of the reliquary (reverent display of sacred objects, whose impor-tance lies in their very being) and the role of the teacher (instruc-tive display of informative objects, whose importance lies in their ability to inspire questions).'

Gould saw this as a paradoxical problem and asked how the 'awe of reverence can mix with the scepticism of learning'. Let us look at some more relics before asking some questions of our own.

Ball 1
A mounted ball is donated to the museum. It is significant because it is associated with a special performance and is inscribed in the following manner:

Pres to
GORDON B. INKSTER
by J.F. TRAVERS
on securing 9 wickets
as Wicket Keeper
South Australia v Victoria
Melbourne Cricket Ground
Jan 1, 3, 4, 5, 1927
in Match (c4 st5) = 9 Record in Representative
Cricket in Australia
2nd Inns (c4 st2) = 6 Record in Sheffield
Shield Games

Ball 2

A second ball on an ornate art nouveau stand is presented by the secretary of the Prospect Returned Services League to the museum for examination. It has been in the club's possession for many years and has already been viewed by Christie's Australia with a view to auction. But Christie's cannot establish its provenance and cannot price it beyond its ornamental value. It is inscribed as follows:

Presented by
A.M. AMBLER
to Prospect S Branch
R.S.A
This ball was used in the match
at Melbourne, 26.12.34
in which S.A. retained The Ashes

Test Pitch

World-famous Adelaide Oval curator Les Burdett once gave me a piece of Test pitch. It is 11 centimetres long, five centimetres wide and five centimetres deep. Only the top three millimetres is grassed. The rest is heavy black subsoil. It looks like a piece of mudcake or a block of hash depending on one's preference. Very occasionally I remove it from a display case and allow visitors to handle it. People most often ask where the subsoil comes from: Athelstone in the Adelaide Hills. But a Test pitch is more than this.

What do we have thus far? Relics but no education, the shrine without the university, to use the subtitle of Gould's paper.

Why would we want to exhibit Colin Miller's blue hair and why would I caption it 'Funky Blue' when he, later on the English tour of 2001, coloured his hair (if not every colour of the rainbow) at least orange, yellow, pink and green? What is so important about Miller anyway? In seizing something from a moment am I trying to give it significance it does not merit? Possibly, but let us go further.

Miller's singular act established him as a character at a time when 'characters' are rare in modern professional sport. The talent identification programs, sports academies, university scholarships and so on, with all the benefits of sports science, nutrition and psychology, may produce high quality athletes but their narrow focus gives us greyer men and women. Apart from Shane Warne's occasional excesses, the Australian cricket larrikin has been overtaken by line and length men.

Miller is also worth celebrating and remembering for the reason that he proved that good cricketers can still emerge from outside the current fast-track system. A journeyman medium-pacer who plied his trade for his native Victoria as well as South Australia and Tasmania, it wasn't until he reached the age of 34 that he remade himself as an off-spinner and revealed himself a highly competent Test cricketer with 69 wickets from 18 matches. 'Funky' is/was thus more than a cricketer with coloured hair. His story can be read as the triumph of a man who two matches before captured 10 wickets in an Adelaide Oval Test; and whose perseverance and ingenuity can inspire others, even those who might be ready to hang up their boots.

The Gordon Inkster ball contains one obvious mystery. Who was he? Gordon Bradford Inkster had a varied if sporadic sporting career, dictated by the pressures of business. For a big man, standing six foot two and weighing nearly 15 stone, it is not surprising that he should have made a senior appearance as a follower with Port Adelaide in league football. What is surprising is that he was a remarkably fine wicket-keeper, particularly adept at handling slow bowling.

He was born at Port Adelaide in 1893 and attended primary school in the area before going to business college for a commercial education. He first worked for a firm of customs agents in the Port before moving to Wilcannia, New South Wales, as an assistant accountant. In the First World War Inkster joined the 10th Battalion in Egypt; he was invalided to England in 1916, and attached to the headquarters staff of the Australian Imperial Force in London where he remained until the armistice.

Inkster's A-grade cricket debut came in April 1913. That was, however, the end of Inkster's participation in top-level sport in the city for several years, except for his period of war service. Inkster was an original member and wicket-keeper for the first AIF side in England before the official tour began in 1919, playing alongside Test players Charlie Macartney, Charles Kelleway and Johnny Taylor. His return to Australia allowed for his replacement by Bert Oldfield, who went on to become Australia's legendary gloveman in the interwar years.

Back home Inkster re-appeared with Port Adelaide briefly in the 1919–20 season, but then moved to a sheep station in New South Wales where he played cricket for Balranald. He was back with Port (again briefly) in 1921–22 before becoming secretary of the Renmark Hospital and playing a major role in sport and community bodies in the Riverland district over the next five years.

On his return to Adelaide Inkster joined the sales staff of a financial underwriting firm, and aged 32 resumed district cricket with Port. Inkster was quickly rushed into the South Australian side and immediately revealed his class at the top level. In his second game against Victoria, starting on New Year's Day 1927 at the Melbourne Cricket Ground, he grabbed national attention. While the home side enjoyed a monumental winning margin of 571 runs, Inkster's glove work was superb in claiming an Australian record of nine dismissals, stumping three batsmen off

Clarrie Grimmett in the first innings, and then stumping two and catching four in the second innings.

Inkster's three dismissals in his third game was a modest contribution to South Australia's 340-run win over New South Wales in Sydney, but it was the decisive match which enabled the side to capture the Sheffield Shield for the first time since 1912–13. At the end of the season Inkster played two more first-class non-Sheffield Shield games against Western Australia in Perth, which South Australia won. In these he took a further six dismissals for a total of 23 from five matches. It might have been expected that after his impressive start Inkster would retain the South Australian wicket-keeping position for as long as he wanted it. However, the following season when Victoria made 8 for 646 to defeat the home state by an innings and 310 runs in the first match, Inkster came under fire in the press. Despite his previous excellent form he was replaced and his state career was over after just six games.

The ball brings great credit to a cricket might-have-been; a man who could have played Test cricket, but who placed work and community service above mainstream sport at a time when the financial rewards to top cricketers were meagre. Yet in one match he outshone all the great Australian glovemen before him – Jack Blackham, Jim Kelly, Hanson Carter and Bert Oldfield – and though his record would not stand for long, it would take the superb Don Tallon to leap pass it with 12 dismissals for Queensland against New South Wales at the Brisbane Cricket Ground in November 1938. Inkster's feat remained a South Australian record for 35 years, however, until Barry Jarman surpassed it with 10 dismissals against New South Wales at Adelaide Oval in February 1962.

The ball from the Prospect RSL contains some delightful mysteries. Certainly, no Ashes Test match was played in Melbourne on Boxing Day 1934 and nor did South Australia's Sheffield Shield team play Victoria on that date. What can we learn from it? The most important thing is that the term 'The Ashes' has often been extended well beyond Anglo-Australian Test cricket matches. In fact, it has been used informally to cover a wide variety of contests between sporting teams. Once that is known it frees up all sorts of possibilities.

More clues about the ball lie with the name of the person to whom it was awarded. A.M. Ambler was Albert Mark Ambler, who was born in Murray Bridge on 27 September 1892 and died at Prospect on 27 November 1970. He kept wickets in 22 matches for South Australia from October 1920 to December 1925, making 57 dismissals (28 catches and 29 stumpings) besides averaging 10.83 with the bat.

Ambler was a member of the Prospect branch of the Returned Sailors, Soldiers and Airmen's Imperial League (RSSAIL), played for Prospect in district cricket and was captained there by his South Australian team-mate, the former Test player, C.E. 'Nip' Pellew.

During much of the interwar period Pellew captained the RSSAIL teams against those from Victoria in annual contests. My hunch is that it was one of these contests that was held on Boxing Day 1934 and that Albert Ambler was the wicket-keeper on that occasion and possibly other games as well. The ball makes an interesting exhibit alongside a sword which commemorates South Australia's record of being undefeated in these matches.

A piece of Test pitch can be flexible in terms of both space and time. It depends how it is seen. It can have a life of five days or many years. It can be a small patch on a large area or a part of the main stage. I like to think in big pictures and so the piece Les gave to me is part of a wide stage showcasing great cricketers of the years 1956 to 1990, from early in Arthur Lance's time as curator to well into the Burdett era. A short title could be Benaud to Border, but if one wants to be more expansive it conjures up images of superb performances by other heroes such as Lindwall, Harvey, Davidson, May, Cowdrey, Trueman, Statham, Sobers, Kanhai, Hall, Gibbs, Simpson, Lawry, the Pollocks, the Chappells, Walters, the Richards, Lloyd, Lillee, Marsh, Mallett, Boycott, Underwood, Bedi, Gavaskar, Imran, Kapil, Thomson, Knott, Botham, Gower, Border, Crowe, Hadlee, Roberts, Holding, Marshall, Garner, Wasim and the Waughs. This can be a vivid movie reel of the mind as one holds the turf in the palm of one's hand.

And people ask me about sub-soil!

Baggy Green, October 2003

A MEMORABILIA IDEA FOR TONY GREIG

Tony Wilson

It was the golden summer of 1993–94 and while recovering from a knee scrape, I had my orthopaedic brace signed by a young, psychologically traumatised Daryll Cullinan. This was the era before SMS, and so Shane Warne's fingers were undistracted from the task of bowling deliveries of a quality we may never see in this country again. Certainly, the record books suggest that Cullinan didn't see them that well the first time, and when I held the foam brace over the mid wicket fence at Adelaide he'd batted five times for 26 runs at 5.20. Daryll signed with the blank stare of a man who had seen too much horror. Appropriately, the 'i' in Cullinan was dotted with a big round 'O'.

My proposal to Greig and others at *Wide World of Sports* (*WWOS*) is that for this the 10th anniversary, we frame the brace and below it a photo of a bewildered Cullinan padding up to a straight one. Beneath that, we splash the famous Warne quote 'I could bowl to him for a living' and then call the whole thing – 'Lame Duck'. Beautiful. In the words of another famous Darryl, '*That* is going straight to the pool room.'

Obviously one 'Lame Duck' is not particularly lucrative, so I propose we contact Cullinan and get him to sign 519 more foam braces. If he wants a fee, we pay it. If he asks too many questions, they're for a polio charity in India. Then we unleash 'Lame Duck' onto an eager public. Limited edition of just 520 (his average without the decimal point). Unit price – $1499? An extra hundred perhaps if we can't get the braces second-hand.

Some readers might argue that 'Lame Duck' is flawed; that no one would be interested in an orthopaedic brace which has never been a part of Shane Warne's career and was only a part of Cullinan's for the few fleeting moments it grazed his signing hand in early 1994. They might argue that for memorabilia to obtain any value, it needs to have been touched by the stars, sweated on by champions. That simply put, my right knee hasn't done enough.

These people clearly haven't been watching the cricket the last few summers. The graze of a signing wrist is the new way in sports memorabilia. Take a mounted shirt signed by Mark Waugh that has been continually flogged by the Channel Nine commentators this summer. They talk about the deluxe showcase, the signature and the PricewaterhouseCoopers certificate of authenticity. They mention the fact that this offer will never occur again. They express surprise at the low, low amount payable each month, without particularly talking about the total purchase price, which just happens to be $2,055.00.

And there are 349 of the bastards, in all their pristine, lily-white glory. Greig and the other *WWOS* spruikers do always take care to state the edition number (for example, 'this is one of just 349 on offer'), but equal care seems to be taken to avoid the words 'replica' or 'copy'. From the sheer numbers, we assume that they are replicas, for even a punter as notorious as Mark Waugh is unlikely to lose his shirt 348 times in a summer, but the language is confusing. Take this description on the ninemsn website:

Mark Waugh's Australian Test match [sic] is now available to collectors. The Test shirt features the number 349 beneath the ACB Coat of Arms which is Mark Waugh's unique cricketing 'fingerprint' … The Test match shirt is fashioned by Fila Sport, the official uniform supplier and is the exact same shirt and size as worn by Mark Waugh in Tests complete with sponsor markings and the distinctive signifying marks introduced by the ACB in the 2001–02 season. Now collectors can acquire the

Test shirt of one of the team's batting mainstays of the past decade. By special arrangement with Mark Waugh and the ACB, this is the ONLY release of Mark Waugh's Test match shirt to be offered.

Nine Network lawyers have obviously OK'd this, and decided that 'Mark Waugh's Test match shirt' is not a misleading and deceptive description for a shirt that was never worn in a Test match by Mark Waugh. Equally, 'the exact same shirt and size as worn by Mark Waugh' was deemed to be within the bounds of the *Trade Practices Act*. If all 349 sell, gross revenue will be $717,195.

The Mark Waugh shirt is just one of thousands of items in the *WWOS* Shop. The similarly misleading 'Nathan Buckley Brownlow Jersey' could gross $311,250. A small battalion of Matthew Hayden 'On Top of the World' signed bats *did* gross $583,300.

My first question is whether I can have a cut. I'm also wondering whether the commentary team's loudest salesman, Tony Greig, gets one. His is the face on the *WWOS* Shop website. He's 'proud to recommend … these limited edition collector items'. Certainly, money must be flowing to the player (the trend now is only to sign a full name for paid gigs), the ACB and the Nine Network, but whether Greig spruiks on the commentary as an employee of Nine or as an interested party is difficult to determine. Is it Greig's business being given respectability by the Nine name, or is it Nine employing Greig to endorse a range of products that might just take some of the shine off that respectability? Either way, the *WWOS* Shop is just the next trough that has been set up by Kerry Packer to thank Greig for lending the legitimacy of the England captaincy to World Series Cricket following a handshake at Bellevue Hill way back in 1976.

I wish I had 1976 stunning Pro Hart prints of that handshake.

The Age, 31 December 2003

THE MEANINGS OF FOOTBALL

*Everyone knows that Australia supports more codes of
football than any other nation on the face of the sporting
earth. If we can't play it, we watch it. We have to give
them different names in order to differentiate between
what other places might just call plain old football. We
have Australian (Rules) football or footy, American football, Gaelic football, International Rules, soccer, Rugby or
Rugby Union, Rugby League or League, and probably
others. They all have different meanings, rituals, codes,
grammars, heroes and lexicons. Here eight writers look at
four codes.*

THE MEANING OF FOOTBALL

Martin Flanagan

In the year 2000, a Dutch journalist came to Melbourne to see the AFL Grand Final as part of a book that was being written on the great sports events of the world. He went to considerable trouble to track me down but when he finally succeeded he had only two questions. Two very good questions. The first was this – the Netherlands and Australia have roughly comparable populations. Furthermore, the number of registered soccer players in Holland approximates to the number of registered Australian footballers in this country. The difference, he said to me, is this, and I am quoting him direct: *'Here everyone talks about your game. Why?'* His second question related to female attendance at matches. In Holland, the percentage of women at major league soccer matches was 13 per cent. Here, he had been told, it was about 45 per cent. Again, why?

One answer to the first question is because it's a great game, but, as the song on the footy show says, it's more than a game. Take, for example, the two biggest footy stories of last year – Bali bombing victim Jason McCartney's return match and the death of Collingwood's Bob Rose. To reduce the importance of Jason McCartney's return match to a mere scoreline would be nothing less than foolishness. That night the game was a mirror in which people around the country looked and saw an image which consoled them at a time of national grief. Jason McCartney's behaviour at the time of the blast embodied certain selfless qualities we like to think of as Australian and which many people fear are being lost. Similarly, with Bob Rose. We weren't just mourning the loss of a Collingwood champion. We were mourning the loss of a man who could impose his presence on 35 other players on a football field but was humble off it, who was sincerely egalitarian, who came to Melbourne as a 16-year-old during the Great Depression to fight at Festival Hall because the money was needed, in his own words, 'to keep his brothers in shoes'. Bob Rose's story was more than a football story. It was a story which said something about Australia, its history and customs. And that was my first answer to the Dutch journalist. By the traditional measures of television, cinema, books, music, theatre, Australian culture is in retreat, but I believe passionately that Australians still want Australian stories with Australian characters, values and humour. Australian football provides them, and that's why I think a lot of people in this part of the world talk footy a lot of the time.

The second question, about the number of women at Australian football matches, underlines a considerable irony. Australian football is intermittently attacked for being violent as a result of which middle-class parents, particularly mothers, are swinging their children into soccer. But soccer, perhaps because it is less violent on the ground is violent in the stands in a way our game is not. Our game offers a more wholesome environment to watch sport in. But I also think part of the answer to the question about female attendance at our game lies in football's origins. For the first twenty years, the game was played on the slope between the present MCG and the Hilton Hotel and in other public parks around Melbourne. Admission, initially at least, was free. There was no ladies enclosure, no members'. Everybody mixed as one, Catholic and Protestant, squatter and larrikin, barmaid and lady of the night. The game was open to all. It was played passionately and organised on a local basis and people attached to it in that way so that football became intertwined with families and generations of families. In 1986, the year after I came to Melbourne, *The Age* sent me to Whitten Oval, then called the Western Oval, to report on the proposed merger between the Fitzroy and Footscray Football Clubs. That day, a middle-aged Bulldogs supporter called Cec Sargent pointed to the Western Oval and said to me, 'I know it sounds funny but when I look at that ground I see my father.' It didn't sound funny to me because I was brought up in a football family.

I could outline my relationship with football by listing events I have observed or been part of, like the first time a team I supported won a premiership. The team was East Devonport, the competition was the North-West Tasmanian Union, but I'm confident if I told that event in detail today I would be easily understood. Another event which influenced my view of the game occurred in 1993 when the then Footscray coach Terry Wheeler invited me to spend a year with the Bulldogs and write a book on it. Wheeler said the Dogs were going to win the premiership. I told him I doubted it but I accepted his offer all the same. I wanted to write a novel on football. In particular, I wanted to learn more about the experience of playing it at that level. In the event, I did learn something about that but it was almost incidental to what I ultimately extracted from the year. Previously, I had taken football for granted. It had never occurred to me that the game was historically vulnerable, but watching this fine old club battle for its existence it all became clear to me. Australian football is a nineteenth-century game. It was built on the principles of community and local pride. I once asked Fitzroy legend Alan 'Butch' Gale what it meant to play for Fitzroy when he was a young man. He replied, 'It meant you were a god in your street'. We now believe, not in community, but individualism and instead of having local ties and affections we pride ourselves on our mobility. How many of us live in the street, town or suburb where we spent our childhood?

People ask me all the time, 'Who do you barrack for?' I answer honestly. I say, 'I barrack for Australian football.' The truth is I barrack for Australian culture generally, which is not an argument about race but it is an argument about place. What comes from this country, what grows here, interests me more than what grows in other places, and few things in this country have grown as prolifically as Australian football, or have such deep roots. I have never said Australian football is an Aboriginal game, but I know a lot of Aboriginal people around Australia think it is; the footy field is one place where black and white legends stand alongside one another in a spirit of comradeship. In the early years of the twentieth century, rugby divided on class lines. Our game never did. My favourite post-match interview last year was with Barry Hall after the Swans had won a totally unexpected victory over Port Adelaide in Adelaide. A TV reporter had come running up to Big Bad Barry, or Harry as he now prefers to be called, and gushed over Adam Goodes's game. Barry's response was all of five words. *Goodes? Brownlow. Get on him.* And, with that, he turned and trotted off. You don't see characters like Barry Hall on *Friends* or any of the other American television shows that crowd Australian TV. Nor do you hear that minimal use of words that was a characteristic of the Australian language. I go into video stores and see any number of recklessly violent Hollywood fantasies. Where's the film with a character as real as Jason McCartney?

Several years ago, I received an email from an American who had picked up Australian football on American cable TV and become a Carlton supporter. After 10 years, as a wedding anniversary present, his wife had given him a return ticket to Melbourne for him to check out the home of this game he had come to love. And so, in the course of visiting as many grounds as he could, he went to Arden Street where, to his surprise, he was taken into the rooms, shown around and introduced to Byron Pickett, with whom he had his photo taken. When he got back to the United States, he sent me an email. 'There is nothing like this in America,' he wrote. 'Do Australians know what they've got?' He couldn't believe that a club that was involved in an elite sporting competition could be so welcoming, so accepting. He sensed the old egalitarianism that is still a part of most footy clubs, the sense of belonging and community. What he was saying was that Australian football still has a charm, a depth of feeling, that is lost when sport simply becomes a function of the entertainment industry, when players become performers employed by a franchise known to their fans through staged media events, when people go to see games as they might otherwise go to the cinema with the exception that they cheer for one side.

Our game will never lose its lustre as a spectacle for the simple reason that it is spectacular. Over the past century, a variety of visitors to Australia including Sir Arthur Conan Doyle, the creator of Sherlock Holmes, and C.B. Fry, the gifted amateur who represented England at three sports, have attested to its wonder as sport. The quandary facing Australian football is that we have a world-class game played, and followed, by only a tiny fraction of the world's population. That can work both for us and against us. The reason we weren't raided by Rupert Murdoch in the way that rugby league was a couple of years ago was because there wasn't a sufficient global audience for our game. Similarly, I don't believe our code will ever be seriously challenged by the National Soccer League while the likes of Harry Kewell play in Europe; part of the magic of sport is the belief that you're watching the best. But the world of global entertainment is upon us. Australian football evolved in the same sort of cultural isolation that created West Indian cricket. The current state of West Indian cricket shows what can happen when that isolation is breached.

I know of no exact replica to Australian football anywhere else in the world. It's unlike Irish sport which is amateur and strictly local. It's unlike American pro football and basketball which rest on the platform of college sport. Our game has a unique place, not only in Australian sport, but in Australian culture which, in my experience, is obvious to outsiders. I can admire the Australian rugby union team and enjoy watching them play, but at the end of the day it is a British game they're playing. Australian football is a marvellous sporting invention that found its way into the hearts of people and infiltrated other aspects of their lives so that it became something by which you knew families and suburbs and towns and, more recently with the national competition, different parts of Australia. I realise that each of you, as presidents and CEOs of AFL clubs, have concerns and worries of which I am not aware. While I do not see football essentially as a business, I do understand it has to be run in a businesslike manner. Guiding a game like ours through the times now confronting us will require a fine balancing act, but it is one that must pay regard to the web of connections that make up this greater entity we call the game. Your task is not an easy one but it is a proud one. Our game has lived for 150 years. May it live for 150 more.

The Age, 20 February 2004

RETURN OF THE MAGNIFICENT SIX

Roy Masters

There's always a game behind The Game. When the NSW State of Origin team assembled at a Randwick restaurant on Monday night, coach Phil Gould invited everyone to stand up and describe themselves.

The staff spoke first, with manager Chris Johns explaining his rolled-up tracksuit collar was to hide the rope marks left by the noose by which he was almost hanged after he was deemed responsible for players leaving the team hotel at 3 a.m. before Origin I. 'My name is Christopher Shane Johns and you blokes almost got me sacked. Don't f—— up this time,' he said.

But Willie Mason stole the show with, 'I'm Willie Mason and I've got ADHD. I've got a slight alcohol problem and I don't go to brothels any more'.

As an icebreaker, Gould's move was brilliant. The recall of veteran Brad Fittler was always going to distract debate away from the ignominy of the Origin I camp but some closure was also required. Fittler, never one for speeches, simply acknowledged his senior status and said, 'It's good to be back.'

His return promises to be the most scrutinised since General MacArthur stepped ashore in the Philippines, with Fittler admitting he wants to atone for his exit from Origin football three years ago, when the team he led was humbled. Joining him in the recall from that embarrassment in Brisbane are halfback Brett Kimmorley and prop Jason Stevens. Centre Matthew Gidley, second-rower Andrew Ryan and prop Mark O'Meley also played in that game.

If Origin II is all about exorcising the demons of 2001, the new NSW team is not without some sorcery, judging from the way the ball swept almost magically across the ruck during training at Wentworth Park midweek. Like a high-speed teleprinter shifting across a page, tapping into short spaces and then swooping across with long carries, the ball moved first right and then back, speeding to the open with clever cut-outs and decoys. It was far more sophisticated than the way Origin games are often played, like a Barbary ape taking a lead cosh to the typewriter keys. But perfection is the noble aim of all coaches and Gould was clearly in charge, calling the players together and rebuking them when the dropped-ball rate became unacceptable.

Gould has said Origin II is Kimmorley's show but really it his own. When Gould presented two flat footballs and a pump to Kimmorley on the first day of camp in a reference to a previous remark from the Sharks camp that Gould believes his importance to rugby league is such he even controls the air that goes into the football, it wasn't an invitation to Kimmorley to run the show. It was more an offer to contribute, a reminder to everyone that NSW's preparation is a team thing.

In any case, Kimmorley's style suits the way Gould wants his Origin team to play short advantage-line passes with plenty of players in motion, setting high-speed recognition problems for a retreating defence.

And it wasn't only Kimmorley taking the first pass off the ruck, with Craig Wing and Fittler also assuming the role. The Wentworth Park training session was different to the ones run by missing injured half Andrew Johns, who sometimes resembled the conductor of an orchestra, majestically waving the baton at his enthusiastic players, other times playing the role of a dispirited band leader, flicking it miserably at musicians who didn't belong on the same stage.

At training this week, Gould first divided the players into two groups, the left-hand-side players and the right-hand-side ones. Rugby league remains a regimented game. Given that the majority of players are right-handed, the ball inevitably heads more to the left, meaning it is better to put the defenders on the right-hand side.

Fittler will play on the left and his Roosters team-mate and lock Craig Fitzgibbon on the right. However, in attack, Fittler will float, with Kimmorley taking the first pass. Confirming this after training on Thursday, Fittler said: 'The half pretty much runs the show. He will do a lot of the ball playing. The way we've trained, he's been in charge but hopefully I'll get more say than Timmo [Shaun Timmins] did in the first game. He's basically a lock and the first game was very slippery, so hopefully I'll get more ball.'

Like Johns, Fittler can clear the forwards with one pass, a distance most club halves would need two passes to cover, and he can do it equally well orthodox or southpaw. He can also step off both feet, although his left is the more prodigious.

'I'll be on the left-hand side with Lewie [centre Luke Lewis] and Andrew Ryan and hopefully they'll get more ball,' Fittler said. 'I'll be definitely calling for it but I plan to get over on the right-hand side, as well. I find that if you stick to one side, you can fall out of the game.'

Queensland five-eighth Darren Lockyer is also a left- and right-side player, although he is a better runner than Fittler and will try to go the short side, running wide to hit wingers Billy Slater and Matt Sing with the ball at top speed.

The bottom line is this: despite the hype surrounding the meeting of Fittler and Lockyer, they won't clash that much during the 80 minutes of Origin II at Suncorp Stadium. 'The way the modern game is played, it's not as though five-eighths can line themselves up,' Fittler said. 'There's a good chance we will not play against each other at all in the game.'

Queensland would love to have a player like Gorden Tallis terrorising Fittler, running at him constantly, tiring his 32-year-old legs and stinging his battle-weary shoulders. The Maroons' best option for a player to fulfil this role was Fittler's Roosters team-mate Michael Crocker, who is suspended. Crocker is the type of player to whom a coach can assign a task, running at X, cleaning up Y. But the Maroons have gone for size, with five props, so they don't have the wide runners to flatten Fittler.

Origin I was a tight game for three reasons: no ball-moving five-eighths, slippery conditions and referee Sean Hampstead's skinny 10 metres. ARL chief executive Geoff Carr has spoken to Hampstead about opening up Origin II. 'On behalf of both leagues [NSW and Queensland], and given the nature of Origin I, we were keen to let him know the 10 metres needs to be observed,' Carr said. 'If he has to blow his whistle early to achieve this and sets that trend early, it will be a great game.'

Fittler said: 'It will be interesting to say the least.' And asked if he could play 80 minutes, he replied: 'If my body doesn't let me down. There's a big chance of that happening.'

The Sydney Morning Herald, 12 June 2004

THE CHANT OF JIMMY KRAKOUER

Martin Flanagan

In 1985, when *The Age* held a lunch to present the news-paper's Footballer of the Year award, I was seated beside the winner, North Melbourne's Jimmy Krakouer. The first things I noticed about him were the softness of his voice, the way his gaze was habitually cast downwards. He said neither 'yes' nor 'no' to anything placed before him. Soup, main course, dessert, wines – all were duly put in front of him and taken away untouched.

Nonetheless, I didn't find him hard to talk to. I asked him about his on-field relationship with his brother, Phillip, the one that had Melbourne sportswriters making uncharacteristic forays into poetry. 'It's confidence,' he said. 'That's all.' When I asked him how he dealt with the problem of fame, he was equally to the point. 'You never forget where you're from.'

Jimmy Krakouer is from Mount Barker on the southern tip of Western Australia. I made the trip to Mount Barker earlier this week, detouring about an hour out of Perth to see Karnet Prison Farm, where Jimmy is now being held as he serves out his sentence for trafficking amphetamines.

The prison is on the edge of a state forest. We got there about dawn, crossing the Serpentine Dam just as the rain cleared and a valley of white fog was rising in the morning sun. I also nearly hit – on three separate occasions – five kangaroos, big grey ones known as yongars to the Nyungar, the Aboriginal clan whose traditional lands extend from the south of Western Australia beyond Perth to Geraldton.

Jimmy Krakouer's a proud Nyungar. A remarkable number of prominent Australian footballers have been, among them Polly Farmer, Nicky Winmar, Peter Matera and Derek Kickett.

One not known to Victorian audiences, and possibly the greatest of them all, Stephen Michael, said it was hard enough to get his family to move to Perth from Kojunup without getting them to move to the other side of the country. Kojunup is half the distance Mount Barker is from Perth. Placed on a map relative to Melbourne, Mount Barker would be somewhere south of Launceston.

That far.

My companion on the journey, Sean Gorman, was a former wool classer who decided to get himself an education. He has a hearty, generous manner and once worked in the same shearing sheds as Jimmy's father, Eric Krakouer. Gorman says Eric was 'a really good shearer'.

There are two pubs in Mount Barker. The top pub is aligned with North Mount Barker Football Club, for whom Eric, Jimmy and Phil played. So did Gorman, and for the past four years, he has been working on a Ph.D thesis titled 'Moorditj Magic: The Story of Jim and Phillip Krakouer'. Moorditj is a Nyungar word meaning especially good or, to use another indigenous expression, 'deadly'.

It was about four years ago that Gorman arrived at my home with questions about articles I had written on the Krakouers in their North Melbourne days, and a videotape of the 1981 WAFL Grand Final between South Fremantle and Claremont. This game deserves inclusion in any catalogue of great grand finals.

South is being coached by Mal Brown, whose deeds and tactics are legend. South's hard man, Basil Campbell, a blackfella from the Northern Territory, duly shirtfronts a Claremont player at the opening bounce, the Claremont man going down as if struck by a club.

Jimmy Krakouer, one of the smallest men on the field, then leads the Claremont attack, not on the ball, but on Basil Campbell, who stands waiting for him like a heavyweight boxer. Given Jimmy's importance to Claremont, it looks suspiciously like a set-up. At the climactic moment, however, Stephen Michael steps between them. Michael is one of Campbell's South Fremantle team-mates but, like Jimmy, he is also a Nyungar. The game is on Nyungar land. This could lead to a much bigger fight.

The above insight is Gorman's, not mine, and that's why it's a privilege to make this trip with him. He knows the place, has studied its dual histories.

I'm soon aware I'm a long way from Melbourne, with its urban preoccupations, and remind myself that the journey I'm making the Krakouers made in reverse as young Aboriginal men in their early 20s.

On my previous visits to Western Australia, I've travelled north of Perth. Into bare red country. The area around Mount Barker is not unlike Gippsland and parts of Tasmania, scrubby, semi-cleared, pale blue mountains in view. Going for a walk atop Mount Barker, I find myself knee-deep in wet shrubs and bushes, with green moss underfoot. The town, by mainland Australian standards, is hilly.

Having previously agreed to talk to me, Jimmy's father Eric has decided to go away for the day. Eric's house is a new, yellow brick place. Having discovered Eric's absence, Gorman calls me over to look over a high side wall. There, tied against a wire fence, is a freshly gutted yongar, still with its fur, head flung to one side, its insides bright red and bony. In a nearby pen, four kangaroo dogs that look like greyhounds are baying.

We go to the top pub for a beer. When Gorman was working at nearby shearing sheds in the late '80s, the pub had a special bar for blacks only. A sliding door would open, a black arm would appear with money between its fingers. Slabs and flagons would pass the other way. The only other place blacks could gather in the town was the TAB. Jimmy, who didn't drink or smoke, went there from a young age. There's a thought in Mount Barker that Jimmy got into drug running because his gambling debts got out of control.

Using the pub phone, Gorman tracks down Eric, who's 50 kilometres away in Albany. 'Buddy, buddy, buddy,' says Eric to Gorman. 'I've told you everything. We've done all the talking.'

Eric's apparently decided he's not talking to journalists. Can't say I blame him. I know the request for media interviews with Jimmy's son Andrew had reached double figures by midway through last week. He wasn't talking either. One of the reasons Jimmy won't be getting out on day release to watch Andrew play against West Coast next weekend was the volume of media interest.

I spoke to Tiger CEO Greg Miller, who was at North Melbourne when Phil and Jimmy were there. I had wanted to ask Andrew if he had much to do with Phil growing up. To me, particularly when he started, Andrew played Phil's way – highly skilful, face impassive, relying on his superior understanding of the odd-shaped ball.

Miller vigorously resisted the idea, saying Andrew has become, like Jimmy, an 'in-and-under' player. But he agrees Andrew doesn't have Jimmy's fire. Jimmy was even known to throw punches on the training track. He'd ring the individual that night and apologise. Miller says it was because Jimmy couldn't bear to be beaten.

Victorian football had never seen anything like the Krakouers when they appeared in 1982. There'd been great Aboriginal players before, but they'd been individuals. When Steve Hawke wrote his biography of Polly Farmer, he found not one reference to Farmer's Aboriginality in the West Australian press before 1985. The Krakouers played as a pair, thereby dragging ideas of Aboriginality onto centre stage with them.

Good players are often one thought ahead of the play. The Krakouers were two – Jimmy's thought and Phil's thought, based on what he knew Jimmy was going to do. They unravelled games in the way that people unravel knots and it was once calculated that North won 62 per cent of its fixtures with the brothers playing together and only 38 per cent without.

The passions aroused by the Krakouer brothers went way beyond the norm. In fact, the worst racism I've ever heard at football matches was directed at the Krakouers, particularly Jimmy, and later, West Coast's Chris Lewis. One day at the MCG, in the members' enclosure, I saw a young man with a pink face standing whenever Jimmy came near, screaming: 'Hit him!'

I have a history of Aboriginal sport in which Jimmy is quoted as saying, 'Once you know what you want, they can't hurt you,' but his record argues this is not true. In an appearance before the VFL Tribunal in 1982, Jimmy claimed all his on-field offences were retaliatory. 'It has been in my make-up since I was a kid not to let people stand over me,' he said. 'I will be like that till the day I die.'

Jimmy had his own law. Phillip never got in fights but then he never had to. Jimmy, the older brother, handled that, even hitting a Carlton opponent at an after-match function for something done to Phillip during a game. Even in Melbourne, far from Nyungar country, people realised the Krakouer story had an extra dimension, although no one knew exactly what that was. In his whimsical way, Greg Champion provided the most abiding image when he called one of his songs 'The Chant of Jimmy Krakouer'.

Gorman calls Jimmy 'the great anti-hero of Mount Barker'. He was sent away to a boys' home for fighting while still at school, was imprisoned at the age of 16 for rape (Gorman says Jimmy is deeply aggrieved at his conviction for this crime, claiming he only pleaded guilty because told to do so by a lawyer). Three weeks after he got his licence, he was chasing a car in which some youthful companions were travelling when he slewed off the highway and into a road gang, killing one of the workers. It is hardly surprising to learn there are locals who say Jimmy Krakouer was always going to come to a bad end.

Gorman takes me to meet a stalwart of the North Mount Barker Football Club who has a newspaper clipping from the 1960s, saying what a popular fellow Eric Krakouer was and the winner of two club 'fairests and bests'. As a player, I am told, Eric was nothing brilliant but he was persistent, 'always there'. He played in every position he was asked, which ended up being every position on the ground. In those days, Eric and his family were living in a shack between the stockyards and the railway track outside town.

Gorman's thesis analyses the race laws enacted in Western Australia, particularly the grossly paternalistic protectorate of A.O. Neville. Their radical impact on Aboriginal families, particularly of Eric Krakouer's generation, is virtually inconceivable to non-Aboriginal Australians. The Krakouer name comes from a Polish Jew who became the mayor of Kojonup. Eric, who was born in Kojonup, came to Mount Barker in 1947 and married into a local family, the Millers, about 10 years later. Locally, the brilliance of Phil and Jimmy as footballers is seen to have come from the Millers.

The old whitefellas I met in Mount Barker expressed a genuine liking and respect for Eric Krakouer, although one said he'd 'hardened' in later years and another struggled to find a polite way of saying he'd become more assertively Aboriginal. Both used the word Nyungar, one of them saying in a slightly concerned way: 'You know it's not a term of abuse.' I do. It's a term of respect. In how many parts of southern Australia do Aboriginal people get called by their tribal name?

Phil Krakouer is well remembered around Mount Barker and there's by no means a single view of Jimmy. One old whitefella said Jimmy's a subject people just don't talk about. The last man I meet is a local grazier. Eric Krakouer lived for a time on his property and for many years the family received a Christmas card from Phil. 'That accident out on the road could have happened to anyone,' he said. 'I'd shake Jimmy's hand if he came in here now.'

It was a long drive back to Perth but we did a lot of talking. Gorman's research has taken him everywhere – to former administrators and team-mates at North Melbourne, to WAFL figures, to junior coaches and classmates, to other family members. Among those Gorman spoke to was John Kennedy, one of Jimmy's coaches at North. Kennedy described Jimmy as 'an enormous footballer' and said 'there was something pretty honourable' about Jimmy's habit of settling on-field disputes on the spot rather than brooding on them. But he also said you can't conduct football games in that way.

Kennedy is a legendary figure in the game, a strict disciplinarian, a magnificent orator, a man who paid no heed to pain. The day we met in *The Age* boardroom, Jimmy indicated his respect for Kennedy. I didn't realise at the time quite how significant an utterance this was; Jimmy's respect is like something carved from wood. I have never heard of anyone answering John Kennedy back. I now learned Jimmy Krakouer did – Jimmy, who more commonly averted his gaze in the Nyungar manner, and from whom some people in Mount Barker say they never got a word. At the time, Jimmy had just been suspended again and Kennedy was talking to the team, saying one of their number had let them down.

Gorman includes a version of Jimmy's speech in his thesis. It needs an actor to deliver it, one who can put the force of his being into the words, but basically, Jimmy said he'd copped shit all his life and what did Kennedy want him to do, lie down like a dog and take it?

Some people told Gorman that Jimmy's the best footballer they've ever seen, among them his sublimely gifted North Melbourne team-mate, Matthew Larkin. Jimmy is generally well liked by his former North team-mates because, being the total footballer, he was for the team. In an interview during his playing days, then-club president Bob Ansett mused on Jimmy's discipline in the way he approached games compared with the lack of discipline he displayed with gambling.

The coach with whom his career at North ended, Wayne Schimmelbush, told Gorman Jimmy's inability to disregard taunts was his great flaw. It meant he could be 'got in'. Jimmy's playing days were nearly over by the time he left North, but the final issue was Schimmelbush insisting Jimmy do his pre-season in Melbourne and not, as was his way, Mount Barker. Gorman showed me the hill on the edge of town that Jimmy and Phil used to run up and said they also trained by chasing 'roos.

Traditionally in Australia, race relations have been seen as a simple matter of black and white, but in between, there's actually been this grey space called the footy field. For years, we interpreted it in a whitefella way. That changed for me with the Krakouers and I know I wasn't alone. That's when signs saying 'Black Magic' started appearing at the footy.

Once, when I quoted one of those signs in an article, I was called a racist, but when the Nyungars made a film about footy, they called it *Black Magic*. And that's where I first saw the start of the 1981 WAFL Grand Final, Phil and Jimmy's last game before coming to Victoria to change the way we saw footy and more besides.

The Age, 22 May 2004

HOW RUGBY'S BID FOR JOEY WAS SUNK

Greg Growden

Eddie Jones wanted Andrew Johns. NSW wanted Andrew Johns. Johns was intrigued. But, in the end, the Australian Rugby Union, which had originally led the charge for the Kangaroos captain's signature in a drive that included two recent clandestine meetings with Johns, made an about-turn and said, 'No'.

The Johns saga is a complex, often bewildering affair, with a fair share of intrigue, which has ultimately undermined relationships between NSW Rugby Union officials and the ARU. The *Herald* last week revealed NSW had made Johns their No. 1 target for the 2005 Super 12 season, but rugby has been pursuing the world's best league player for some time.

The first serious indication the ARU was interested in Johns was in 2000, when its then chief executive officer John O'Neill said the Wallabies were keen on several high-profile league players. Johns was high on the hit list.

And it again became an ARU issue just before Johns injured his knee in late March, when the first of two meetings, involving Wallabies coach Jones, ARU high-performance manager Brett Robinson and Johns, was held at the Sydney home of Johns' manager John Fordham.

The meeting was so secret that a special code was used in any contact between Fordham, Jones and Robinson. Johns' name was never used in correspondence. Instead, Johns was referred to as 'Player Y'. Fordham yesterday confirmed to the *Herald* the two meetings had taken place and the letter 'Y' was used because it was the last letter of Johns' nickname, Joey.

The second meeting between Jones, Robinson and Johns was held just over a month ago, again at Fordham's house. Both were 'curiosity' sessions, at which Jones and Robinson discussed rugby with Johns, but never got to the negotiation stage. The meetings were a 'question and answer, getting to know you' exercise.

Chasing Johns's signature again became a priority a few weeks ago, when after another up-and-down NSW season, Waratahs officials decided they would fail in the Super 12 unless they found a consistent, match-winning pivot. Someone like Johns.

NSW officials knew they had the forward pack to win the Super 12. But they needed midfield authority to unleash the exceptional attacking talents of former league players Lote Tuqiri and Mat Rogers. And they were aware several key forwards were becoming irritated that all their good work up-front was being wasted because the team did not have an authoritative five-eighth with the required kicking game. Good ball was being wasted. Poor kicking options in several Super 12 matches had afforded the forwards little respite from making tackle after tackle. The Waratahs were concerned a divide could form between the forwards and the backs if the situation continued and the team would be doomed.

Knowing that Jones wanted Johns, NSW, confident they had the backing of the Australian coach, started the process of trying to speak with the Newcastle Knights player. However, NSW soon discovered there was considerable opposition in the ARU ranks. Several officials, including Robinson and at least one ARU board member, had raised doubts over whether Johns would be a good investment, especially as he had just turned 30 and had suffered several serious injuries. Robinson's support was crucial, especially as he is intimately involved in all contract negotiations. The old guard at the ARU was also worried rugby was becoming a lucrative retirement home for former league stars, the code having already signed Tuqiri, Rogers and Wendell Sailor.

The ARU was unimpressed that the NSWRU had gone public over its eagerness to get Johns, arguing there was a proper process for the recruitment of all players, and that was not through newspapers. An ARU official told the *Herald* on Wednesday: 'This is not the proper way to conduct business.' The *Herald* has learned that on Wednesday a high-ranking NSW official was chastised by an ARU board member.

NSW were in a tricky situation: they needed the ARU's support for top-up funding to be able to provide an attractive financial package for Johns. Buoyed by the Wallabies coach's interest, they kept pushing for a meeting with Johns. However, barriers kept being put in their way. ARU officials offered little support and NSW's bid to have a meeting with Johns finally failed. This angered several NSW officials, who had been told that Johns 'genuinely wanted to join Rogers and Tuqiri at the Waratahs'.

They rightfully believed a golden opportunity to snare Johns was being ruined through higher intervention and conflicting voices from within the ARU bunker. NSW, aware of the growing division between several ARU employees, became wary of at least two ARU officials. Following a demand from Fordham, all the parties met on Thursday. Those at the meeting included ARU acting chief executive officer Matt Carroll, Robinson and NSWRU chief executive Fraser Neill.

Well before the meeting, the ARU had made up its mind. On Wednesday night, the ARU media staff had drafted a media release, stating the union would not be 'seeking to contract' Johns. However, Carroll decided to delay the media release until the following day. On Thursday morning, and before the start of the meeting, an ARU media staff member told the *Herald* the media release would be made public at 2 p.m. that day.

At that stage, Fordham said Johns remained committed to rugby league. 'I went to the meeting to see if there was any genuine interest in Andrew Johns,' Fordham said yesterday. 'I wasn't there to negotiate a contract.'

At the meeting, Carroll explained why the ARU was not interested in Johns, giving several reasons, including the player's age and recent problems with injury. Carroll made it clear the ARU would not add any money to NSW's offer. Neill was asked if the NSWRU could finance Johns on its own. Neill was not confident – he knew the Waratahs were sunk without ARU support. All the Waratahs could offer Johns on their own was $155,000, the average wage of a Super 12 player. Fordham shook his head, before uttering: 'What am I doing here?'

'I left the meeting very angry,' Fordham said yesterday. 'That meeting was like going to visit Fort Fumble … it was embarrassing. Based on what has gone on over the last few days, I now have no confidence in dealing with the ARU high-performance unit. And I can understand why there are now serious moves to have that unit dismantled.'

The ARU was surprised that 20 minutes before its statement was to be released to the media, Fordham gazumped them with an official release that said Johns was staying in league. Cleverly,

Fordham had stolen the ARU's thunder. But the fact remained the ARU hierarchy did not want Johns, as the union pointed out in its press release, which arrived, as expected, at 2 p.m.

The upshot is NSW have missed out on Johns and are worried it may adversely affect their efforts to keep Tuqiri, who has yet to decide whether to remain in union or return to league next year. Tuqiri was genuinely excited by the prospect of playing alongside Johns at NSW. As was Rogers.

Senior NSW players contacted Johns on Thursday and were told that although he was originally interested in the NSW proposal, he was now 'out'. A particular ARU official was blamed.

The deadline for Tuqiri's decision about where he will play next season was originally yesterday. That deadline has now been extended and the Waratahs are praying the Johns saga does not make Tuqiri predisposed to returning to league. They are hopeful, but not overly confident, Tuqiri will be with the Waratahs in 2005.

And so NSW are still looking for someone, anyone, to become their match-winner at number 10. They are getting desperate. The high-priority names are Julian Huxley, Manuel Edmonds and Shane Drahm. Huxley is again in favour, and Edmonds and Drahm would have to be lured back from overseas.

And, once again, the relationship between NSW and the ARU is tense. As a NSW official said last night: 'There are going to be serious ramifications over this whole mess.'

The Sydney Morning Herald, 29 May 2004

BELIEVING IN THE IMPOSSIBLE

Tony Wilson

Shaun Dockery 1990

Shaun Dockery only ever gave one truly great three-quarter-time address, but that's not bad for someone who's never actually coached. The match was Hawthorn versus North Melbourne at Arden Street, and if the year had have been 1976, this story might have been coloured with screaming fans, traditional rivalry and searching Mick Nolan runs. As it was, the year was 1990, and about 300 people had come along to watch Denis Pagan's Kangaroos teach Russell Greene's Hawks what under-19 football was all about.

What the clubs believed under-19 football to be all about was producing senior footballers, but from the look of Russell Greene's jugular vein as we trudged into the three-quarter-time huddle, it was clear he also had a passing interest in winning. He'd indicated as much at half-time when he'd said, 'If you're going to keep playing like that, don't bother coming in at three-quarter time.' It was supposed to be the game where we secured the double chance, but now we'd fallen 55 points behind. If Greeney was true to his word, he didn't particularly want to see us.

'I don't really have anything much to say,' Greene began. 'Any of you blokes got anything to say?'

He was quiet, he was angry and it was absolutely, definitely nobody's cue. A glance at my team-mates revealed that staring at the Arden Street grass was the preferred way of weathering this storm, followed closely by picking at strapping. The most important thing was not to make eye contact and not to speak. On the opposite flank, Pagan was screaming at his players, which given they were nine goals up, only made things feel all the more ominous in our huddle.

'We can fucken win this, Greeney.'

I'd like to say that I looked up and saw Shaun Dockery ringed by haloes of sunlight or as a mystical silhouette against the Arden Street gasometers, but at the moment Doc started speaking, there was no indication that he was embarking upon one of the great football addresses. It was just a standard Shaun Dockery sentence. Expletive, check. Volume of low-flying jet, check. Black mouthguard impeding some of the more difficult vowel sounds, check. Nonetheless, there was an intensity in his tone that made you think that Doc might actually believe we could win. Greeney seemed to pick up on it too.

'Doc reckons we can win it, so Doc can bloody well talk to you blokes.'

With that Greene picked up his clipboard and exited the huddle, leaving us in the hands of an oiled-up 17-year-old in a helmet. These were the first things you noticed about Shaun Dockery on a football field. He had enormous muscles for his age, which he accentuated firstly by walking around with clenched fists and then by oiling his arms several times a quarter. He also wore one of those black, padded, buckle-up helmets; something his opponents might also have chosen to wear if they, like Doc, knew how much of their afternoon would be spent punching on. Not that Doc was deliberately dirty. It's just that accidents happen more frequently when you run around with clenched fists.

Doc moved to the middle of the huddle, undid the strap on his helmet, and went to remove his mouthguard before deciding against it. His teeth were gritted, his eyes wide and furious. Shit. Maybe he was going to deck a couple of us? Finally, he extended as far as his six-foot frame would allow, turned his face an alarming shade of red, and started screaming.

'We're going to fucken win this! ANYONE RECKON WE'RE NOT GUNNA FUCKEN WIN THIS?'

Nobody spoke, but Doc must have sensed that at least some of us were concerned about our prospects of kicking 10 goals to nothing in the last quarter. Throw in the fact that we'd so far sneaked just three goals for the game, and we were at least

justified in asking Doc to explain his case. As it was, Doc didn't
need any prompting.

'TEN GOALS IN 30 MINUTES! ONE FUCKEN GOAL EVERY
THREE MINUTES! CAN WE KICK A GOAL IN THE FIRST
THREE MINUTES?'

At this point, the huddle collectively squeezed out a 'yes'.

'SO WHAT REASON IS THERE THAT WE CAN'T KICK
ANOTHER FUCKEN GOAL IN THE NEXT THREE MINUTES?'

We murmured. The consensus seemed to be that there was no
reason. Doc's torso was shaking like a jackhammer as he gathered momentum.

'THERE'S NO FUCKEN REASON. WE'RE GOING TO KICK
A GOAL EVERY THREE MINUTES! AND DO YOU KNOW
WHAT WILL HAPPEN IF WE DO?'

'We'll win!' shouted a few of the blokes with growing
enthusiasm.

'OF COURSE WE'LL FUCKEN WIN!' screamed Doc. 'AND
DO YOU KNOW WHAT ELSE WILL HAPPEN?'

There was some scratching of heads as we wondered where
Doc was taking us. We didn't have to wait long.

'THERE'LL BE SO MUCH FUCKEN TIME-ON, THAT BY
THE END WE'LL HAVE HAD MORE THAN THREE MIN-
UTES TO SCORE EACH GOAL!'

And that was basically it. Russell Greene's approach had
tended to focus on the so called 'one-percenters'. Tackling, chasing, smothering, unrewarded running. 'Goals,' Greeney said,
'would look after themselves.' But that hadn't worked and
now the game plan was in the hands of a back-pocket from
Doveton. And from what Doc had just said, that game plan
seemed to be: we kick the first 10 at approximately three-
minute intervals, then if we miss out on the last couple, we rely
on additional time-on generated from our opening burst to
mop them up later. No mention of unrewarded running. No
mention of the opposition. Still, the mood in the trench had
improved considerably, and we were all now looking to Doc for
inspiration.

His next move was to jump forward and grab Azza by the top

of his jumper. Azza had bleached blonde hair, played in the forward pocket, and hadn't handballed for two seasons. Even today, Azza remains one of the most smackable people I've met in my life. For a moment, I thought that Doc was going to sacrifice Azza to demonstrate his commitment to the cause. But then he revealed his grand plan. We were all to be grabbed violently around the collar and shaken.

'Everyone's gotta look into my eyes and say we can fucken win it.' Doc spat. 'Azza, can we fucken win it?'

'Yes Doc, we can fucken win it.'

'LOUDER AZZA, SAY IT AT THE TOP OF YOUR VOICE,' Doc shrieked.

'YES DOCCA, WE CAN FUCKEN WIN IT!' shouted Azza.

Doc moved on to Macca and after Macca another bloke we called Macca. Both were loud, both full of resolve. 'YES DOCCA, WE'RE GOING TO DO IT!' Rowdy had only said about 30 words since he'd come down from the bush, but now Doc's black mouthguard was only centimetres from his face. 'We'll do it Doc,' he said at a volume that was a revelation for everyone. Bickers fell quickly into line, and it wasn't like Crazy Dave wanted any trouble. One by one Shaun Dockery took his turn with each of us, and one by one we committed to the cause. Finally, he came to me.

'Willo, can we fucken do it?'

Before I looked into Doc's eyes, I honestly didn't believe we could fucken do it. But at the moment I looked up and saw the face of the man who was holding both of my ears and spitting over the front of my jumper, I was a convert.

'YES WE CAN DO IT DOCCA!' I yelled.

'GOAL EVERY THREE MINUTES WILLO!'

'GOAL EVERY THREE MINUTES DOCCA!'

The team was electrified. There probably wasn't a player amongst us that had touched the ball more than 10 times all day, but a rant, a rave and a bit of Shaun Dockery inspired whiplash, and suddenly we felt like world beaters. Spontaneously, we all ran as hard as we could into the centre of the huddle so we could smash into one another and scream some more. We were going to make football history, insofar as football history can be made in the under 19s.

To say that Doc completely out-coached Denis Pagan over the course of the next six minutes would be somewhat of an over-statement, but we did kick the first two goals of the quarter. On balance though, the points probably went to Pagan as his boys slammed through the next eight, bringing the final margin to 85 points.

Doc was right when he predicted the length of that quarter. It went for ages.

Read at the Victorian Writer's Centre
Football Spoken Word Night, Grand Final week, 2003

THE VIRGIN COACH

Paul Connolly

My first soccer coach, John, had a moustache, smoked like a crematorium and drove a diarrhoea-coloured Datsun 120Y. His private life, like the private life of all adults, was a mystery I never contemplated. Being six, I assumed his entire existence was devoted to ferrying kids around in his car, dousing bloody knees with the magic sponge and combating the junior player's inclination to surround the ball like a herd of hooligans with the scent of blood in their noses. Unquestionably, I loved him for it.

All of this came fondly back to me last year when I was asked to coach a newly formed soccer team of, ahem, mature-aged women, bursting with an enthusiasm inflamed by the 2002 World Cup. Here, I figured, was a tempting opportunity to emu-late John and perhaps even make a mark on the lives of others in the same way he had made a mark on mine. The problem, however, was that while I'd played soccer with some degree of competence for much of my life – and it's true what they say, the older you got, the better you were – I'd never coached. Did I, like John, have it in me? Or would I be as useless as one of John's successors who, having hoisted the white flag some time earlier, spent training sessions half inside his Kingswood station wagon listening to the latest from Kembla Grange?

Reassuringly, none of the prospective players, whose average age was about 32 (with three in their mid-to-late 40s), had played competition soccer before. In fact, many in the squad (comprising, in part, working mums, social workers, sexual assault counsellors, a graphic artist, a Chinese medicine practitioner, an engineer and a medical student) had never played organised sport of any persuasion and couldn't be accused of being athletic. A broader, more inventive range of running styles I'd never seen; from one who seemed to be tiptoeing over burning coals to another who ran hesitantly, almost apologetically, as if streaking through St Peter's basilica during an Easter service yet somehow hoping to pass unnoticed. These weren't, with all due respect, the dexterous sylphs of *Bend It Like Beckham*.

Though mindful of the 'old dogs-new tricks' adage, I decided to give it a go, figuring that in the event of disaster they'd be too inexperienced to blame me, let alone notice me staring from the sidelines as blankly as a monkey at a trigonometry term paper. But what model of coaching would I look to emulate? The encouraging, *in loco parentis* model favoured by John? Or that of the mega-successful Sir Alex Ferguson of Manchester United, known as the hair dryer for his withering half-time blasts?

Of course, like Liberace, I hoped to develop my own distinct style that I realised should take into account the relevant factors: we were a team of ageing novices playing in the darkest fathoms of Melbourne's Open Women's league. This was not The Big Time. So, all things considered, patience and positive reinforcement would get more out of my players than arse-kicking fury. And a good thing too. On the sliding scale of intimidation book-ended by Mike Tyson and Woody Allen I'm rubbing shoulders with Michael J. Fox.

Just as my coaching philosophy hoped to consider the above factors so too, I discovered, at a pre-season get-together, did the team's philosophy. While I'd mostly played in teams where winning was paramount and, as such, team-mates competed with each other for starting positions, we decided to do something different.

Simply, it was argued that the same bums shouldn't have to warm the bench week after week. In this case, everyone, regardless of ability, would get equal time on the field.

Perhaps, I feared, this egalitarian system would emasculate me in a way no self-respecting coach would countenance. Perhaps, too, the removal of competition for starting places would hinder the rate of individual improvement since there were no adverse consequences to mistakes, laziness or complacency. But considering we were consenting adults with no previous experience it didn't seem to matter.

Of course, we all hoped to win every game but this venture was primarily about participation and pleasure. Legendary Liverpool manager Bill Shankly once said, 'Football isn't a matter of life and death, it's much more important than that.' I guess we took the view that that's just bullshit.

We were, we joked, a motley bunch; comparable with the bumbling jumble of misfits, cast-offs and ne'er-do-wells that made up those teams in Disney movies like *The Bad News Bears*. Of course, according to Hollywood, these teams always overcame their ineptitude and various impairments to defeat, in the dying seconds of the championship game, to become a smug, athletic and physically imposing team drilled with military precision by an autocratic coach trying to make up, vicariously, for his own shortcomings. Pure malarkey, of course, but if you look hard enough, you'll find a worthy message in there somewhere.

At least that's what I told my team in a cliché-riddled address before our opening game. 'Passion and determination can make up, in some way, for deficiencies in experience,' I told them, as they sat in their wrapper-fresh playing strips (which, to a woman, they found dreadfully unflattering despite the slimming vertical stripes) nervously clicking their studs against the concrete floor of the dressing shed.

'Besides which,' I went on, noticing a faint whiff of liniment that will always conjure for me (and now perhaps them) the comforting, preparatory rituals of sport, 'the result doesn't matter. If you give it your best you should come off pleased with yourselves no matter what. We just have to concentrate, encourage each other and show some ... um ...'

'Balls', clearly, wasn't about to cut it with this audience. So, I improvised, rather grandly I thought, with 'intestinal fortitude.'

Instead of beating their chests like adrenaline charged silverback gorillas they sniggered behind their hands. Clearly, I was no Martin Luther King. Nevertheless, they left the dressing room – led by our energised captain, Liz – with equal measures of apprehension, excitement and determination. Watching them run into the unknown, I longed for them to be competitive, for their bravery to be rewarded and, yes, to prove to myself and them that should they replace me with a turnip they'd be worse off. Please God, I thought, don't let them be thrashed.

Accentuating our age in that first game we faced a team of teenage girls with more make-up and attitude than a revue of transvestites. A disharmonious bunch, they were captained by a strapping blonde with an unholy vocabulary who threatened, in gangster parlance, to take one of her recalcitrant team-mates 'for a drive' after the match unless she got her 'effing' act together.

Though shocked by their feistiness (one of them called our flying winger, Brita, an 'animal' which intrigued everyone) we tried valiantly to put all we'd learned into practice. This was complicated early on by an apocalyptic turn in the weather when coal black clouds began haemorrhaging sheets of rain so thick at times I couldn't see across the pitch. It was as if the gods wanted to help us remember this occasion forever.

But we would have anyway. For despite the odd foul throws, air swings, misdirected passes and shortness of breath, we did enough things right and midway through the second half were leading 2–0 thanks to goals by Annie and Jo. Forget the rehearsed celebrations of today's professionals who expect goals to come, if any goals have ever been greeted with purer expressions of joy I've never seen or heard of them.

But sport cares little for sentiment and, ultimately, we ran out of legs and our two-goal cushion was cruelly neutralised in the final seconds. But the disappointment – theirs and mine – was momentary. As our midfielder, Gemma, pointed out with considerable mathematical acumen: 'Hang on, we scored two too!' While a sporting cliché opines 'a draw is like kissing your sister', we were more than thrilled to come out with honours even against a team who, give or take, were young enough to be our daughters.

And so, for the first of many times that season, we celebrated our effort rather than the result. So used to being around male athletes who would sooner soap each other's chests in the showers afterwards than celebrate a draw (let alone a loss), this was a revelation.

I could, with much affection and detail, recall every game of the season but suffice to say, the opener was one of few statistical highs. Of the 18 games we played, we won one, drew two and lost 15, conceding 60 goals and scoring eight. But that's the thing about sport, the numbers are just a version of the truth. There's a lot they don't reveal.

Like effort. Under the watery lights of our home ground in East Brunswick, my charges trained week after week in biting cold and creeping mist, striving gamely and good humouredly to improve their fitness levels, interpret my gibbering explanations and learn the kind of things a moderately sporty child would take for granted. Not only tactical knowledge like where and when to kick the ball but more elementary stuff like how to kick the ball.

Certainly there were times when I stood in the drizzle and wondered how I got roped into all this. And, sure, there were matches when we were inexplicably listless and conceded horrific goals that owed more to *The Texas Chainsaw Massacre* than *Match of the Day*, when I was tempted to fill my pockets with stones and, like Virginia Woolf, calmly walk into a creek and end the misery.

But these moments were forgotten when, against an undeni-able and soul-warming trend of continual improvement, I wit-nessed the kamikaze-like determination of Sue, Tami and Jen, or saw a smooth one-two between Fiona and Alicia, or a sharp shot on goal from Lucy or Nat, or even just an attempt at a judicious pass from anyone which showed, mentally at least, we were learning, even if the body couldn't yet, or wouldn't ever, exe-cute the play.

But more appealing still was the consistent buoyancy of the team's mood. Perhaps no one felt skilful enough to sport a righteous ego (not that that stops many men) but not once did they turn on each other, even after the kind of blunders that would make Jesus weep. Rather, this group of women stood by each other and, led by our goalie Deb, dished out more sup-portive hugs than you'd see in a lifetime of watching Oprah. They all felt part of something bigger which is surely one of sport's main purposes.

My reward was the privilege of accompanying and guiding them through those moments, good and bad, that John guided me through. Moments which one day they'll look back on with a deserved sense of pride and nostalgia: the muddy training sessions, the road trips to unexplored suburbia, the dressing-room banter, the shock of shorts in winter, the tremulous first glance at the opposition, the shrill cry of a whistle, the first dry-mouthed gasp for breath, the wet crack of an ankle buck-ling, the exhilaration of a smoothly executed move, the abject, head-hanging frustration of a goal conceded and the sound of a ball you've struck hitting the back of the net.

Twelve of my team got to hear that sound. Of course, for five of them, it was their own net. But in the greater scheme of things, it hardly mattered.

The Big Issue, 6 September 2004

THE SPORT I HATE

Anthea Henwood

There I was. Standing there, freezing to death, trying to become enthusiastic about the spectacle that was unfolding before my eyes. And what a spectacle it was. Pale-skinned men in shorts, with goose bumps so large I could see them from beyond the fence, running towards a ball while the 10 people who had showed up to watch said nothing. That was how I spent my first weekend in Ireland. Freezing to death while taking in my first real experience of Gaelic football.

The freezing to death was to remain fairly constant during my time in Ireland, but I was to blame for that. After all, I went there during the Irish winter. However by quarter time of my first game of Gaelic football I had decided that I wasn't spending my entire trip at a football pitch, even though through my boyfriend I knew half the guys on the team. Here are a group of guys, who look as though they really want to be at home in front of the heater, following a ball around a rectangle football field, while at the same time trying to figure out exactly what the rules governing the game are.

Ah, Gaelic football. The sport that some Irish genius came up with and some people in America whose great-great-great-grandparents came from Ireland are hugely enthusiastic about. Let the Americans have this stupid game! Gaelic football has to be the worst code of football there is, except maybe American football. Maybe that's why the Americans have taken such a shining to it?

It is like every Irish joke you ever heard was combined and played out in front of you. As I stood there trying to make sense of the activity happening before my eyes I could almost see the guys who came up with the rules.

'You know, Paddy, I think we should base the game on Aussie Rules.'

'Ah Seamus, let's not do that. Let's just complicate it, that'll make it easier for everyone.'

'To be sure it will.'

'So you like speccies? Let's get rid of them. They're a bit dangerous. Hey, let's get rid of marking all together. Who needs it? Now, do we want a soccer goal or Aussie Rules style goal posts?'

'Let's not make a decision on that one, let's try and put the two of them together. Take off the point posts, add a net to the goals and there we are. What else can we change?'

'Hmmmmm. That oval ball just has to go. I mean, how could we chase that? It wouldn't work very well in the frost. But what do we change it too?'

'Let's borrow a soccer ball from the guy across the road and use that. And while we're borrowing from soccer let's use their style of "throwing in".'

'Yeah, and we'll make the field rectangle and call it a pitch! That'll make shots at goal easier, as there won't be any snap shots from the wings.'

'An excellent idea, Paddy. But you know, bouncing a ball on wet grass, and I mean VERY wet grass, doesn't work very well.'

'Right you are, Seamus! Well, we'll make the guys bounce the ball on their foot as they run, that ought to make it easier!'

'Then just to keep things really simple, we won't name any of the teams after the towns where they're from. We'll name them after people!'

'And these people will just be any random person. They won't even have to contribute anything to the game.'

'Sounds good. And, the finishing touch … what will we call it?'

'Let's call it Gaelic football. We'll make it the central point of the Gaelic Athletic Association. One day it will be more popular than hurling.'

If this game is the pinnacle of Irish champions and competitiveness, if this is what Irish pride is based on, then remind me to never go to a game of hurling.

In my mind I could even see what Seamus and Paddy looked like. I guess it doesn't say much for me or them (I haven't decided which one) that they bore a striking resemblance to Dougal from the *Father Ted* TV show.

Halfway through my first game of Gaelic football, between the Keiron O'Reilly's GAA Club and the John Mitchel's GAA Club, and I was only a spectator, I decided not to completely waste the afternoon. I looked around the ground for the place that I thought everyone would surely be: the bar. But my search yielded nothing but a perimeter fence. Could it be that there were really only 20 people here? There was no warm, cosy bar where all the sensible people were watching the game from?

'John, where's the bar?' I asked my boyfriend.

He pointed to a small grey building that looked like it had been thrown together sometime in the 1920s and everyone had decided to just leave it that way since. And I hoped that the pitch had been built after the bar, otherwise there were a lot of Irish jokes that suddenly got a whole lot more credit.

'There's no point going there yet though,' said John. 'It won't open until after the match has finished.'

I looked at him in disbelief. This game was boring me to death and there was no hope of going and sitting in front of a heater while downing pints of Heineken, which would have been the best bet for livening up the crap that I was being forced to watch. Failing that, it would have made it a hell of a lot easier for me to feign an interest in the match.

Finding it increasingly difficult to watch the game I began to look at other things around the ground. There were no signs, so where did the team get their money? What do the sponsors get? An inscription on the back of the toilet door? Where were all the women? Don't they come and watch their sons, boyfriends, brothers, uncles, cousins, friends anyone? Looking around the ground something else dawned on me.

'John,' I said, tugging on his arm. 'Isn't this the local derby?'

'Oh, yeah,' came his reply. 'But this is a cup game. Everyone's only interested in the premiership.'

Oh so that explained it. Of course. They only like the premiership. What was the difference? Wizard Cup or premiership season, there are still people at AFL matches. Could it be that most Irish people think this game sucks as much as I do?

My theory was thwarted when the game ended. Suddenly there were people everywhere. They filed on to the field as the Keiron O'Reilly's GAA Club was awarded the perpetual trophy. But where had they all been during the game? Could it be that I had found the sensible people in Ireland: the ones who chose to stay away until the end of the match and then arrive to join in the piss-up that follows? Or were these just the bandwagon supporters, who are literally only there when the boys win?

Finally it looked as though we were heading to the bar. I couldn't wait to get in there and slam back a few shots of something, anything, as long as it got rid of the frostbite that I was sure I could feel in my toes. But my boyfriend had other ideas. We remained in the cold, outside the change rooms waiting for his friends to appear. I managed to peel him away and into the bar after much sweet-talking. I was all ready for a shot of vodka, or whiskey, hey I was ready to settle for metho, when another disaster struck. They were only serving Guinness or the world's worst beer, Harp Lager. I settled for Harp, as I am at least able to keep that down. Settling into the corner with a pint of Harp I was ready to drown my sorrows and pretend that I was sorry the boys had lost. The place was jammers, but if I timed it right I would be able to get the pint to my mouth without much spillage. Then another disaster struck. The boys came into the bar. They were less than impressed that we were drinking in the opposition's pub, despite the fact that they knew everyone that was there anyway, and demanded that we leave ASAP. So there I was. Trapped and forced to throw back a pint of world's worst lager.

However, I must admit that things got decidedly better from there. As we walked along to the pub that sponsors the boy's team I turned to my boyfriend's best mate, Paul.

'Bad luck today, Paul,' I said. 'Who do you play next week?'

'Na,' came his reply. 'That was the last game of the season.'

Write Out of Left Field (*WOOLF*), Victoria University 2004

THE GAME THEY PLAY IN SYDNEY

Gideon Haigh

Rugby might well be, as is alleged, the game they play in heaven. But it is also the game they play in Sydney – which is why it isn't, and will probably never be, the game they play in Melbourne.

There will undoubtedly be some whose Rugby World Cup has runneth over in the past week or so. But football in Australia is distinctly tribal. It fosters not merely allegiance to one's own code but an active disdain for others. Melbourne is the *locus classicus* of Australian Rules, that all-in mud-wrestling game which to its followers comes like a second language – for some of them, a first language. Contempt for rugby, like suspicion of all things Sydney, is bred in the bone here. Some of us would not cross the street to see it for free.

Promotors of the World Cup doubtless drew heart from the reputation of Melburnians as a great sporting population. This is a city where horses are known as 'he' and 'she' rather than 'it'. The Melbourne Cricket Ground has hosted Test cricket crowds exceeding 90,000, and three years ago was sold out for games of Olympic soccer.

It was curious, nonetheless, to be part of the crowd on the night of Australia's contest with Italy – apparently the Games' great drawcard. Patrons talked among themselves while a prefatory women's international was played, then sat in what can only be described as rapt incomprehension through the main event.

Led to expect a species of Olympic 'Supersport', they slowly realised they'd been conned: it was still bloody soccer, that roundball code where the players fall over like they've been shot by a sniper and the goals come fortnightly. In the great tradition, the friend I'd accompanied returned from the Gents just as the only score was being fished from the back of the net.

The Australian sports fan, it should be said, is more ecumenical than he was. Rugby has even made some inroads into the vernacular here. One hears pub conversations in which the expression 'built like a prop' is being used in preference to the traditional Australian idiom for a solid physique ('built like a brick shithouse') and various emergent global alternatives ('built like the Governor of California').

During major sporting events, Australians can also usually be relied upon to lose perspective. This tradition was maintained by Prime Minister John Howard in his benediction at the opening ceremony of the World Cup when he exhorted his audience 'to remember that, of the more than 200 people who died in Bali just a year ago, 132 of them came from rugby-playing nations'. Those Jemaah Islamiah fiends will stop at nothing, it seems, in their Islamofascist crusade for ball sports domination; look out for the forthcoming Bali telemovie *Target: Rugby*.

So dressing the next few weeks up as a World Cup may convince some that they're missing out on sport *in excelsis*. But it's not so much that Melburnians think Aussie Rules superior to rugby – it's that we know it is. Near Melbourne's Flinders Street gateway are giant billboards advertising 'I Am Blood' and 'The Age of Unbeauty'. Although these are dance performances scheduled for Melbourne's International Arts Festival, they might have been inspired by rugby's local reputation. The organisers have even betrayed their event's inauthenticity by staging it at the gimcrack Telstra Dome rather than the venerable MCG. This is a bit like the Three Tenors coming to Sydney and saying: 'Opera House shmopera house. Let's go find a pub with a karaoke machine.'

Aside from the usual obstacles of regional affiliation, the World Cup seems to fail two crucial antipodean tests. For one, you can't dress up rugby union as something inherently Australian. It's not ours – and that matters here. A history of the growth of Australian Rules by our finest historian Geoffrey Blainey bears the title *A Game of Our Own*. The best essay collection about the emergence of rugby league is *A League of Our Own*, edited by David Headon and Lex Marinos. And while historians contend that we did not invent cricket, W.G. Grace sure sledged like an Aussie.

Two, it would seem this is a tournament in which Australia might not triumph. This is a disastrous design oversight. Like most countries, we distinguish crisply between the world's important and unimportant sports by the classic rule of thumb: the significant ones are those at which we succeed, the trivial those at which we fail. Or those in which England win.

While Australians love sport, furthermore, more than that they love winners, whether they be our Steve, our Nicole, or our Kylie. At losing, we are not nearly so accomplished, especially when we don't have perfidious Albion to blame (cf Gallipoli, Singapore, etc.). So while the Wallabies might be essaying the game they play in heaven, purgatory seems their likelier ultimate venue.

The Guardian, 17 October 2003

WORLD CUP THOUGHTS
FROM THE SIDELINE

Michael Morley

It was that noted sportswriter Albert Camus who once observed: 'All I know most surely about morality and the obligations of man, I know from football.' While he may have had in mind that other world game played with a round ball, as a cultivated Frenchman he would have been well aware that the real game played with an oval ball occupied just as important a position on the French sporting scene.

It might be going a little far to suggest that the weekend of the Rugby World Cup semi-finals brought observers of the sporting scene into closer contact with morality (though any Kiwi would be sure to argue that the completely undeserved loss to Australia demonstrated yet again how cruel morality in practice can actually be). But any observer of crowds with a set of eyes and ears could have picked up enough anecdotal insights into human behaviour to fill a couple of volumes on social anthropology.

Take, for instance, the two tall and solidly built English supporters quietly sipping beer in the barred Novotel enclosure at Sunday's match. You could tell they were English by their narrow scarves and Union Jack badges, though not from the delicate salmon-pink of their rugby shirts. One of our party – as a Kiwi, I felt my best chance of future revenge was to turn from black to white – also English, otherwise the response might have been rather different, greeted the pair derisively with the remark, 'So whose knickers went into the wash with whose nice white English shirts?'

The taller of the two (and I do mean tall) thought (I thought) for a moment about the possibility of taking both umbrage and a poke at the questioner, but then calmly told my companion to take a look at the monogram on his shirt. It read: 'Ditchling Wild Pigs Rugby Club', the words stylishly entwined around what heraldic commentators might describe as 'a swine rampant'. While we never did get to find out either how pink pigs became wild (pink) pigs or whether that was the way they played the game, we did learn that Ditchling is just down the road from what the shorter of the two referred to as 'Burgess Bloody Hill' – which just so happens to be the very town where my daughter is currently on a gap year, and for which she has roughly the same regard ...

Not too far away from the pink pig pair, and seeking to catch anyone's attention through the bars round the enclosure, was a rather portly figure who looked as if he'd stepped out of some surreal French pantomime. On his head, one of those close-fitting blue felt items of headgear sported by the 1789 revolutionaries, topped by a screaming red rooster's crest; below that a very large French rugby shirt, trailing strips of ribbon; the ensemble rounded off by a ballerina's short white tulle skirt and white stockings. I thought at first he'd been banned by the vigilant Maori bouncers (shorts OK; mini-skirts on large Frogs, not OK), but all he wanted was 'five verres vides – empty glasses'. (We got them for him and he scuttled off into the distance, uttering some very natural-sounding chicken and rooster cries on the way back to his presumably Continental coop.)

In another group close by was an emphatically moustachioed figure, clad in beret, striped sailor shirt, various combinations of the French *tricolore*, and clutching a large, paper-wrapped baguette. One of our number, having worked for a French company, and determined to reactivate his conversational French, hailed the figure with a series of variations on 'Bonjour … D'ou venez-vous?' and 'Vous autres Francais ??? – Pas de chance!!' The addressee of these remarks, whose moustaches, on closer inspections, revealed themselves as thick black eyeliner, looked at the speaker in blank, then puzzled silence, before declaring in broad Strine : 'Sorry mate. No idea. Just thought one or two of us Aussies oughta support the Frogs.'

If in terms of (even borrowed) outfits, the French carried the day theatrically, they also did so when it came to matters of culture and style. Before the game itself got under way, the stadium's sound system offered its usual mix of the bland and the nationalistic (though, thank God, not a note of the ineffable John Williamson). But when the ground began to ring to the sounds of Edith Piaf in 'Non, je ne regrette rien', a group of eight French supporters behind us not only joined in, but sang the song through to the end, note- and word-perfect. I wonder how many English-speakers could sing more than two consecutive phrases of, say, something like 'My Way' (even as a singalong with, God forbid, John Williamson) or, infinitely preferable, 'You Gotta Have Heart'? Of course, the real Rugby supporter should be able to join in 'Frigging in the Rigging' or 'My Grandfather's Cock' at the drop of a jockstrap: but great anthems as these are, they're not quite in the same league as Piaf's signature song.

And as for style? Splendidly demonstrated by the French supporter in front of our group of less-than-restrained English supporters, who, whenever Jonny Wilkinson potted yet another goal, stood up, turned to us, curled his lip, mimed the act of kicking a tiny goal, before shaking his head and sitting down again. He never varied his performance for all eight kicks (mind you, nor did Wilkinson), though at 18–7, he did add the brave assertion 'ce n'est pas fini.'

A shame his optimism turned out to be so misplaced. Nevertheless, 10 minutes before the end, he took his girl-friend's hand, stood up to leave, turned round to us once more, and, instead of the expected final aside, held out his hand and said: 'Bonne chance pour samedi.' Perhaps even Australian supporters might learn just a little from such a display of grace in defeat …

But sport isn't always full of happy stories. Spare a thought for the group of five Kiwis who, on the way back on the train from the England–France match, didn't seem too homicidal or suicidal – until they came to ask us if we knew anyone who might like tickets for the final. After the All Blacks' defeat, they were flying back to the Land of the Long White Shroud on Tuesday, but still had 12 tickets to dispose of – at NZ$800 each, together with an IRB overall tax of $1000. These were not accountants, doctors or bankers, but working men, who had laid out the amount some time before: I just hope they got on to eBay in time, where tickets for the finals were being sold at any-thing up to four and five times their face value.

Most sobering of all was a conversation the next morning with what we took to be an English supporter in a pub packed with exuberant, but not over-the-top pilgrims on the trail of a Union-Jack-draped Holy Grail. 'Robert' (the reason for the quotation marks will become clear later) had slightly greying hair, the build of a back-row forward, and a slight Scottish burr. (It was the accent that made us think that lumping him in with your standard English supporter might be a slight misjudgement – and so it was, though not in the way we'd imagined.)

He was indeed a Rugby supporter, now wanted England to win (having flown out only 10 days previously from the UK): but a phone call summoning him back to the UK now meant he had to miss the final. 'Hope it's not a family emergency,' I com-mented. 'Oh, no, just work,' he replied. 'Work? What sort of boss would do that? And what sort of job?' 'I'm in the army,' came the reply, 'and I'll be on my way back to Iraq.'

What was it that Camus said about the obligations of man? Rugby no longer seemed the most pressing topic of conversation. It emerged that he was based in Basra, had been on a tour of duty since the start of the year, spoke two other languages (not Arabic, though two members of his 'group' did), and had joined a Scottish regiment as soon as he left school in 1979. His conversation was smart, measured, not completely forthcoming, and considerably more perceptive than most of the reporting from Iraq the newspapers choose to carry.

He clearly knew more about the problems of dealing with a native population on the ground in their own country than, to take a random example, Donald Rumsfeld or his gung-ho master. 'We try not to display our weapons to the population,' he said, 'and, where possible, the soldiers are encouraged to wear tam o' shanters or berets, rather than battlefield helmets.'

'And what about flak jackets or protective gear?' I asked.

He paused. 'Well, these days I'm mostly in civilian clothes, and tend to carry my weapon at my side, out of sight.'

'How likely is it that British forces will be exposed to the same sort of attacks as the Americans?'

'In the south, where we are, it's a lot different from Baghdad. I think we've got good relations with the population, and we work at it. The Americans go for in-your-face tactics, parading their weapons, and kicking down doors, trying to intimidate the population. It doesn't work.'

'And what next?'

It was the only time his manner turned sharp. 'We'll probably have to move up to Baghdad. Bush has got an election coming up, and he doesn't want body bags coming back next year. So they've suddenly changed the "process" they've been following. I'm betting they're now looking at wanting out – and that's why I've been called back. The British may now have to go to Baghdad as well. Would have been great to be at the final, but …' He shrugged.

There were dozens more questions we could have asked him:

but I suspect he'd said as much as he felt he could say, given the place, and his questioners. A shame, however, that our own sports-tragic PM and his hangers-on, rather than cradling their champagne in the corporate boxes, couldn't occasionally mingle with the people to whom the game also (actually?) belongs. They'd learn something about character, culture, obligations and, maybe, even, morality.

ABOVE THE SHOULDERS, BETWEEN THE EARS

If sport is played 90 per cent above the shoulders, it is because that is where your ears are. Warwick Hadfield and Radio National's Sports Factor swing through the musical background of sport with the legendary Paul Kelly. Chip Le Grand gets inside the head of Andre Agassi, Matthew Ricketson writes on the scientific construction of athletic bodies, and Michelle Griffin gets inside sports psychology.

ANDRE THE MASTERMIND

Chip Le Grand

There is an Andre Agassi match that Craig O'Shannessy has watched 200 times. It is not one of the Agassi–Sampras classics. Not even an Agassi–Rafter epic. It is a match against Scott Draper in the final of a relatively minor ATP tournament six years ago, a match Draper probably wishes he hadn't seen the first time.

O'Shannessy is a tennis coach from Albury, NSW, now plying his trade in the US. Every time he takes charge of a new player he sits them down to watch the Agassi–Draper match.

It is not to show them Agassi's phenomenal return of serve or precision forehand. Anyone who has watched Agassi can appreciate these things. It is not to teach them about footwork and fundamentals, though Agassi's are as good as anyone's.

It is to show them how Agassi thinks through a point and out-thinks an opponent. To reveal the workings inside that neatly shaved head which some time today will be plotting the demise of another hapless opponent en route to another Australian Open title.

Any player can do the work Agassi does; the work on court, the work in the gym, the work dragging tyres up that oft-mentioned hill behind his Las Vegas home in preparation for another Australian summer. But even if they did the work, it would not be enough. Just like the generation of basketballers who wanted to be like Mike, today's players need to think like Andre.

'If I could take off his skull and look inside his brain at what is going on, that's when you'd understand where every shot goes, why it is going there and how well he understands his opponents,' O'Shannessy said. 'He understands his opponents much more than his opponents understand their own game.'

If only. Like the rest of us, O'Shannessy has no direct access to Agassi's inner thoughts and processes. But what O'Shannessy has been doing this Australian Open, along with fellow coach Alan Curtis, is to chart with computer software the patterns in Agassi's shots and strategies.

They are no closer to finding a foolproof way to beat Agassi. For all the hours spent in the stands of the Rod Laver Arena, they have exposed no glaring weakness in his game.

What they have discovered is a better understanding of what Agassi does and why he does it. Against Czech qualifier Tomas Berdych in the second round, for example, O'Shannessy and Curtis discovered an extraordinary grouping of Agassi returns whenever he was receiving on his backhand from the deuce court. Nearly every return landed slightly to the backhand side of the Czech, and well inside the sideline. He did not hit one winner.

What O'Shannessy and Curtis realised was that the game's best returner of serve had decided not to attack the serve directly, but to draw his opponent into rally after rally. From there, the percentages were always with Agassi. With every shot, Agassi would slightly improve his position and Berdych would lose ground. And so on until he faltered, or Agassi found an open court.

Against Thomas Enqvist yesterday, one of only a few current players to have a winning record against Agassi before this match, the plan was brutally simple. Computer grouping of his return revealed his key objective was to rally on the backhand side. Then at a moment invariably of Agassi's choosing, Enqvist would be sent scurrying across court. Enqvist has a great forehand, but he only got to use it at the least opportune times.

Enqvist did not win a point until the fourth game and ended up in a 6–0 6–3 6–3 rout.

'Usually I have been able to play pretty well against him,' Enqvist said. 'Against another player, he is going to give you a few chances to get back into the match. When Andre is up, he will not give you anything.'

What both these examples show is the depth to which Agassi constructs his points.

After Agassi beat Yevgeny Kafelnikov to win the 2000 Australian Open, he was asked about the points he had won with two stunning drop shots. The answer provided a glimpse into the Agassi psyche. 'He's a good mover and plays five metres behind the baseline. I thought if I could get him to come in a bit, it would make my power game more effective.'

The endgame was not the drop-shot winner, it was keeping Kafelnikov closer to the baseline in rallies so Agassi could hurt him with his ground strokes. With Agassi, it is not the winner you see which is necessarily doing the damage. For every shot a purpose, but the purpose is not always immediately clear.

The great advantage Agassi has is that not many players think about tennis this way. They think mainly of their own game. They come into post-match press conferences and speak of it in isolation, as if one opponent is interchangeable with the next.

With Agassi, no two game plans are the same. Paradorn Srichaphan beat him in their only meeting at Wimbledon and will require a different strategy altogether when the pair meet tomorrow. Agassi's game starts with the weaknesses of those he plays. For him, tennis is a zero-sum game. When he comes into post-match press conferences, he talks about his opponents, for they are foremost in his mind.

'You go out there with a real clear awareness as to what it is you need to do, what it is you need to worry about, the dynamic you want to set up from the baseline,' he explained after thrashing Enqvist. 'When you play each other so many times, you are sensitive to those subtle changes that happen throughout the course of a match. You constantly feel like you are making adjustments to get it back to the terms that you are looking for.

'I felt like when he hit a good ball, I was staying strong on my shots. I wasn't letting him back me up. When I got control of the point, I felt like I was keeping control. Thomas has a big game. If I'm not hitting the ball sharply and I'm not moving well, he can let one ball go and get a big advantage in the point.'

Agassi can be beaten, even at Melbourne Park. When Pat Rafter played here in 2001, he matched Agassi shot-for-shot and thought-for-thought before severe cramping set in. But to find the last time Agassi did lose in Melbourne, you need to go back five years. Too long you might think, for a tennis player to have any recollection of how it felt.

Not so with Agassi. In that neatly shaved cranium, there is a special compartment even for this. 'I'm way too experienced not to realise how on the line you play, you walk, every single match,' he said. 'I don't know how it looks from the outside. I can tell you that it is hard work and I'm absolutely relieved every time I put together a good match here.'

The Australian, 24 January 2004

THE ROLE OF SPORTS SCIENCE IN AUSTRALIA'S SPORTING SUCCESS

Matthew Ricketson

In the toddler pool, babies are gurgling and blinking determinedly in the arms of young male swimming instructors. In the heated indoor pool, older women taking a water aerobics class splash and stretch to the strains of 'It's Raining Men'. Outside, in the 50-metre pool, a handful of primary school children are doing time trials for their coming school sports. Some swim purposefully, but others, whose tummies and thighs wobble as they walk, underscore the growing disquiet about rising obesity levels. About 20 seagulls in a line are dipping and drinking from the pool's edge. On this clear sunny morning at the Monash aquatic centre in Melbourne's south-east, none of these people have taken much notice of the group of national swimming squad members who alternately glide or churn up and down the outdoor pool.

Why not? Maybe because in the water everyone looks pretty much the same, but what about the array of equipment set up by sports scientist Megan Jones so she can measure the swimmers' height, their weight, their skin folds (how lean they are) and their lactate levels? (Lactic acid builds up in the blood when the body is working hard at speed.) What about when after every set of several hundred metres, the swimmers draw themselves out of the pool in one flowing movement so Jones can take a pinprick of blood for the lactate measurement? It shouldn't be hard to miss the superb physiques of the elite athletes, muscles sculpted by hundreds of hours training, but barely a head turns. Social commentator Craig McGregor once wrote that one of the great things about Australia was its egalitarian beach culture where judges and plumbers could sit side-by-side, wearing only their Speedos, without a flicker of self-consciousness.

Perhaps that is what was happening on this February morning leading up to the national swimming trials for the Athens Olympics; more likely it was something else, a new wrinkle in the ever-developing Australian story. Australians are famously passionate about sport, but largely incurious about the importance of sports science in the nation achieving its extraordinary level of sporting success.

Brooke Hanson, one of the national squad members training at Monash, is passionate about sport and its science. After each skin-fold measurement, Hanson records the result on a waterproof board resting on the pool deck. She and Megan Jones have been monitoring her skin-fold levels since 2000; what they have been searching for is her optimum combination of muscle, bone density and fat. The less fat the better, you might think, and to the observer Hanson appears to be carrying not a gram of fat, but if her fat level drops below a certain level she becomes prone to illness or injury. As she turns to start a new lap, her coach, Mark Thompson, mutters to Jones, 'Can you shoot those seagulls?' Jones turns to me: 'Thommo's worried about the amount of illness among his swimmers and he's wondering whether the seagulls might be causing it. He's calling it "bird flu",' she said, referring ironically to the flu then affecting chickens in south-east Asia as Thompson shoos away the offending birds.

Hanson is unequivocal about the importance of sports science to her career. 'I've gone from ranking 20th in the world in my event to sixth.' The 26-year-old Hanson first represented Australia at the 1994 Commonwealth Games. She did not represent the country at either the 1996 Atlanta Olympics or the 2000 Games in Sydney but she won a silver medal at the 2002 Commonwealth Games in the 100-metre breaststroke and another silver at the 2003 World Championships, in the 50-metre breaststroke.

Lauryn Ogilvie is similarly enthusiastic about the benefits of applying scientific methods to her sport – shooting. Already chosen as one of Australia's representatives at the Athens Olympics in skeet shooting, Ogilvie has been using the heart-rate monitoring technology pioneered by her partner, Russell Mark, leading up to the Atlanta Olympics (where he won gold). Ogilvie was a world-class shooter in practice but faltered in the cauldron of competition. 'The competition controlled me rather than the other way round,' she says.

By monitoring her heart rate closely she found that for her the crucial indicator of success was not her actual heart rate when shooting but whether it was rising or dropping. If it was rising she shot poorly, if it was falling she shot well. 'It has been a huge advantage for me. Knowing that I can perform as well in competition as in practice means I can take my shooting to the next step.' From being ranked 16th in the world, Ogilvie is ranked fifth in 2004. She won a silver medal at the World Cup final in 2003 and is a strong medal contender for Athens.

Applying science to sport does not guarantee success. There is no substitute for high levels of natural ability, technique, training and tenacity. As Russell Mark says: 'If you haven't got the fundamentals it doesn't matter how much sports science you've got. But for me sports science was the last 10 per cent that got me over the line.' (He missed a second Olympic gold, in Sydney, by the narrowest of margins). 'Lots of people competing at the Olympics are 90 per cent excellent. To win a medal you need to be 98 per cent excellent, or more. Sports science gives you hints on how to fool your brain. It helps you think you are in a practice round at the Werribee clay target club instead of competing for a gold medal.'

Science is becoming increasingly important in the progress of sporting performance worldwide, though, as it is the last variable in the equation that can be finessed. People's natural ability to perform the purest athletic events of running, jumping and throwing has not altered much over the years; in 1936 Jesse Owens set a world record in the 100 metres that stood for more than 20 years, and even today his time would probably gain him a spot in the Olympic final. On the eve of the Athens Olympics the defining feature of sports science is just how finely calibrated it is. The most precise attention is paid to the seemingly smallest details. Technology is being used to measure and improve every possible aspect of sporting performance, from technique to training to equipment to psychology.

There are many talented and creative sports scientists working around Australia, in universities, at the Australian Institute of Sport and at the various state institutes of sport. The Victorian Institute of Sport, headed by Dr Frank Pyke, is perhaps the most successful of the state bodies; at the last two Olympics Victorians have won 46 of the 99 medals, including 11 of the 25 gold.

The head of the institute's sports science unit is Troy Flanagan, an affable former swimmer who joined the VIS in 1992, two years after it opened. His background is in physiology, but he chose to do a Ph.D in aerospace engineering. 'I'm not building rockets but I have been looking at the aerospace engineers' technology and seeing how to apply it to sport. You could say I've been raised by wolves. My approach has not been to go to academia and ask them to create something for sport but to work with coaches and see what they need. Lots of our ideas have come from us standing on the side of the track with the coach. They say, "If only we could do this," and I go off and try to come up with something that does that.'

Flanagan and his team of eight full- or part-time scientists have come up with some remarkable things. The heart-rate monitor, mentioned above, came from Flanagan; he did not invent the monitor but he was the first to apply it to shooting where he learnt not only that it was critical for shooters to have their heart rate dropping as they shot, but that even though shooting is not an aerobic sport shooters' heart rates jump from an average resting rate of 70 beats a minute to 160 or 170 under competition pressure. (He also found that the heart rate of cricket umpires exceeds 150 beats a minute when there is an lbw appeal. Who would have thought standing still could be so demanding? 'It's the fright reflex. It brings a surge of adrenalin,' says Flanagan.) The shooter, Russell Mark, then worked on developing such control over his heart rate that it would be beating at 130 even during an Olympic final.

At his VIS office in inner-city Melbourne, Flanagan plays on his computer to bring up an underwater video shot of Olympic gold medal-winning swimmer Michael Klim. Coaches have been using videos for 20 years, but Flanagan has exploited digital technology to give coaches and athletes almost instant analysis. Historically, one of the greatest disadvantages Australian sportspeople have faced is that most world championships are held in the northern hemisphere. Athletes have had long distances to travel, often cut off from their support staff as well as their families. After 18 months development work at the VIS, now when Michael Klim competes overseas film of him can be fed into a standard laptop computer, transmitted via the internet, downloaded and analysed in Australia by his physiotherapist (looking at his range of movement), his biomechanist (analysing technique), his physiologist (looking at how to improve his performance through training methods) and his strength and conditioning coach. Flanagan says: 'Michael can pull into an internet café in Germany and look at this stuff. All it needs is Windows Media Player 9, which is pretty standard technology.' What this means is that Klim can get feedback on his heat swim in the morning in time for his final in the evening.

Klim can also be guided to look at a particular spot by a

white circle on the screen that follows, say, his hand or his kick as the video plays. 'Sometimes when you show athletes or teams like the Hockeyroos a video it can be hard to get them to focus on what you want them to focus on. They're saying, you know, "Does my bum look big in this?" The circle draws their eye and they concentrate on the particular movement or play you want them to.' The next step is to use computers to analyse team sports, which Flanagan can do through a system he calls 'Pattern Plotter'. He demonstrated it for me one Saturday morning recently at the Victorian hockey centre where a state team that included some national women's squad members played a practice match against a scratch team made up of state league women and men. Flanagan sat in the stands at the end of the field with an assistant, a sports science student, who videoed the game.

Flanagan sat with his laptop perched on a seat. A graphic of the hockey field showed on the computer screen and he used the touch mouse pad to trace every movement of the ball. 'It's taken a bit of practice but I'm pretty precise now. Today I'm only tracking one team but I can do both teams if need be, though it gets a bit hectic.'

The computer can analyse the data instantly, bringing up screens showing a team's paths to attack, which attacking moves had been successful and which hadn't, where the ball was being turned over, how effectively the ball was being brought out of defence and, of course, all the same analysis of the opposition. Video footage of particular plays can be isolated and replayed straight away, to complement the graphics on the screen. At half-time Flanagan took the laptop into the dressing-rooms at the request of state and VIS coach, Toni Cumpston, where he held it up for players to look at, though they probably did not absorb all it had to offer as they were melting from a traditional low-tech 'bake' from the coach. 'I don't know why some of you bothered to turn up today. You're not leading, you're not running ...'

Watching footballers run led to another of Flanagan's innovations, which he has developed with colleagues David Castles,

Kendal Hook and Jeremy Oliver. As a consultant to Essendon football club in 1998, Flanagan recalls thinking as he stood at the side of the oval, 'How can we see how much work these guys are doing?' Television sports commentary teams monitor the distance players run during a game, but it is not done with precision, Flanagan says, nor can they track anything other than distance travelled.

There are three ways to meaningfully analyse a player's performance, he says, drawing an analogy with a car: how fast the car can go, how much petrol it consumes and how much wear and tear there is on the car. Flanagan and his team have developed a remarkable gizmo he calls the vector elite tracking system. 'The US defence people have been working on a similar system for soldiers, and we got there ahead of them.' Smaller than a matchbox and weighing 19 grams, the prototype of the tracking system is attached to the athlete's shoe with gaffer tape (in the future it will be built into the sole of the shoe). The tracking system takes up to 200 samples per second showing where the athlete is in space. When the athlete stops a USB cable can be run from their shoe to a laptop and the data analysed immediately. 'It will show us acceleration and deceleration. We will be able to tell (400-metre hurdler) Jana Pittman at exactly what point in a race she starts to decelerate, or when her running gait begins to lose form.'

The limitations of video analysis prompted a colleague of Flanagan's, Stuart Morris, to develop a three-dimensional game simulator. Working with academics at Swinburne University's departments of astrophysics and super-computing, Morris has adapted virtual reality technology for sport. He allowed me to try one variation where, after putting on a pair of 3D glasses, you watch a Brett Lee-like cricketer thunder in and bowl at you, but just before the moment the ball takes off-stump, or the fleshy part of your thigh, the film freezes and you are given the chance to say how you would play the shot. Morris has similar simulations for hockey.

The 3D simulator helps players develop their ability to pick up and quickly analyse the hundreds of cues provided by, in cricket, the position of the bowler's arm, the angle of the delivery, etc., and in hockey, what the players around you look like they are about to do. The difference between you and I and a Hockeyroo is their ability to 'read' the myriad of cues as they fly all around. Flanagan recalls watching an elite-level hockey match with Jim Irvine, who had represented Australia many times and was now coaching. 'At one point Jim leant over the stand and called down to a player, "Hey, just move to your left two metres." The ball was on the other side of the pitch going into attack but a couple of seconds later the defence got it and hit it out the other side – to exactly where this guy was standing.'

For the sports-mad Aussie, is this scientific approach way too much information, as Uma Thurman famously remarked in *Pulp Fiction*? Don't we love our sports heroes sun-drenched and laconic, like 'Snowy' Baker who in the early years of the twentieth century played 26 sports and represented the fledgling nation in no fewer than seven: boxing, rugby union, fencing, diving, swimming, water polo and polo. Sport is something you enjoy, and what separates you from Olympians is natural ability and buckets of elbow grease. Not any more, as the work of Flanagan and many others amply illustrates. What is most curious is that it was a mortal blow to our sporting pride that spurred this shift.

Sport developed quickly in colonial Australia, according to long-time sports scientist and administrator, John Bloomfield, in his recently released book, *Australia's Sporting Success: The Inside Story*. In the 1830s there were excited reports in the press of 'currency lads', the sons of the convicts, winning cricket matches against British regiments stationed in the colonies. Historian Helen Irving has said that cricket matches against Mother England united the colonies well before Federation in 1901. The organisation of sport occurred early; Australian Rules football set up leagues in Victoria and South Australia 11 years before British soccer associations were established in 1888. For many years Australians' huge passion for sport enabled them to be competitive internationally, but in the second half of the twentieth century many other nations began pouring millions of dollars into developing sport, whether through the college system as in the United States or through centrally commanded agencies as in the Soviet bloc during the Cold War.

After the success of the 1956 Melbourne Olympics, Australia's record at the Games gradually declined but few took notice until the 1976 Montreal Olympics, when no Australian won a gold medal and only five medals were won in total. It was the country's worst performance since the 1936 Berlin Games and it provoked a national outcry, with headlines like 'Australia's Golden Days Have Gone' (in *The West Australian*, 23 July 1976). A study quoted by Bloomfield showed that Malcolm Fraser's coalition federal government spent $1.86 per head on the arts compared to nine cents a head on sport. From this almost negligible base of about $1.5 million, the government began putting in more money and set up the Australian Institute of Sport in 1981, but it was the Labor government of sports-loving prime minister, Bob Hawke, that really drove sport's development by massively increasing its funding. The Howard coalition government continued the funding increase in the lead-up to the Sydney Olympics; in 2003 it spent nearly $150 million on sport. Since the Montreal debacle, writes Bloomfield, Australian sport has been transformed from a loosely structured amateur system into a highly organised but cost-efficient system that 'is the envy of many nations around the world'.

Envy spurs imitation, not to mention poaching; after the success of the Sydney Olympics about 30 top-flight sports coaches and scientists were lured to the United Kingdom. Bloomfield warns that the perhaps inevitable letdown after the euphoria of Sydney spread to funding levels as well. 'Australia's closest sporting competitors in Europe are already allocating at least five per cent of their sports budget to research and development (in sports science), which is two to three times more than Australia currently spends.' Whether rival nations are about to leapfrog Australia in the quest for sporting gold or whether the current system is structurally sound and will continue improving is difficult to predict.

Historically, the host nation does not do particularly well at the next Olympics, but Troy Flanagan is quietly bullish. 'Yes, we have lost some pretty good people overseas but we've kept good ones too. We're working on some new projects now that we should be able to use before Athens.' Like what? 'Can't say too much.' It is a fine irony: sporting rivals may regularly visit Australia to plunder the fruits of our sports scientists, but Australian sports fans, who should applaud their work, remain blissfully unaware of it.

Griffith Review 4, Winter 2004

THERE COMES A TIME WHEN TOO MUCH SPORT PSYCHOLOGY IS BARELY ENOUGH

Michelle Griffin

It's 48 days until the start of the Olympic Games, and in training camps around the world Australian athletes are preparing to enter 'The Zone', that magical high where the moves are automatic, the energy unlimited and the mind clear and calm. By now, bodies have been honed and every move is almost automatic.

But now more than ever, the Olympic Games are mind games, too. When competition results are often measured by an nth of a second, any flicker of doubt could cost an athlete the prize they've been training for.

'I think that at an Olympic Games, the person who wins the event is the person who mentally handles it the best,' says Kieren Perkins, who proved himself the poster boy for mental toughness when he swam to 1500-metre gold at Atlanta. He told the ABC's *Sports Factor* program that the real challenge wasn't physical fitness but facing demons: 'The demon of getting up on the blocks and knowing that when the time came, would I freak out and not be able to handle the situation, or would I be able to pull it together and do the job?'

Even golden boy Ian Thorpe, after his tumble from the blocks in March, understands the price of hesitation. 'I don't think there's any fault in my start, none whatsoever,' he said at a high-altitude training camp in Arizona three weeks ago. 'I've worked too hard for there to be any faults. I won't change anything. Now the only thing I have to get out of my mind is the hesitation I have on the blocks. It sticks in your mind. Hopefully, by the Olympics that will be gone.'

Jana Pittman, the 21-year-old 400-metre hurdles world champion who carries the gold medal hopes of Australian athletics, 'flushes' negative thoughts from her mind by 'pulling a chain'. It's a trick she learned from her coach's wife, Debbie Flintoff-King, who won gold in the same event at the 1988 Olympics in Seoul. 'Every time a negative thought comes into your mind,' Pittman says, 'you press your temple to flush the bad thought out and replace it with a good one.'

But it's not just happy thoughts, repeat viewings of *Rocky* movies and medal-winning mantras. While sports scientists scrutinise heart rates and skin folds for optimum physical results, sports psychologists and coaches are also working harder than ever to develop mind-over-matter techniques.

'There will be some athletes who believe they should be switched on the entire time, but they can't sustain that,' warns Jeff Bond, a sports psychologist who has worked with Olympians for the past 20 years. 'Elite athletes can flick the switch when they need to.'

Gavin Freeman, a psychologist at the Australian Institute of Sport, says: 'We need to create the failure and the mistakes and see them crumble, but with a solid debriefing process. They have to learn how to recover. Good athletes can fail but work through that.'

What our athletes are discovering about the mental game has ramifications beyond the cloistered world of elite sports. It is often rapidly adapted by life coaches and management consultants for the corporate world and then trickles into daily lives through pop psychology. Many gold medallists move on to careers on the corporate speaking circuit: Perkins, taekwondo champion Lauren Burns and Winter Games skier Alisa Camplin, to name but three of dozens who urge Australian corporate workers to go for gold. Almost everything you've heard about motivation, focus and self-belief originated in sports.

'Sports are sexy,' says Michael Martin, the newly appointed head of the psychology department at the Australian Institute of Sport. 'The metaphors that come out of sports are accessible for people. A sportsman like Tiger Woods says he writes down five positives about his day every night. That's easy to do; anyone can think, "I can do that."'

But can the techniques used to finetune Olympic athletes be applied to the corporate sector? Most people in the office don't go for gold every day, they go for coffee.

Bond thinks normal people can be trained to perform like Olympians. Earlier this year, Bond left the Australian Institute of Sports after 23 years as director of psychology to take up a position with Lane4, a British company that uses sports psychology to train corporations. 'There's less and less opportunity for coasters out there,' he warns. 'Right across businesses and public service, this notion of high performance is everywhere.'

One of the most successful athletes on the speakers' circuit is 29-year-old beach volleyball player Natalie Cook, who won gold on Bondi Beach in 2000 with Kerri Pottharst. She brings her own triumph-after-setback to the training seminars: it's the story of how she created her own 'gold medal reality' after she was relegated to a bronze medal finish at Atlanta in 1996.

For Cook, belief isn't something that blooms organically. It has to be custom-built for her purpose, just like the body she puts through its paces 40 hours a week on a rectangle of white sand in the corner of a playing field in Brisbane's West End. After 10 years training in a tiny bikini, Cook's body is as bronzed as that first medal, and probably just as hard. After she dives in the sand for the ball, she looks as if she were dusted with icing sugar, like one of those deep-fried doughnuts she never ever eats.

Cook's new Olympic campaign has a large crew. There's her new partner, a 28-year-old, 183-centimetre Amazon named Nicole Sanderson, who moved to Brisbane with the express purpose of teaming with Cook for gold in Athens. Then there's Cook's coach of the past nine years, Steve Anderson; her chiropractor; her masseuse; her kickboxing guru (for endurance); and her yoga master (for calm and flexibility).

Her Dream Machine, as she calls her pit crew, also includes Kurek Ashley, an Anthony Robbins-trained success coach, and Marcia Pittman, a nurse who discharges negative emotions from the body using a derivation of kinesiology and naturopathy she calls neuro-emotional therapy. The only person Cook doesn't have working on the machine of her dreams is a regular sports psychologist.

'The standard sports psychologist teaches positive affirmation,' Cook says. 'It's what I used to do. We had a psychologist [who] taught us some good fundamental textbook techniques, and that's all great, and then I needed something more. Everyone knows about that. It's about that little point of difference. That's what my people do. Kurek is different, Steve is different. We work with crystals with Marcia. Anything that's going to help get that one per cent of difference.'

Cook has been working with Ashley since she attended a seminar in 1997. 'I said to him that day, I want you to take me to win a gold medal in Sydney,' remembers Cook. Over the past seven years, Cook has changed volleyball partners twice, but she has stuck with Ashley, a former Hollywood actor and stuntman whose bantam boxer build and tough guy stare won him bit-part roles such as 'Tattooed Lowlife' and 'Psycho Rocker'. In 1990, he survived a helicopter crash on the set of the Chuck Norris film *Delta Force 2: Operation Stranglehold*. Five other crew members were killed. In the redemption story he tells his audiences, he spent the next two and a half years suicidally depressed, 'a gun to my mouth every night, I pumped drugs up my nose, I smoked too much and got drunk every day'. Then he started looking for answers, and found them in the motivation work of Anthony Robbins – visualisation, positive energy, and yes, walking on hot coals.

The firewalking is the most controversial element of Ashley's teaching. He says firewalking is about tapping into 'dormant resources' and elevating 'the frequency of your energy to that of the fire – fire can't burn fire'. However, all the scientific studies of walking on hot coals suggest that firewalking is possible because wood and coal are poor heat conductors – a coal can glow bright red below, but those walking quickly across the ashy surface of a properly raked and prepared pit will feel no more sting than on a very hot beach.

'That's not true,' insists Ashley. 'Natalie and I have done the Tibetan fire walk, where there are flames coming through the coals. It's hot. There's no trick.' So you could walk across a hot grill? Absolutely, he says, 'but you need to have a purpose and a reason for doing so'.

Whatever the factors, a successful fire walk does give participants a powerful buzz. 'The fire for me is [being] pumped,' says Cook. 'You did something you thought was impossible and you wonder what else can you do that you once thought impossible. It's like superman: you can do anything.'

Cook and Pottharst were the golden girls of the last Olympics not just because they won the medal, but because Cook bought a gold-rimmed fish tank and filled it with gold-themed trinkets. She had a gold toaster, washed her face with Palmolive Gold soap, brushed her teeth with gold toothpaste. She still does. And she drives a gold four-wheel-drive Nissan decorated with sponsors' logos. But now everybody knows about gold, 'so I've had to go to the next level: platinum'.

But isn't it risky convincing athletes that they will win a gold medal? What if they don't? Cook's success coach, Ashley, says: 'That's something average people say. An elite person believes in their goals and makes them happen.'

'It is a conundrum,' Bond says. 'If you don't believe you're going to win the gold medal, and tell yourself that, and tell others, you won't win it. But by the same token, if the belief becomes all-consuming, it may be so pervasive it compromises the performance. It's a balance thing. Many medal winners have said they were so focused on the process they didn't realise they'd won.'

*

Self-belief is the double bind of every gold medal contender competing at the Olympics. Everyone who makes it to a final must believe they are going to win, but only one of them will. The others have to cope with the psychological backwash of their defeat. 'The athletes can be extremely traumatised if they perform poorly at the Olympics,' Bond says.

He estimates that between a third and half of Australia's 620 Sydney Olympians were disappointed with their performance. Who can forget sprinter Matt Shirvington, visibly distraught after he failed to make the 100-metre finals? Or the tears shed by pole vaulter Emma George when she failed to make the final after setting 17 world records in her sport?

And now it appears that even the winners can suffer from what Bond describes as a form of post-traumatic stress syndrome.

When Cathy Freeman retired last year, she wrote in *The Daily Telegraph* in Britain that, looking back on her career, 'the ups [were] always followed by huge swooshing downs, like not even making the semi-finals of the Barcelona Olympics when I had gone there believing I would win the whole thing.

'And climaxing with that night in the Sydney Olympic Stadium when I won the 400 metres and then just sat there on the track, hardly daring to open the window in my mind that would let me experience all the feelings that were fighting to get in my head. I don't think I ever really did open the window fully.

'I boxed myself in. I had to be so focused that I forbade myself to feel deeply. That is another reason I know it's time to retire. I am not so good at not feeling any more. Things get to me. I'm happier and sadder, more involved in others' lives.'

Another athlete who knows all about the highs and lows is Melbourne rower Drew Ginn. With his rowing partner James

Tomkins, Ginn is the world champion in the men's coxless pairs event, and a hot favourite for gold at Athens. Tomkins, an original member of the Oarsome Foursome who turns 40 just before the Games, has contested the past four Olympics and has two Olympic golds and a bronze in the trophy chest already. Ginn, 29, was a BMX champion as a child and won gold when he was recruited for the second Oarsome Foursome for Atlanta in 1996. But 10 weeks before the Sydney Games, Ginn was forced to drop out with a back injury.

'It was the strangest thing,' he recalls. 'For the first time in my life, I'm quitting. As soon as I said I couldn't do it, my body shut down immediately, and the pain flooded in. I'd held it off for eight months and now it was like, OK, hit me.'

While Ginn's wife and parents and Tomkins all offered their sympathies, he was still in for a rude shock: 'I was told by the selectors [he was dropped from the Olympic team] at Munich Airport. They told me in front of 70 athletes in an airport lounge. I broke down at that stage.'

Once Ginn returned to Melbourne, he let go completely. He was never, ever going to row again. 'I wallowed in it for many weeks.'

Ginn returned to competition after 18 months of recovery from spinal surgery. In his time off, he had started to reflect on the way he approached competition. Like Tomkins, a merchant banker, he'd always strived for balance in his life, working (as a children's coach with Blue Earth, a non-profit physical education program), relaxing, surfing. Both men became fathers in 2002, the year they were on the comeback trail. And Ginn decided that an all-consuming focus on winning was not, ultimately, the best way to win. 'I remember standing in the Olympic village, and you see a whole host of athletes who haven't achieved the results they wanted, and they're almost like zombies.'

His heretical new idea was to let go of ego. 'The majority of athletes have huge egos, and they need them. Dominating your opponents is pure attitude: I will win, no matter what you do. And in the real world, relationships can be very difficult – friends, partners, families find us extraordinarily selfish.'

Ginn wants to try something different. 'I've had 20 years involved in elite sport, 12 years in rowing. I'm starting to realise you don't need to be selfish. You can have self-belief, but you can have balance. It's a balance between who you are inside and what you show, a balance between yourself and the people you love. I've been married five years and I have a three-year-old daughter, Kyra. She demands I pay her attention – it's not about me or my sport.'

Focus, Ginn says, can be turned on and off like a switch, as needed. 'Don't sacrifice things, include them. Accept your competitors, accept your family. So when you sit on the starting line, you've got so much more to draw upon. If you succeed or don't succeed, you're still whole.'

Sun Herald, 27 June 2004

LEAPS AND BOUNDS

Warwick Hadfield

Warwick Hadfield: This week, the fascinating relationship between musos and sport. Sport and the arts are not always viewed as natural bedfellows. There are many in the arts world who are critical of the profile, and of course the money, given to leading footballers and cricketers. But for Paul Kelly, regarded these days as Australia's premier songwriter, going to the cricket provides moments of deep contemplation, as well as the inspiration for the odd great song.

Paul Kelly: I find watching cricket can be meditative, in a way. You can switch off from everything else you're dealing with and find plenty to occupy your mind watching a day's Test cricket – what the ball's doing, how it's moving off the pitch; all the statistical elements of cricket suit my mind as well, so you're thinking about how fast the runs are being scored and how many overs are left at the end of the day. You know, I could fill my mind up with these things very happily.

The other thing I really like about sport is that you don't know what's going to happen, so that's one of the great things. That's one of the analogies with music, especially with jazz where you have highly skilled performers acting together and where you don't know the outcome. I think that's why you can watch the same sort of scenarios over and over again, because you just want to know, how's it going to turn out this time.

Also, sport is full of cruelty, and I think we still like participating in cruelty or watching it, because sport is cruel, has a winner and a loser. I think that satisfies something in all of us, watching that. Playing sport also gives you a chance to measure yourself up against someone else. You kind of get some satisfaction one way or the other. Art is much more, it's competitive, sure, but it's much more debatable.

WH: Singer-songwriter Paul Kelly can be inspired as much by football – well, some of the shenanigans that go with football these days – as by cricket. His song 'Sure Got Me', which is from his latest album, *Ways and Means*, is based on the love triangle involving AFL footballer Wayne Carey, his former team-mate Anthony Stevens, and Stevens' wife, Kelli.

It's not just honouring a hero, though, or looking at love gone wrong in the goal square, that have brought sport and music together. In the corporatised and televised world of modern sport, no replay of a goal, a try or a catch, can be broadcast without the musical accompaniment.

And whenever a champion retires, there must also be the slow-mo images of their moments of glory, complete with a soundtrack, possibly Green Day's 'I Hope You Had the Time of Your Life', or Crowded House's 'Don't Dream It's Over'.

Paul Hester was the drummer in Crowded House, and before that in another famous trans-Tasman band, Split Enz. A talented runner and footballer as a teenager, he says he has no problems mixing his art with his love for sport.

Paul Hester: Oh no, I find myself hanging around with sportspeople now, sharing a similar thing that reminds me of when I was very young. There's a lot of similarities between sports-people and musicians, in the sense that you can really become quite mono with the one thing you do. There's plenty of guitar-ists sitting on their beds all day playing guitar, and getting the muscle memory, the whole thing going, which is kind of similar to somebody training day in, day out, doing a certain event.

WH: So guitar players are into muscle memory … of course you'll see a batsman play an imaginary shot before he goes to play the real thing in a Test match. So guitarists do that as well?

PH: Yes, but the point is, guitarists don't realise they're doing it, and they don't have a name for it, and they're not very technical, but you find yourself realising similar things, particularly when you get into a business, sort-of-successful type of musical band, and then you can relate to other sportspeople in their fields and how you're promoted and marketed. Brad Pierce down at the Hi Fi Bar, Brad used to play for Carlton, and we were having a good old yak after the show, and he was saying, 'It's funny you know, every musician I meet they have the same thing, they always wanted to have been a sportsperson, and every footy player I know has always wanted to do what you guys do, just be up there and flang it out for a night.' And there's this mutual kind of thing that you get going with it. But for musicians and creative people in general, we're in the minority, that's where it ends. Sportspeople very much come from the majority of Australians' support and love and there's a football match on the weekend, there'll be a board of seven or eight men discussing that match in all sincerity at six o'clock that night and then there'll be a replay of it, and then on Sunday they're going to take that whole thing apart again for four or five hours. So imagine if Barnsey did a gig and at six o'clock that night there were eight blokes from bands that kept on there and discussed it in all sincerity, and then the next day they're going to get back and just pull it all apart, all the gigs over the weekend for hours on hours.

WH: A lot of sport is used in art to create images. I think you were quite moved by the sight of the footballers kicking a football in front of the pyramids in the film *Gallipoli*.

PH: I think it's a really psychological play. That scene is about these young boys kicking a footy, saying 'This is what we really like to do, but we're here and we've got to kill people and we might be killed soon. There's something about this trip that's going to be big.'

WH: What sports are you involved in now?

PH: I've come down with a virus called golf, the widow-maker. Yes, I've been furiously hammering away at it. I got turned on to it by the Melbourne Tigers basketballers. I used to go and play with Mark Bradtke and Leonard Copeland.

WH: They're so much taller than you.

PH: Yes, we used to play every Wednesday morning in Albert Park, and from a fairway away you could think, 'Isn't that nice, those lads have taken their son out for a game.' And they got me into it. I did get my handicap down and I'm playing off eight now, so I'm giving it a red hot go.

WH: That's quite exceptional.

PH: And I'm feeling like I want to – my dream is by the time I'm 50, to see if I'm good enough to get into a qualifying round for the Seniors. I don't think I'd be good enough to get in, but I just wonder if I could get into that qualifying part of it.

WH: Well, tennis player Scotty Draper has doubled his chances, he's gone and done some qualifying with golf, but I would think that a drummer who got onto the pro circuit, even at the qualifying level, I think that would be even putting Scotty Draper in the shade a bit, wouldn't it?

PH: Well you know, Alice Cooper's pretty good and a pretty serious golfer. There's quite a few of them around.

WH: You're destroying reputations here. I mean this is the man who bites off chickens' heads, and he's also a golfer.

PH: But he can putt. There's a lot to be found in it that's similar to writing, and for me there's like a Zen connection. With golf, that film *The Legend of Bagger Vance* has that line in it, 'You can't win this, you can only play this.' Now for me coming from a musician's point of view, that really speaks to me, that makes a lot of sense. If I go out and try and win that day at the golf club, I usually am very frustrated, or I can't really enjoy it on a certain level. But if I just go out to play it and play my game and try and feel it, it's another day out.

WH: Do you think sportspeople and musicians might gravitate towards each other because they both understand the fame thing, and what it is to perform in front of a huge crowd of people?

PH: Yes, there's that point where you go in, when people say, 'How did you do that? There were so many people there, you must have been nervous, what were you thinking, how did you do that?' And I understand that from being on stage in front of 70,000-odd, 100,000, 200,000 and being able to go into where you need to go, and execute this thing, make this team process work. A band is a team, a team is a good band, a good team has good support, a good band has good roadies. It's all very similar in the way it's put together. The only thing that bands don't have the benefit of is good coaching. It would be great if you could sub people during a gig and put them on the bench for 10 minutes for dropping a bum note or – you know, it's not played that way, and you don't win or lose at music, or plays, or art or film, you don't win or lose. You go to feel. Whereas when you talk to sportspeople about the big picture they have a much different sort of feeling about it. For them it's win or lose or suffer the consequences. With bands, or music, it's much more gentle.

WH: When with the young Neil Finn, the brother of band leader Tim Finn, Hester joined Split Enz, he discovered the big container full of sports gear was as important a part of the touring equipment as all the speakers and amplifiers.

PH: Well, in Split Enz, it was very particular, because they were an incredibly competitive bunch of people. They'd known each other for a long time, most of them had gone to university together and when Neil and I turned up later on, we were quite young and quite keen to compete on any level at anything at any time, anywhere. So the games box, the road case that you mentioned, was quite a sincere gesture towards competing on the road. There were a lot of frisbee competitions in Split Enz. I remember one time we're having a meal in Tararonga in New

Zealand, just before going down to the gig that night and Neil appeared in the restaurant in a cold sweat with this frisbee in his hand, and walked up to Eddie Rayner's table and stood over him and pronounced that he'd just beaten Eddie's record, which was set earlier in the day across the road at this oval, and they had these distance records that Split Enz would do for hours. So Eddie, in the middle of his meal, dropped tools, turned straight to Neil and took the challenge and went straight out there. We had to pick him up from the oval to take him to the gig because he was determined to stay until he beat Neil's record, and things were righted again, and the band could go on. And there was always that insane competitive things between those guys.

WH: And you had baseball mitts, you had footballs.

PH: Yes, softballs, yes, lots of things. Depending on the venue. If you were in an indoor sort of sports venue, then you might be able to get them to put a hoop down and a backboard and play a bit of ball, or just do some –

WH: That's basketball?

PH: Yes, or generally with Split Enz it had to have some spiteful nature to it. It wasn't good enough just to compete, there had to be some other – like there used to be a game where we'd have the football and we'd be kicking it from side to side but somebody had to be going in between on rollerblades, and you had to actually try and hit that person. So that was the sort of way it came about.

WH: Would that help though, when you're on the road with a bunch of musicians and there are lots of tensions, and when you're in a band with brothers in it there can be lots of tensions, was that sport a way of getting rid of some of those tensions from the music?

PH: Oh clearly. You know, it was a way of surviving the day-to-day moving. You're never actually anywhere when you're on tour, you're either leaving or arriving. So to have that little moment somewhere in the afternoon where you play. Music is also a big play thing, but when you get down to doing a tour, it becomes quite a job to undertake and there's a lot of effort to be able to appear like you're not trying very hard on stage every night. So to have something in the day that would break that down, certainly sport provided that. There was a furious activity after gigs in Split Enz where we'd go to one person's room and make paper aeroplanes and helicopters till the early hours of the morning, and hordes of people would come back sometimes and be slightly disappointed at the goings-on of the Split Enz boys, rather than sex, drugs and rock 'n' roll. It was paper aeroplanes at ten paces.

WH: Now when you were in Crowded House and you did a lot of tours of the United States, on some of those tours you actually covered the Paul Kelly song 'Leaps and Bounds'. What did American audiences do when you sang 'I'm standing high on a hill overlooking the MCG'? Do you think they had any idea about what Neil was singing about?

PH: Well you've got to understand now, some of these kids are looking up at us as gods. You sang anything. They're not really dissecting it.

WH: Neil Finn of course is a New Zealander, you're an Australian through and through and grew up playing Australian football; was there any sort of banter between you two in particular about New Zealand and Rugby and Australian Rules Football in Australia?

PH: Well, being from Victoria I never got sown the early seeds of the Rugby life, so in a funny way it was frustrating for Neil that he couldn't really bait me or Nick with any sort of Rugby talk, because we just wanted –

WH: This is Nick Seymour, the bass player?

PH: Yes. We weren't really turned on to the Rugby.

WH: Right. Now he wrote a song for the New Zealand All Blacks, not the World Cup just gone, the one before that, and it didn't do them any good because they didn't win that World Cup either. Have you ever written a song about a sport?

PH: I did write a song about Little Athletics. I used to have the fear of God of running the 1500 metres because I was quite good at it, and had the record for a while and there was a lot of pressure on me as under-12.

WH: You had the under-12 1500 metres record?

PH: Yes, at Waverley, for quite a while. And I had this nightmare of going every Saturday to run. I'd have to take on Graham Hinton, who was the other record holder, and it was either him or me, and we ended up becoming good friends, because I think we both shared a similar thing. So I wrote a song about it years later, 'Last Call for the 1500 Metres', which would come over the PA at Little Athletics, and it would haunt me, send shivers up my spine when I heard that call, the last call, meaning that I had to go up to the start and put my toe on the line, smell that lawn and run my little 12-year-old butt off, and it was very scary.

WH: Drummer and former Little Athletics champion, Paul Hester.

If you're a regular listener to *The Sports Factor*, you may have heard this song. It's called 'Jimmy Stynes', and it's named after the youngster recruited from Gaelic football who became a champion ruckman with Melbourne in the AFL.

Stynes' wholehearted approach to his football caught the eye of diehard Demon supporter David Bridie, who is also the lead singer in the fabled Australian band My Friend the Chocolate Cake. David Bridie, thanks for joining me on *The Sport Factor*. Now people say when they hear that song they can see Big Jimmy Stynes lumbering and puffing his way round the field in his Melbourne colours. When you wrote it, was that what you were thinking as well?

David Bridie: To be honest, no, it was an instrumental that was written and it had a vaguely Celtic feel to it, and it did have that lumbering quality. We were looking for a title for it. Andrew Carswell, the mandolin player in My Friend the Chocolate Cake, and myself are both passionate Melbourne supporters and we kind of followed Jimmy Stynes' career from the beginning, from a Gaelic football recruit who had very little idea to a stoic veteran who held the team together at the end. And the song is probably more reminiscent of the latter days of his career when he was carrying injuries. But even when Melbourne were getting quite beaten, he was still trying his heart out. Yes, so it does have that quality of that sort of lumbering along, keep going, and the energy's still there.

WH: Jim of course has become not just a great footballer, Brownlow Medallist and 244 games in a row, but he also has become very much a part of the humanitarian scene here in Australia. Is that something else that would have attracted you to him when you came to name this song after him?

DB: Oh yes, and also to identify him as one of the players we like to go and see. I mean, footballers are a pretty boring lot, and we spend a lot of our time, sports lovers, listening to our footballers and cricketers saying the most inane statements in their interviews, and they take up a lot of media space.

WH: They do one press conference at a time, just like one match at a time.

DB: Jimmy from the beginning, there was something about him that was very interesting, there was something that the football thing was more than just winning, it was a life experience. I remember reading his biography which as opposed to all the others as read to whoever, some *Herald Sun* journalist, he wrote it himself, and a lot of the book talks about Irish nationalism, talks about his love for his grandmother and the strength of family, and about issues outside of that, you know, caring for the younger generation. Some of it's slightly crackpot, but a lot of it is very passionate and very humane, and that's obviously very different for an AFL footballer.

WH: Now as probably the prime lyricist in My Friend the Chocolate Cake, you bring a lot of social issues into your lyrics and address them that way. Given the place that sport has in our society – for many people it defines us – is it a little bit strange that there aren't more songs written about sport, using sport as the idiom to describe Australia?

DB: Yes, look, sport is such a moral plane. The good side of sport is to go there and not hero-worship but to go and enjoy the highs and lows; there's a certain sector of sports fans who like the maverick players, those that don't fit in, that aren't the mullet-haired, tight-torso'd, who can do all the skills, taking it one week at a time, but are kind of Stewie McGills, the Jack Iversons of the world.

WH: We should explain. Stuart McGill, of course, is the current

Australian leg spinner, who they say doesn't quite fit into the current XI because he drinks red wine, instead of beer; and Jack Iverson from a different time, who taught himself to bowl with a ping-pong ball while serving in the Army in New Guinea, then came back and bamboozled the English. You like those guys who come from left field, as they say.

DB: They're interesting characters, and I think they're the people that are interesting in all walks of life. There are sporting people who do use their public profile to push things outside of the narrow mains of a sport. I thought Ian Chappell's comments about *Tampa* were really telling, and quite an amazing thing because I guess Ian Chappell's always been regarded as this blokier-than-bloke ex-Australian skipper. I'd always thought, especially coming from the elite in South Australia, that he might have been quite conservative, but his heartfelt speech about *Tampa* and also about giving due recognition to the first Aboriginal cricket team that went to England, yes, were wonderful comments, and I think because they come from a sportsman, people do prick their ears up a little bit and listen to it a bit more.

WH: One of the things I've often noticed when I've seen elite sports people and very, very high-profile talented musicians get together is they seem to immediately have an understanding of what each other is about, whether it be because they play in front of a lot of people, and understand the mass adulation that comes, or because they understand high performance. When you meet sportspeople, do you feel you have an instant rapport with them?

DB: Not when it comes to physical fitness. But there is that thing we talk about sometimes, when you're feeling, on the day of a performance, you're feeling not well or you're just not motivated for it, but as soon as you walk on stage, it is kind of a white line fever that as soon as you're there in front of the crowd, your performance level picks up amazingly. You have to perform under pressure, because when people have paid good money to see you, they don't care if you've got a headache or if you missed your tram and you're running late.

BARRY DICKINS: A SPORTING YEAR

*A little known fact about Melbourne's sentimental chroni-
cler Barry Dickins is that he is a pretty ferocious tennis
player. Better known is that he has a deep passion for
football as it used to be, when Fitzroy's Kevin Murray
was king of the kids. Now he has one of his own, learning
the game. In this series of pieces we view his year in sport,
from the Melbourne Cup to Auskick.*

GREY CUP WITHOUT THE CRIMS
AND FATHERS

One wonders whether the Cup will ever be the sporting miracle it certainly was when Melbourne boasted a few more remarkable characters, and I don't merely mean the horses. It used to be the defining melting gold pot of amusing murderers and crooked coppers who took the first Monday of November off because of the pressures of work.

Famous flamboyant punters such as the suavely, savagely spoken Father John Brosnan, wandering around with a whisky in one palm and the other around 'Putty Nose' Nicholls, joking with Christopher 'Rent-a-Kill' Flannery, then giving a betting slip to Rent-a-Kill's half-brother, Ed, telling him to shove three thou' on the Mighty Manikato for a win-place.

The drunkard bookies laugh, all in a cluster under their hang-overs and umbrellas, because Manikato is old and had the Richard, so a few emus say. Emus, in my day, were the no-hopers of Flemington who turned all the bet slips over in the slippery slime of the betting ring, hunting about for a holy not-paid-out winner.

Roy Higgins is sipping some sort of appalling pink Porphory Pearl fizz through a hot straw, laughing with Twiggy in her outrageous get-up, and Ronald Ryan, who was later hanged for murder, is sipping a flat stout waiting with an intellectual colleague for a plunge upon Peter Pan. It's over 50 years since that horse won the cup, but the ongoing romantic dream of its history is quirky, and endless.

Father Brosnan shouts petty crims pots, as well as floating each of them a quid each to lash out on a few roughies, the coppers cannot do much because Father has done nothing much wrong, except hang around with scum. But Christ forgave sinners such as bookies and mug punters.

Bill Collins used to call the Cup, or Alf Brown, who I once saw call it without the need of his great big, black binoculars, because he lost them, and when Bill Collins called the Cup it was Called Right!

One Flemington call, he interrupted his broadcast to tick off some drunken hoons who were trying to pull down the lavatory stinkpipe. Collins swore his head off briefly – it would never occur today because there are no public characters left. We exist in a vapid world where nobodies describe nothing to nondescript other nobodies, and nobody cares a stuff.

Racing writers want to be seen as screenwriters doped upon stats. Statistics are the new poems of Flemington, and people talk numerically rather than abstractly, therefore nothing outrageous is said, broadcast or remembered. Blandness rules the racetrack today, and eloquently spoken criminals aren't invited to go on the record, even though their stories would cut the mustard in a second, or less.

Today, we see the bizarre costume, but not the incredibly beautiful pinstripe suit of Bill Collins strutting by the lovely, honest, fresh, gleaming horse shit, his remarkable top hat on, winking lasciviously at Abigail.

We get the bored rich, but not the equals of Oscar Wilde, like John Hindle cracking a gem with John Hepworth and Michael Leunig, who is pouring all of them chilled 10th-rate Pink Bodega, and now they dance arm-in-arm with Bert Newton, who thinks he is John Brosnan, and probably is.

I am putting a boozy bob on Beldale Ball in 1980, with Robo, my youngest brother, and my mother Edna decides for her happy-go-lucky sons to whack 10 or 15 bucks on Beldale Ball also, and as I give the bookie, named White, my dough, and he proffers the greasy bookie's slips to me, a thief steals all my bet-cards, and without missing a beat, White the bookie says to me, without looking up: 'It's perfectly OK, mate. If Beldale Ball comes in, I'll pay you out, no worries about that.'

I hurried back to my family pozzie at the packed hot barrier, as the field thundered up. It won by a short half-head. My brother Robo and I ran to the bookie, and he paid me out without bothering to look up from his squashy pile of 50s and 20s, with pie-covered shrapnel at the mildew end of the bag. I gave the winnings to Edna and we all had a big drink and feed in Lygon Street after.

Most Novembers I turn up, but not today, for some reason my ticker's not in the new way of it. The Melbourne Cup used to be sacredly odd and full of the most original morons, but today it is a vast sea of upwardly mobile cretinousness.

I loved it for its legion of chuckling, light-hearted souls such as Dame Zara Holt and the human cello, Athol Guy, who drank as well as he played. I loved the North Melbourne housing commission poor, who once had enough dough to get in and do their dole on some 200–1 glue-hoofed galloper slower than the pots in the grandstand.

It's too good now, too important and commercial, with sponsors calling their predictable shots. Too many Irish millionaires and Emirates millionaires. Not enough Father Brosnans for my liking.

The Age, 4 November 2003

GREYHOUNDS WITH CHIPS STOP YOU GOING TO THE DOGS

Yesterday, I strolled up Smith Street, Collingwood, to bung a unit on a virtual greyhound at my favourite watering hole, the Albion. Lots of fellow mug punters awaited me there, and although the mood was extremely sombre, even suicidal, I felt inspired to sit on a fresh pot and review my revenue. Last week I won at the Dapto dogs, six units on the moist and eager nostrils of a dead cert. The week before I did my dough on a Melbourne canine, and unlike my usual calm and collected self, I swore.

It was pension day yesterday and lots of desperate characters either sat staring stupefied back out at Smith Street, clutching weakly a stone-cold spring roll, or tried to come at a feebly-rolled Havelock rollie, while nursing a Farmland moselle hangover. I felt good. I gazed up at what appeared to be actual likenesses of dogs, and assumed I was watching a televised dog race at Harold Park or Sandown, or possibly upon the planet Neptune, but the truth was I was looking straight down the guts of computerised greyhound racing. I was aghast, but interested. You could bet on a laser-chip implant dog without going to the dog track. You could enjoy the bewitching sight of all their slobber clinging to their synthetic tails and digitally remastered whiskers, without dipping out on your shout.

A few terribly relaxed punters half-heartedly looked up at the computer menu, in order to comprehend the colossal IQ needed to shove a coin in a slot. I bought an old mate a Scotch and myself a jar and together, in the most enjoyable manner possible, we bet on anything that moved. It was absolutely incredible how realistic the hologram hounds were – you expected the idiotic things to bay at you, as they got in the frame.

After a few delicious braces of effervescent beers and lots of scrumptious inhaling of tobacco, I started to really take it easy, and in fact the cyber creatures galloped through the bar and breasted the winning line in the most agreeable way you could imagine.

I remembered chatting to lots of people in the underworld at Sandown out at Noble Park, and laughing with fellow mugs at Olympic Park, where Father Brosnan and his brother, the bookie, used to go. I am old enough to vaguely recall the sight of chimps being put on greyhounds' backs as jockeys, 50 years ago.

Marvelling at the new world available to all keen sportsmen at pubs, I ordered a parting jug for the pie-eyed pals, shouted them a bag of Korean cashews, and reluctantly hit the toe. How do virtual dogs get rewarded, I wondered as I waited for the Johnston Street bus to gas me. I always remember greyhounds of yesterday being real, and exercised in their revolting muzzles around the block. You don't have to feed a hologram mongrel, so you kick a large goal there.

The city bus eventually chugged to a halt and I got on with all the losers on it. When I got home I couldn't explain to the family where I had been. It's 50–1 they wouldn't believe me, anyway.

The Age, 28 November 2003

COURTING THE GOOD OLD DAYS OF GLORY

It was scintillating, of course, the other day to watch Mark Philippoussis clean up that wily Spaniard Juan Carlos Ferrero, to go on the better against his mob at the Davis Cup. Not many mortal tennis players can handle a serve at the speed of sound. Or withstand a Scud orang-utan primordial scream. Rather off-putting, to say the least.

Grunting gloominess married to an unconquerable iron will to win is the way to go, even suburban newsagents scream these days, and do a whole lot of Americanised air-punching. We are all practising egomaniacs, especially schoolchildren, who are delighted to give their exhausted parents the finger.

Brute force wins the point every time, and the illiterate heroes of tennis garble and snigger their way through half-hearted news conferences. It's not worth their time.

Watching Philippoussis strut his supersonic stuff during a robotic encounter with someone equally unamusing, I remembered watching Lew Hoad play his old cobber Ken Rosewall at White City in Sydney 40 years ago. It was like looking into an impressionist painting, their crisp brushstroke shots rather like blobs of light on a lake. Hoad had a serve that was more like serving up a chop at a birthday party barbecue. He volleyed like a praying mantis with a hangover. He laughed a great deal and in his autobiography *Aces and Places*, he said he liked a couple of nice cold bottles of Tooths before he won the toss. He skipped around the surface of the court like a moth with peripheral neuritis. He won Wimbledon as a boy with Rosewall, fluttering the ball across the net as though it were nothing but fun. Fun is not the go today, ego is.

I watched Hoad play with Rosewall once at Kooyong. They were still quick but old, and when the notoriously slow serve of Rosewall drooped towards the net against Pancho Gonzales and Arthur Ashe, Hoad yelled out: 'Don't come into the net on that serve. It'll hit you on the back of the head.'

Pancho was inimitable. I used to say 'Eeh hah' all the time, as if I was Mexican, or was he Spanish?

Once I met my hero Hoad in Brunswick Street, Fitzroy. He was smoking outside a filthy fish and chip shop, and he hopped on the St Georges Road rocket with me. It was a pretty hot sort of a day and the connie put her shoe into the canvas slide-up door, and it shot up to the roof like a rocket. Lew looked at me and I asked him if I could examine his right runner. He took off his runner and sock and there was no big right toe. 'You did the damage long back, dragging your toe on the serve, didn't you, Lew?' I said, politely. He had written about his missing big right toe, and I just wanted to have a captain's.

His famous grin intact, the wicked big handsome wisecracking jaw the same, just about, he wore an out-of-date vanilla suit and crimson spotty tie. At his Spanish tennis ranch, he was coaching Sean Connery, and I thought of them bowling over a foaming VB.

His autobiography is funny. The pics are good, and depict him leaping about like a quivery five-quid note, playing the likes of Roy Emerson and Vic Seixas, defeating some Egyptian in 123-degree heat in the fiery days before tie-breakers. Hoad did not work the crowd, air-punch or blaspheme or stare anyone down.

When Harry Hopman coached the Davis Cup in the old days, he did not have to sneer or swear or resemble a werewolf to get his points across. His protégés got a few bob a game and were innumerate, especially when it came to shouting the man who just did you 6–0.

I am still on that sweltering old West Preston green tram with him, Lew Hoad, and he is putting his right Dunlop runner back on, and telling me he needs a jar.

The Age, 5 December 2003

THE REMEMBRANCE OF WALLY GROUTS PAST

Out they magnificently strode on to the turf and amid the thrips and mozzies and annoying Poms to front drunks who bayed out the holy curse of triumph, 'howzat'. All the Australian green, floppy caps with boastful noses and sunburnt earholes, Wally Grouts the lot of them; barnacle-buttocked, towrope shouldered, adjusting the sweaty but necessary box to ward off the likes of Freddie Trueman. Scum, Poms.

My father Len is gripping hard his dilapidated kitbag containing our family's beloved tartan thermos full of Bushells tea, plus Mum has remembered to also whack in the bag her trusty old Dexal bottle that she always put the milk in. Chicken sandwiches just about on the curl in century-degree heat. A hundred degrees we used to call sweltering Boxing Days at the MCG. Dad is sharpening half a black-lead pencil, and he is quietly whistling something anti-British as Ian Redpath plays a leg glance for a boundary.

'Good bat, that bloke,' he murmurs, not bothering to look up at me. He knows I'm OK for a chook sandwich. Richie Benaud grins a great deal out there; the savage sun glint of his bridgework would give you a headache if you're too sensitive.

My peaceful father gives me a 'captain' through his father's binoculars; I can see Freddie Trueman's testicles through them. He is actually right on the boundary, the mythic Yorkshire paceman, flirting with a breasty South Yarra lass. To my considerable surprise O'Neill's clocked a six and Freddie Trueman catches the ball right in the centre of his beautiful cricket hat. The incredibly sensuous sheila he's been amusing gives him her phone number. O'Neill's yorked.

It is about 40 years ago now, and the crowd, as you dreamily take them in, all resemble polite children. The men never swear and they get up for the women to sit down. The cricketers don't pat each other's bum when they hit a six or get an lbw.

It was a time when the men would innocently offer salt or pepper to their wives' salad sandwiches. The children could run on to the jade green grass to excitedly have their autograph albums signed by players such as Peter Burge. It was an era when even Bill Lawry could manage a smile, even when Rod Marsh was right on the ton. Perhaps that's not 40 years ago. I still hear us booing Bill Lawry for declaring.

I am contentedly sipping the most amazingly scrumptious Marchants soft drink that cost Dad one and fourpence. It's Passiona, and I can just about detect the bloody passionfruit pips in its uncanny fizziness. Cowper's run out. Dad ticks him off on his tiny scorebook. 'Hopeless,' he mutters.

Above all, the cricket was cheap and you didn't have to be an arsehole to go to it. About 20 years ago, my father took a mate of mine and me to the cricket during all the Bay 13 mayhem. It was really humid, with chronic deafening swearing chanted like voodoo amid the cyclonic vomit, stone-cold dimmies and yuppies chucking empties at seagulls.

A little girl with adorable blonde-coloured plaits was hit on the head with a dirty big hunk of beer ice, turfed down from the drunk's perspective. Blood came out of her head, and my father admitted that Kerry Packer killed the thing he loved. The exhausted St John ambos carted the wounded infant away. No one cared less.

I have met lovely old blokes at the cricket who knew Victor Trumper, and I have amiably chatted away with a woman once in the bar; she shouted me a jug we shared, she cried like buggery when Grout kicked it. 'Jesus Christ is as close to Wally Grout as a wicket-keeper can get,' she blubbered in her cups. And that's quite right, lady, he is.

Cricket is bullshit now, and it is money got up as patriotism that makes the lobotomised, monied patrons shriek for Warne and Ponting and the others, who may as well put on their pullovers for Mephistopheles. The Mexican wave goes one way and the remembrance of clean, poor, honest wicket-keepers like Wal Grout, the protégé of Don 'the claw' Tallon, go the exact opposite way.

Humble cricketers of the old days are bullshit in the beery eyes of today's cricket barbarians, who kick over their million-buck motorbikes with their old boys. I remember the excitement of Neil Harvey hitting a brilliant four, 40 years ago, and the eagerness and gratefulness of the working-class crowd standing up for him.

Going home to Reservoir on the train we swept ever onwards past Pie Park, where there was a cricket match on, and although we only stopped there for a fraction of a second, a drunkard yelled, 'Have a go, ya mug!'

The Age, 26 December 2003

WE FOUGHT THEM ON THE BEACHES, AND WE NEVER GAVE IN

The former infantrymen of my father's battalion used to play beach cricket down at Sandringham in the '50s. Len Dickins served in 57/60th unit, saw action in New Guinea and what was called 'the islands'. He was demobbed back in 1946, and brought home with him a Japanese execution sword. It was the size of a guillotine. I remember seeing it hung up in our sombre garage. It wickedly twinkled.

Cricket was religion in my home town of Reservoir. We belted the Christ out of skinned Slazenger tennis balls up on Rathcown Road, where we were born. We used a burnt dirt tin for a wicket in the middle of the gravel, and everyone in the neighbourhood played with the most passionate intensity. You couldn't poof-terise 'round.

Folks of our town were so fanatical about cricket that they pretended to be Don Bradman or Slasher or Neil Harvey. They even spoke like them if they could, and ran frantically between fruit box wickets in the same graceful and athletic manner.

We listened to the radio on the beach train from Reservoir to Sandy, following the drama of each transmitted full-toss or lethargic leg break with the true devotion of saints about to go for a tumble.

We arrived at Sandringham armed to the gunwales with badminton feathers, badminton racquets and togs that were never called bathers. You kept a bit of old torn-off Aspro packet over your nose to ward off unwanted sunburn, and after pressing the freckled flesh of his fellow soldiers, my father got out the buggered old cricket bat and organised the hunt for the tennis ball.

Five breakers out were the boundaries, from memory, with some old blokes dangling their bowed legs over pumped-up black Dunlop tractor tubes – these were boundary umpires who sipped from a bottle of beer with a straw in it. The wicket was a few sticks scrounged from the shallows with a length of revolting yellow kelp draped over it by way of bails. A one-legged digger dragged his stump along the chopped-up sand to make the pitch. He did it every single year at what was called 'the Gymkhana'. Why it was called that eludes me entirely, but it was great fun, I have to tell you.

There was a great big dug-up sealed-off area of sand, I remember, with red rope around it, and tokens or coupons were hidden there, and after a pistol got fired, the deliriously happy pent-up children tore into it like mad things. If you dug up a ticket, you ran off to the kiosk and cashed it in. The sweating jovial or stroppy lady there, in a perm and No. 1 Pimms hangover, swapped it for an icy pole. You then bit it and screamed.

I see easily before me a bandy-legged veteran of war atrocities patiently re-wrap a bit of stinky old kelp round the cricket bat as if it were real pigskin. Men keep jumping up and down flattening the beach cricket pitch. The mums couldn't give a stuff.

Some mums are sipping a shandy and gasping an Ardath,
shielding the razor-sharp sun from their un-mascara'd eyes.
Kids are fielding intently, certainly in too close, and as surely as
God made the Darebin Creek, they shall be nauseous after
receiving the ball violently in the tum-tum. And there shall be
no pity for any of them. Beach cricket is deadset, to say the least.

A digger hits an immaculate six and a squall starts up.
Lightning is duly noted, of the sheet sort, and it is also noted
that the tennis ball has broken clean in half after too earnest a
whack. I am given a bowl and with one particular sea-weedy
delivery, my ball hits the soldier in his right knee. The bowling
side explodes. 'Owzat, you mug!'

Alas, my right thong was a little bit ahead of the crease and
my delivery seen as a no-ball.

A minute later, I clean bowl him and knock his kelp wicket
right over, and he violently blasphemes. He kicks the pathetic
impromptu wicket over and he looks mighty crestfallen as he
wanders back to the niner.

My father has the uncanniest eyesight and I cannot remember
ever seeing him miss a ball of any kind in his life. They can't get
him out, no matter what they pitch up at him. He clouts one
over long-on, which is the kiosk, and men cheer him. Me, too,
and my brothers, John and Chris, both sunburnt just like me.

A soldier trashed the sandy wicket, but later I heard him crying in the cool kiosk, confessing the horrors of war to a cleaner.
It was a sad day in some ways, the old Gymkhana, the annual
battalion 'do'. It was, of course, the chance for soldiers to see
each other and meet the newborn babies. Some blokes drank a
bit much. Only because, I suppose, going to war is a bit much.

After the match is over and hooroos said, my father and
mother stroll arm-in-arm up to sweltering Sandringham railway station, where we wait an eternity for a Flinders Street
rocket. Dad reads *The Herald* and laughs at Weg. John and I look
at smouldering seagulls stuck to rusty overhead electricity
wires. Chris considers an electrocuted crow.

It took two long, hot hours to get home again to Reservoir, but
there is a cool change eventually, and Mum and me sit together

on the back porch and watch the lightning fall not far off. 'Hope it doesn't go on my new washing,' she says in a deadset sort of way. Dad gives her a nice hot cuppa and we all sit there half-asleep, while the beautiful sudden rain paints away the unbearable heat.

The Age, 3 January 2004

A HAIRCUT, A TOUCH OF STYPTIC AND A ROCKER CALLED BUTCH GALE

Not far from Separation Street in Northcote and a vertigo attack from the West Preston tram, there exists – although it is hard to credit – an old Italian barber shop that needs the ball put through it, bad. You think of Whelan the Wrecker as you pass by its extravagant hideousness, for the pong of the premises is hard on the soul, but possibly good for the heart. It is a tribute to former football heroes; now they'd be rheumatoid ruckmen and Alzheimer rovers.

The grotty door is a wonder of no-longer functioning tin hinges and memory. You venture into this hairdo horror-house and in a complete trance you grope your way into the faded brown leatherette revolving barber-chair, to front a baffling array of photos. Everywhere you squint, you behold Ray Gabelich. Dessie Tuddenham grins down at you from where his touched-up photo is sticky-taped upon the mirror, and you instantly recall him getting into a bit of strife, and the kids I kicked the footy with praying for him. Poor murdered Freddie Swift smiles wistfully at your can of 1970s talcum powder. He is very much alive here, though, and it is as if he is enjoying the sight of kids coming in for a trim. The No. 12 Preston tram rumbles by, and watermelons fall off a rust-bucket of a Kombi Van with the back cut out of it.

The old stroppy barber does not ask you how you want it. He

violently pins a stiff white bib round your throat, and commences to sharpen up the shaving-knife. I have come in for a Dad and Dave, a light trim without too much chat, but he intends to get rid of the whiskers, which have been a bit sprouty lately anyway.

'Do you think about the Old Butcher?' he winks, whisking away some tufts that pile up on his linoleum floor.

He means Alan Gale, the old Fitzroy captain. He was my friend, but I cannot possibly find an answer to his query. I am enraptured in the sight of the slightly bleached hairdresser photos. You remember Bobby Skilton, the way he baulked, marked, pivoted, laughed, tore away from the enemy – as soon as you reacquaint yourself with his haircut. Same exactly with Murray Weideman, who has a big Rocker hairdo today, complete with raffish sideburns, so that he rather resembles a Northcote Elvis, with just a hint of Mephistopheles.

There are two Italian children after I get my ears lowered, and a baby fast asleep in a pusher, with an enormous homemade salami resting on its white plastic handles. Everything feels asleep here, particularly the present. Only the past kicks the footy into life and summer laughter, like in the '60s, when boys did not love their football heroes. They would have laid down their lives for them. Easy.

He slaps my red-raw throat with a funny old thing called styptic pencil, which fixes up cuts, I am reliably informed. It is restful in here, I have to tell you, and in a mid-summer reverie, I can see boys of 50 years ago, doing their hair just like Bill Twomey and Polly Farmer, although that might be a bit later. Christ, he was graceful. He didn't need a light trim, Pol.

Summer footy training was nothing but a horse-laugh, said Gale, when last we spoke in his home in Rathdowne Street, Carlton, where Pat, his friendly wife, made the most scrumptious minestrone, and we all chuckled, mostly about nothing, which isn't a bad thing to joke about half the time. So much of life is so tantalisingly brief, like a fantastic goal you booted upon a prickle-paddock millennia ago, and your father bipped his FJ car-horn.

Butch told me summer footy before it commences in deadly

earnest consisted of a few O.P. rums, then a bit of circle work. Brunswick Street Oval only had the one former aerodrome light hanging over it, and Butch told me if anyone kicked the bladder over the fence, they gave it away. Too dark.

He ran the old Birmingham Hotel in those days, on the corner of Smith and Johnston streets, and kids in my day used to cheer him on when he hobbled down the concrete race, and some of the dads, I suppose, did their hair like him. His was a natural Rocker style, and in truth, his skull was so bumpy it was just as well his tufts developed in their way over all the gouges and gristle-hills of his.

The words 'laid back' weren't invented then, or maybe that catch-phrase was current in The States, but what was the go back then was called, 'So what?' So what we are up against The Pies at Pie Park? So what if Thorold Merrett got both legs broken waiting for a rainmaker to finally land on his chest? So what if I die? At least I beat the big prick they put on me. At least I've got the tram dough home. And there's a coldie in the fridge.

Summer children study the holy portraits of the pilgrims of the Sherrin. They imitate them. They weave just like Bobby Skilton does, only the weaving is done in their tiny Collingwood backyards or Croydon backyards, or they handpass the O So Lite flour box to sleepy Granny in the claustrophobic hallway of their putrescent high-rise flat.

I pay the Italian barber and step into St Georges Road, gazing back at the young boy in the now-vacated chair. He looks not unlike Roy Cazaly in this dreamy January light, the dust-motes mildly spinning towards the bib with the clip catching a sudden prism. Rain has leaked through the window and on sale in it are the hard round plastic combs that were popular in the '50s to maintain your superb new Flat Top. I was never game enough to boast a Flat Top.

I stroll up towards The Hump, Northcote's only night-life, it is the hill trams go over at the intersection of Miller Street and St Georges Road. There's no suffocating tram chugging over it, but in my mind, I can see hundreds of Housing Commission football-hero-worshippers, hugging a scuffed footy under their skinny arms, singing out to men they do not barrack for or even love. They would lay down their young lives for them. Easy.

The Age, 10 January 2004

THE BRAT WHO'S BEEN REINCARNATED AS THE GAME'S GREAT LISTENER

Something is certainly wrong with Australian Open TV broadcasters, apart from their oafdom. All they can manage is stats. All that impresses them is whether Scud serves the Slazenger at 200 km/h.

Fred Stolle is fascinatingly dull, if there's such a quality, and of course the glued-to-telly tennis fanatics idolise him because he is as cosy as five pots of tea rinsed down with a full walnut loaf.

Each summer on Channel Seven, I have sat absolutely mesmerised as the likes of John Newcombe and John Alexander have shrieked and whimpered, analysed and ad-libbed about the likelihood of rain, whether a random hailstone could wreck a racquet, ventured into tennis's vast history lesson, recalling the slice backhand return of serve of Jack Kramer, vividly and intimately revealing the preferred breakfast cereal of Arthur Ashe in 1970.

Always the commentary is pervy. They ogle busty girls in a jokey, low-key manner, designed to enthuse the drongo at home, poised on the lounge room sofa, with a couple of stubbies jammed down his fanatic front.

Stolle says many times the same remarks about when he himself played in The Open, or at Wimbledon; everything reminds him of his serve. I have to say that I have remembered nothing Fred Stolle or Tony Trabert have ever said, but I have always loved their extreme cosiness, as well as their avuncular affability. They're family, after all. Part of summer, like fainting.

John Newcombe, I used to copy his strong, masculine serving

action. I used to ride my bike over to the local primary school of a night, in summer during The Open, and serve just like John Newcombe does into the shelter shed wall, guided by the moonlight, and thinking about his incredible moustache. He looked like a right-wing revolutionary.

And when John McEnroe served at the Australian Open, because of the deranged and corkscrewing way he wound up his taut body, the way he succeeded in hiding the way he intended to hit it, you couldn't really tell if it was satire or drama. The next thing the opponent knew was that it was an ace. He pantomimed the backhand drop-shot at the net. He Houdini-ed the overhead smash and put the ball on charmed notice. It obeyed its uncanny master. McEnroe broke all the uptight old English, all English rules of the great game, and his style was as uncatalogued as the ancient human compulsion to laugh or fight.

His mastery of the serve baffled Bjorn Borg utterly. He had the drama-script of tennis off by heart, and used maximum close-up of that remarkable ugliness and animal innocence to conquer one and all.

Now, of course, tennis is as dull as a weekend in West Preston. A forced weekend there, at that, with the only thing to do being an hour on an old school set of monkey bars. Or get on the drink.

It was McEnroe's unpredictability and operatic panache that filled Kooyong and every other tennis stadium in our country. But he is at his best on telly. He listens better than he ever speaks, and that's rare in the commentary box, and his refreshing spontaneity is as unteachable as his old service action. What I always like about his remarks is the insightfulness. He never forgets a single stroke, and possesses the innate Irish poet's ability to take the TV viewer or radio listener right into the spirit of each blood-struck volley. He can actually replace you with the player about to go into the shot.

His style on court was imperious and remarkably dainty without seeming vicious or selfish. What the Australian media didn't like was his openness and free-association streams of articulated poetry. John McEnroe always played as though it was just breathing.

Cricket commentary is so dull you would think it would put people off cricket, but we Australians love our sport too much to die of boredom, whether it's cricket or tennis commentary. With uninspired tennis chatter, you just have to put up with it until McEnroe comes on, that's all.

The gluey bounce of Rebound Ace is, I suppose, better than when you play on soggy grass and the ball starts resembling an inflated pear or a fluffy quince, but it doesn't leave a mark, so there's no history. Not like the inspired poetic observations of McEnroe, who speaks like he played – inimitably, sardonically, mysteriously. But not endlessly. And he never mentions himself because that doesn't interest him in any sort of a way.

The Age, 31 January 2004

ABILITY AND HUMILITY A DOUBLES TEAM THAT MALE TENNIS NEEDS

I remember getting done like a dinner, a long time ago, in a breathtaking tennis match in Northcote in the under-19 gents' singles. As a result, I cried buckets. I thought I was the new Lew Hoad. Not quite.

I got up early to add the white runner cleaner to my size-seven runners. I did my hair with Brylcreem before I fronted the ugly crushed brick courts in Arthurton Road. I half expected the old people to beg for my autograph. I smiled pityingly at the old girl sponging up the court puddles. I warmed up, with snobbery on my side.

The other bloke hit the first serve so hard that they couldn't get it out of the fowl-wire at the back. I couldn't even see his slice backhand or make out his disguised West Preston lob. He won the first set in, I suppose, 10 minutes. My young throat felt as dry as several sugar bags as I changed ends, then lost the second set 6–0. My opponent shook hands with me, which shocked me. Like an angel's grasp, it felt not arrogant or mean.

I cried in the gents', and he then came in and smiled lovingly at my ashamed and fevered face reflected in the mirror, where I was rinsing my shame and cooling my agony. I had a desire to buy a spade and bury myself alive, but he said, as if he was my friend: 'Don't do that, mate. Can you join up with me in the doubles? My partner had to drop out because he's crook with the flu. Can yer?'

I blew my nose violently and joined my conqueror. We won the doubles together, and after playing better than ever I had in my whole life, he again grinned at me and shook my hand at the net. We won some kind of tiny goldy-coloured thing.

It was a real lesson in humility for my vanity, I suppose, and it proved to me what I'd always suspected about myself. I am always wrong, misreading people and misunderstanding my own perceptions of them. That young guy who creamed me was in no sense my enemy, and when he was humble enough to step into the changing room and have the heart to invite someone he beat to become his new partner, he was, in my opinion, cultivated, even divine.

To be a good sport is not just the appropriate thing, it is paramount in a world off its noggin. I see Lleyton Hewitt winning many titles, earning millions of bucks because he is so strong and young and gifted, but he is always swearing beneath his millionaire breath, and although he needs his mum there to watch him play, he always plays up something shocking, doesn't he? It would really knock me out to see Lleyton get beat and not mind getting beat, stroll gracefully up to the opponent and say: 'You were simply too good, my friend. May your loving God bless you.'

But these days in men's tennis there are no subtleties of love, nor is pity shown – only the fist-spitting hatred of loss is displayed. As a result of masculine poor sportsmanship, we are at war. We are at war with the sweet side of the racquet-face, the human face that has always had grace in its make-up.

In a dreamy reverie, it came true that from now on all male

professional tennis players learnt humility off by heart, came to the swiftest realisation that winning at all costs is absolute rubbish, and that losing with grace is absolute love. I shall now hop off the lecturing fruit box and give another sportsman a go. See you in the final.

The Age, 14 February 2004

THE BOOT THAT SEALED THE ROMANCE OF THE ROYS

Seldom does one really see greatness, apart from the sky at night, or the incredibly beautiful feet of Bernie Quinlan, whom Fitzroy Football Club adorers called Superboot.

He was the twinkle toes of the drop punt. It was uncanny the way Quinlan read the breeze, able to lob the footy right into the eager and grateful palms of his team-mates or his captain, Garry Wilson, or his indefatigable ruckman, Ron Alexander.

Quinlan was dumped by an unimaginative Footscray 25 years ago and picked up by the Roys when they were the Wandering Jews of Football, training in an ad-lib way at just about every paddock available, including Westgarth Oval, which had only an old aerodrome light in it at night, so you could sort of see the emerging Sherrin, but never for long.

Fitzroy also played at the Junction Oval a quarter of a century ago. I can still remember getting in on a forged concession card, then fluttering it over the brick wall into the eager hands of my brother, Robert so he could get in, too. Lots of people back then didn't have enough dough to get in to see the Royboys play. Everything seemed ad-libbed, especially the poverty.

Standing there in the immaculate sea breeze with your mates, you saw this angelic man called Quinlan. He was grace itself and the long, tireless frame loped along rather like a gazelle with Dencorub on.

He was never brutal or selfish, and when his adorers, the children, ran on after Superboot booted his 100th goal for the season, play stopped and joy began – a wild, innocent unconquerable passion for this genial giant who never cut up rough. I never saw him go the knuckle, not once, and I went to see him every single week.

The way he ran was poetry written by the wind and the way he leapt for the ball was effortless as laughter. You actually used to laugh when Bernie got up on his opponent's kidneys and pulled one in. You laughed because the way he leapt was easy as breath. Easier.

He used to get hobbledy at times, pulling up sore from a crook Achilles tendon. Once up in Sydney, I watched Rod 'Bendyneck' Carter run down the race with Quinlan – for some reason Sydney players got mixed up with Fitzroy ones – and dear old Bendyneck kept working on Quinlan's sore, strapped-up shin, kicking it as they ran on.

During the second quarter, an old woman I know, who used to live in the Brunswick Street high-rise flats, saw Carter booting Bernie on the shins. She screamed out: 'Don't just take it, Superboot. Do him into the tin pie sign!' To my dismay, I watched Bernie cast Bendyneck into the tin pie sign a few goes. Then I heard the same woman shriek out: 'Mean it!'

Footscray bigwigs must have eaten crow when Bernie won the 1981 Brownlow, tying with Barry Round, of Sydney, which I still call South. It seems a second ago.

My brother Robert and I went to watch the Royboys each Saturday – rain, hail or defeat. They got done a lot, but they also played exciting, hectic, brainy football, and sometimes I came home completely hoarse, having barracked myself deaf and dumb all day in the outer.

We flew to Sydney if we had the cash, we dreamt about them and I used to write plays about Fitzroy, satirising the AFL and its determination to rub them out. Like a heartless old school eraser, we used to called them rubbers, rubbing out the past.

Then the bad times turned up. They were in terrible debt and doomed to either die or get spot-welded on to North. North

Fitzroy? You have to be joking! Or it was go to Brisbane and become the Fitzroy Bears. Which is what happened to them. All you get in life or death is your name and the speedy forfeiture of their old name was the beginning of their end.

It really looked a dead cert in 1986 they would win the first grand final since the 1944 victory over Richmond, played at Junction Oval. But in '86 we didn't get it, even though we beat Hawthorn and the Bombers in the lead-up to it. Robert and I screamed ourselves just about dead, sitting next to my old friend Leon Weigard. We felt like real toffee apples in the VIP lounge, with Margaret River chardonnays dished up by grovelling wine waiters, instead of barracking out in the wind and rain.

A few seasons tick by and Bernie was made coach, a fatal blue. He was not a great coach – in fact, he was hopeless – and we lost so often we became nothing but a farce.

He was sacked. With three Sherrins in his giant palm, he was given the flick at training. Fitzroy killed the thing it loved. They sacked their Messiah.

I last saw him on Optus TV in 1996 after the Tigers caned us at the MCG. I covered their last Melbourne match for *A Current Affair* and *Today Tonight*. Bernie was doing a vox pop on the boundary line after the final siren and he was crying. It was so beautiful to see him cry as he faithfully spoke of something rather like the end of the world.

A bit later, his old friends at Channel Seven sacked him as a commentator, proving there's no such thing as life after sport. Then his daughter died of ovarian cancer and everything became tougher than belief after a series of unexpected and undeserved catastrophes. It was like the torment of Job from the Old Testament.

I just hope in my heart that the bigwigs at the AFL and at the hybrid Lions set-up in Brisbane take the necessary time to remember Bernie. He made Fitzroy work. He made it popular. He was so loved by its supporters, and still is, that he boosted their membership and their mythology.

The Age, 24 April 2004

THE DAY BIG MICK CONLAN BARRELLED THE VIC PARK SPIT BRIGADE

In 1986, Fitzroy Football Club made the Einstein decision to ground-share with Collingwood at Pie Park, one of the monumental breakthroughs of all time in terms of sadomasochism.

The Woods have always been the arch-enemy of the Roys. Whenever we caned them at Pie Park, you could have fired a cannon down Hoddle Street afterwards – there was nothing but silence to signify loss.

The firing of any weapon is wrong, but sometimes you felt like firing something to break the profound and eerie silence after Fitzroy went one the better. You could hear a Chiko Roll wrapper fluttering in Turner Street, opposite the Woodsmen's oval, and when you ventured over Johnston Street for a charge at the pub, you heard different sounds. You heard language like the groaning of the crucified.

Loyal, tough, galvanised-iron Collingwood supporters wept into their watered-down pots when the Royboys beat them. It was like the end of existence, or trying to believe in justice after your employer has fired you in the loading bay of your factory in front of your workmates. I couldn't believe my eyes that morning, when I read about the plan to share the mud with the Woodsmen.

The first time they met was a rainy, slushy day and overcast, with wall-to-wall Piemen stuffing themselves stupid with stone-cold Four 'N' Twenties, and dramatically chucking back dozens of VBs. I vividly recall the archaeological dig required to prise your unwanted way through hundreds of uneducated, 30-stone, drunk Woodsmen to watch the Sherrin. Their rough noggins were brainless, their nose hairs barracked for Murray Weideman.

Their wives barracked for Rene Kink. All they thought about was Rene Kink. Just the noise of faith and love from the Collingwood fans alone would put you off. It was designed to nauseate your stomach if you dared to barrack for anybody but the Mighty Pie Boys.

I covered the first Fitzroy versus Collingwood match at the newly shared Vic Park. I wrote about the mayhem of that insane encounter for *The Melbourne Times* and aged a year merely writing about the hatred of it.

About 10 minutes before the siren for both sides to run down the old stern concrete race into the brilliance of the glimmering sea of mud, I poured myself a cup of tea and was called a poof by a woman supporter. She was all done up in cheap Collingwood adoration badges and black-and-white hair, and with plastic shades on her head. A real poor Housing Commission thing she was, dead-drunk on scotch mixed with Coke in a thermos with a leak in it.

'Poof,' she said to me.

Her inebriated husband didn't say a thing. He was endeavouring to listen to harness racing on an old Philips tranny that didn't have any batteries in it. 'Poof,' she said again, as I sipped my Lan Choo, and concentrated on my Footy Record match statistics. I didn't like her tone.

I was inwardly cursing myself for not putting on my jumper that day because it was absolutely freezing. There was icy whistling wind all through my ears, giving me an earache, my socks were wet through, and as I gratefully sipped my hot tea, I went and stood right next to the race, where the Roys ran out to begin the battle with the Pies at the same ground. It felt unclean, like incest.

A few hungover assistant coaches waddled through with a few balls and pumps under their arms, looking appropriately hateful. Robert Walls, the Royboys' coach, rubbed his giant palms together. I saw Les 'Tatts' Parish and Bernie Quinlan having a joke together, their arms gleaming with weak sunshine mixed with Deep Heat.

All of my heroes trotted on in the peak of condition, unafraid of anything, especially Collingwood, whom they held beneath their contempt. A whole lot of booing and insulting boys had got up onto the chicken-wire that covered over the race where the Roys were running out, and some of them commenced to jeer at us. Others lobbed flattened cans at us, or else just spat.

Like all Pie Boy slag, it is chiefly composed of ignorance thinned with poverty, and it strikes you right in the face like the ring of truth.

Two blokes in Collingwood colours spat on Micky Conlan, our courageous follower, and I saw that heap of spit hit Mick on his hair and shoulders, and he immediately leapt up at them and hooked at least one of them with a big right paw. It was excellently judged, that revengeful blow – a thing of awe.

I spoke with Mick after the game, which we won by a narrow margin, and over a few coldies he said he wasn't going to accept getting slagged on, and that's fair enough for any Royboy worth his Dencorub.

So when I read about the craven guy spitting on Dan Frawley a month back, I remembered Micky Conlan copping the same thing 18 seasons ago at a place that was obscene and sacred, horrible and dramatic, funny and idiotic.

I go by the old Pie Park these days and it still feels special in a vomitus sort of way. All the Colliwobbles still remain, as do the formidable ghosts of Pie Boys past. Murray Weideman and Len Thompson and Bob Rose and Peter Daicos, who to me was perhaps the greatest Pieman of the lot. Christ, could Daicos read the wind on a sub-zero day.

Micky Conlan also told me the Pies wouldn't give the Roys hot water for their shower after the hate-match. Now, that is Love.

The Age, 15 May 2004

ANOTHER SATURDAY AT AUSKICK

Can it really be the year 2004? It seems more like 1964 to me, but then the way the tiny tykes put in at training this morning, the years play tricks on fossils such as myself. Can that actually be my boy going in so fearlessly, rushing straight into a menacing pack of gum-guarded Herculean infants, to scoop up the Sherrin and roost another major? It seems like he was just born. But there he is, darting like a famous hailstone over vastness of cold mud, paralysing puddles and tussocks of flattened couch-grass. Anything to get his hands on the bladder.

It is early at the W.T. Peterson Oval in Fitzroy. It used to be called the Brunswick Street oval, but nobody gives a hoot what its title really is. Hung-over dads shudder under the remote concrete Gent's in the middle of a mud-pile. Strung-out mums organise the tea urn as if in a trance. One mum sleepily sells muffins in her sleep-vapour. Kids warming up with fit or fat fathers, doing a bit of circle-work with the lifting fog. Little determined men practising drop punts. Poodles for some reason everywhere, yapping at frosty fathers shaking their heads, joking at the talk of rain.

My little bloke Louis doesn't appear to feel the cold; he loves all of God's elements and I can never get a jumper on him. He is excited when he spies our coaches coming. Kevin and Mick are here, like warriors, like heroes carting bags of jumpers, bags of yet-to-be-pumped footies. 'They're here, Daddy!' whispers Louis.

The sun shines straight through gloom or indecision and the mere fact of us being alive brings joyousness over to our side.

An infant weeps because he has slid in mud. A fat boy weeps because he cannot bend. So how will he pick up the footy? It is emotional – life right in front of your sleepiness and fuzziness and ancientness.

The plastic goal-things are shoved in place. The hung-over fathers shiver, remembering possibly where they got on the drink the night before. The kids stamp to keep the cold out. Mums scream encouragement to their gladiator children.

'Go in, Andrew!'

'Too high, Andrew!'

'Go into rehab, Andrew!'

Kevin our indefatigable coach sends a boy off for swearing. He is a clever miniature footballer, but you're not to blaspheme, even on a Saturday. The devastated boy skulks off the mud.

He squats in a real stink nowhere near the forward line, his natural position for another incredible goal. He shows no contrition and sulks but chooses not to cave in. Eventually my son Louis boots a really good torp to one of his favourite team-mates. Kevin blows the tin whistle and a hung-over father winces from the agony of that noise. Louis smiles as his cobber kicks a goal for Fitzroy under-10s. A couple of poodles dry-mount one another. The blaspheming boy bounces on again and immediately swears.

Kevin sidelines him straight away. 'We're not going to tolerate that kind of language. Hop off until you're better tempered!' But the swearing child spits his dummy and casts his trendy gum guard in the big central mud-puddle, saying: 'I'm not going on the back line. I'm too f——ing short!'

But he isn't going on the back line. He's going right off the ground, and weeps unconsolingly. 'You're not to swear, mate,' says big Kev, and that is the end of the matter of language as it relates to the football.

When the siren sounds all the kids swoop on the oranges volunteered by a kind father, all cut up into quarters for easy slurping. Hundreds of orange rinds everywhere as dads congratulate their exuberant or downcast kids. Birds sing like crazy and my little boy does a torp into a tree.

It's not just the kids having a good time each Saturday morning, but the mums congregate and discuss things such as divorce or school fees, literature or muffins, life or death, who got buried after training the other evening. Why she walked out on him was because he followed the Crows.

Louis runs across to thank Kevin and Mick for helping him play better, and Kevin grins and says to Louis, 'That's quite OK, thanks, Louis. See you next week, mate.'

In such a frightening age, with terrorism as common a topic as footy used to be, with so many doubts about our beautiful blue planet, thank God for blokes like Kevin and Mick.

I used to boot a dog-chewed plastic footy on the muddy track outside our home 50 years ago, and in the friendly dark the old man showed me how to do a stab kick. But the Auskick coaches

I've met on these freezing mornings are as kind and gentle and tough as my beautiful old father. They are more than helpful. More like a blessing.

The Age, 31 July 2004

THE PASSING PARADE

This year saw the passing of two great sportswriters, Percy Beames and Peter Frilingos. Bill Mordey, who was great at many things, also died. Colleagues and friends Ron Carter, Ian Heads and Peter Lalor write affectionately of these legendary Australians.

UNIQUE SPORTSMAN AND SUPER
SPORTS SCRIBE TO BOOT

Ron Carter

Percy Beames: sportsman, journalist. Born 27 July 1911, died 28 March 2004.

No other journalist knew the game better or was more qualified to write about Australian Rules football than Percy Beames during a 32-year career with *The Age* that ended when he retired in 1976. It was uncanny how matches would be played out exactly as the chief football writer would predict in his previews, which dealt with the man-on-man duels and the tactics to be adopted by the opposing coaches.

Beames, who has died after a long illness, aged 92, was not only the best-credentialled football writer of his time but a peerless cricket writer. And although he did not write golf or tennis, he was handy at both.

His uncanny insight was derived from a unique perspective of both sports. He was the only member of the Australian Football League and Victorian Cricket Association 200 Club, having played 213 Victorian Football League (the predecessor to the AFL) games and 205 state and district cricket matches.

Beames was an acute analyst with his finger on the pulse of football life. In his day, football was written about in an entirely different way to today. The VFL had only 12 clubs – all local – and, apart from the occasional split round, all matches were played on Saturday afternoons. There was a strong radio coverage but not the television saturation there is today.

By Saturday night the afternoon newspaper and the *Sporting*

Globe had provided kick-by-kick accounts of matches. There were no Melbourne Sunday papers – so the Monday morning football coverage by Beames in *The Age* was an in-depth account that took the readers far beyond the happenings on the field and their repercussions, and included an astute look at what would confront teams in the weeks ahead.

Except for the long weekends, all games were played at the same time on Saturday at the MCG, Geelong and suburban grounds, but Beames tried his best to see as many teams in action as possible. He did this by watching the first half of one match, say at Princes Park, then at half-time he would go to another game, say Glenferrie Oval, to see the second half there.

Beames's football and cricket records are unbeatable. In the past, footballers and cricketers managed to play both sports – Carlton's Craig Bradley was the last man to play football and cricket at state level, in the late 1980s – but nobody has been able to combine both as successfully and for so long as Beames. His unique 200 double is destined to last forever.

Respect for his knowledge in football circles was enormous. League coaches sought his opinion – after matches it was common to see Beames in deep conversation with a coach long after the final siren.

But his favourite spot was at the end of the bar in the committee room of his beloved Melbourne Football Club, having a quiet beer and rehashing the game with the renowned coach of the Demons and premiership team-mate Norm Smith.

Beames roved in the three premiership triumphs of the great Melbourne teams in 1939, '40 and '41, when the Demons beat Collingwood, Richmond and Essendon. And he was captain-coach in 1942, '43 and '44.

Beames, a country lad from Golden Point in Ballarat, played 213 league games, which was then an MFC record, and finished with a career 323 goals. He also represented Victoria in his second year in 1932 and again in '35, '37 and '39.

Although quietly spoken and one of the nicest men you could meet, Beames was a strong and relentless rover who was named in the MFC's Team of the Century in June 2000, alongside such greats as Don Cordner, Jack Mueller, Norm Smith, Allan La Fontaine, Ivor Warne-Smith, Ron Barassi and Robert Flower.

Beames's cricketing life was just as impressive as his football, on and off the field. As a dashing right-hand batsman, he played with the Melbourne Cricket Club First XI from 1932 to 1946, was captain in 1940, and his run tally of 7072 is the club's fourth-highest after Ayres, Armstrong and Ransford.

In 18 games with Victoria, from 1933 to 1946, he scored 1186 runs, with a highest score of 226 not out, for an average of 51.5.

One of his most delightful and prolific scoring strokes was a thunderbolt square drive, and he was a superbly quick cover fieldsman who saved many runs. The story goes that in one game at the Albert Ground he whacked so many sixes into the tennis courts next door that the tennis was stopped while Beames was at the crease. His cricket team-mates included such greats as Bill Ponsford and Leslie Fleetwood-Smith.

When Beames retired from cricket at the end of the 1945–46 season to become the chief sportswriter for *The Age*, he was in the running for a berth in the Australian XI. Joe Kinnear, who played cricket and football with Beames for many years, told his son, Carlton football administrator Col Kinnear, that Percy was the best cricketer never to have played for Australia.

But Beames never regretted his agonising career decision to join *The Age*, and he went from strength to strength with his writing. He had been a contributor, but the offer of the top position in the sports section was too good to refuse. He covered every international cricket tour of Australia during his time as the chief cricket writer, and he went on three Ashes tours to England and had two trips to South Africa and one to the West Indies.

Beames delighted in telling the story of his first trip to South Africa, with Lindsay Hassett's team in 1949–50 – somebody forgot to book the team's passage home to Australia. As a pressman, Beames was included in the touring party and they had to wait six months for a ship! By the time a vessel arrived to bring them home, everyone was an expert beach cricketer.

In the office we loved ribbing him about how he always

returned from cricket trips with a few strokes off his already low golf handicap. 'Do any actual work, Perce?' we'd ask. And he loved relating how he had a couple of rounds with Don Bradman – 'just the two of us' – or a game at St Andrew's with Ian Chappell.

Besides writing football for *The Age*, Beames was a regular on the ABC's *Footy Show* with household names such as Doug Bigelow, Thorold Merrett, Doug Heywood and Tony Ongarello.

He was dedicated to work. On Friday nights during the football season, when all the serious work was done, Percy and I would stay back and sit around for a couple of hours in case there were late team changes or any other breaking news that could affect the next day's matches.

He loved reminiscing about roving to the biggest man in football at the time, Johnny Lewis, who had joined the Demons in 1936 after 16 seasons with North Melbourne, where he gained state selection 10 times. It seemed Lewis was recruited by Melbourne at the age of 35 as a protector for Beames and the other small men. Beames said that during his three seasons with Melbourne, Lewis cleared a path through the packs, and if any opposition player messed with him the offender ended up answering to Lewis.

Beames admired the talent of one of his greatest opponents, Fitzroy's triple Brownlow medallist Haydn Bunton. Ted Whitten won his vote as the best all-rounder he had seen, and he reckoned Carlton's Bob Chitty was the toughest. Chitty was in Carlton's winning 1945 bloodbath grand final against South Melbourne, regarded by Beames as the roughest and toughest of finals.

Another story he loved telling was about his first visit to Melbourne in the Depression year of 1931, as a young man straight out of Ballarat College. Brought to the city by the Demons, he was told to throw a few things into a bag because he would be staying overnight at a boarding house in Jolimont. The youngster was kept awake all night with people coming and going. Next day he learned the place was also a brothel.

During our Friday night chats, Beames would look at the

future of football. Long before the VFL/AFL had an independent board of directors, he advocated the control of football should be taken away from club delegates who were there only to look after their club interests.

He was a member of the AFL Hall of Fame, life member of the MFC, MCC and the Australian Football Media Association.

Beames is survived by his daughter Adrienne, son Colin and grand-daughters Georgina and Justine. His wife Ruth died before him.

The Age, 31 March 2004

A GAME WELL PLAYED

Ian Heads

The recent days have gouged a great hole in the ranks of Australian sportswriters and tellers of tales. The collapse of Peter 'Chippy' Frilingos, 59, at his desk at *The Daily Telegraph* on Monday afternoon came hard on the heels of the death of the immensely colourful Bill 'Bluegum' Mordey, 67, in Newcastle Hospital ten days before. Mordey's death in turn had come in the shadow of the passing late last year of the peerless golf scribe Phil Tresidder, 75.

The Australian sporting scene is measurably poorer for their passing – and especially so the game of rugby league, which had already been nursing its own bruises via the protracted dramas of the current season.

Each one of the trio was closely connected to league – Tresidder through his coverage of the 1948 Kangaroo tour of England and France when he was still a teenager, Mordey as chief league writer for the *Daily* and *Sunday Mirrors* in the 1960s and '70s and Frilingos who, at his death, had recorded the ebb and flow of the game for the two defunct *Mirror* newspapers, and then *The Daily Telegraph* for exactly 40 years.

While Mordey had moved on from print journalism to fresh fields, as a fearless and dashing promoter of boxing, Frilingos and Tresidder were sportswriters for life.

Tresidder's final story, on golfer Stuart Appleby, was faxed to *Australian Golf Digest* the day before he died. Similarly, Chippy Frilingos was right there in the thick of it to the end, in telephone conversation with National Rugby League chief executive David Gallop at the moment of his collapse – undoubtedly with a story for Tuesday morning in mind.

He died in the manner of famous sporting scribes of the past – including the American legends Bat Masterson, gun-slinger and boxing writer, who collapsed at his typewriter at the *New York Morning Telegraph* in October 1921 while penning a column on the subject of luck, and Grantland Rice, in whose typewriter at the *Daily Mirror* rested a blank sheet carrying only his byline when he suffered a fatal heart attack in July 1954.

In a newsroom full of his *Telegraph* workmates, Frilingos died just 65 hours after attending the funeral that mourned the death of Bill Mordey, and celebrated his life. It was an incredibly bitter fall of the cards. The pair had worked together at the *Mirror* for years, Bill as chief league writer, Peter as his hard-chasing deputy. In tribute to Mordey, Frilingos wrote: 'Everything I know about rugby league and journalism, I learned from him. Bill was a champion bloke.'

The Mordey funeral at least provided a cathartic moment for Peter Frilingos, which would have cheered him. After a brisk handshake outside Sydney's St Mary's Cathedral he spent ten minutes in amiable conversation with the former NSWRL general manager John Quayle. It was the first serious conversation the pair had had in almost a decade – the ravages of the Super League war of 1995 and beyond having split them, seemingly irrevocably, as it had with more than a few other friendships.

'The bloke had woken me up with a 6 a.m. phone call most mornings of the week for 10 years,' Quayle mused this week – recalling how Frilingos (*Mirror*) would ring him at that time each morning, followed promptly by Geoff Prenter (*The Sun*) at 6.15. 'I am deeply shocked at his death but happy we at least had the chance to talk last Friday,' said the former league boss.

The Super League years provided the prickliest challenge of Frilingos's long, energetic years as a rugby league scribe. Employed by News Limited, he was perceived to be firmly on that side of the fence as the News-backed Super League and the ARL fought their bloody and destructive battle.

Old friends fell out, and the Quayle–Frilingos split was just one of many in a tense period in which the enjoyment factor drained from the game. But in recent seasons, with the passing of time spreading its soothing balm, much repair work was done.

My own link with Chippy, who I had known for 40 years, was sorely tested for a time too – but genuinely and gently re-established these past 12 months. Last Wednesday we sat together at a CUB luncheon and yarned of football, and footballers.

Peter Frilingos learned his lessons well from his mentors at the *Mirror*, the late Peter Muszkat and Bill Mordey. He was a relentless worker, with many strings to his media bow in recent years, a dogged chaser of a story and a man who showed admirable loyalty to his employer over a long haul pretty much unmatched in the story of Australian sportswriting.

For years he had been a power-player in rugby league's world, wielding true influence and setting agendas with the stances he took. Fiercely intense in the work environment, he was also supremely quick-witted, as footy radio listeners will be well aware, a loving family man – and a fine companion in the context of a football tour, of which he made many.

Unquestionably he passes the test posed by these immortal words of Grantland Rice. So, too, do Bill Mordey and Phil Tresidder with whom Chippy Frilingos shares this recent, sadly premature full time: 'For when the One Great Scorer comes to write against your name, He marks not that you won or lost, but how you played the Game.'

The Australian, 6 May 2004

BREAK EVEN HAD A WINNING WAY

Peter Lalor

Bill Mordey: sportswriter, promoter and horse stud owner. Born Sydney, 1936. Died Newcastle, 23 April, aged 67.

Bill Mordey was not only one of the great storytellers in Australian sporting life, he also somehow managed to populate many of the great Australian sports stories. Mordey died last Friday while undergoing chemotherapy for cancer.

A larger-than-life journalist, punter, fight promoter and horse breeder, he was a man with a passion for life and risk. They called him Break Even Bill because of his penchant for claiming he had 'broken even' on a fight, even when it was obvious to all concerned that he had done considerably better – or worse.

The young William claimed he had his first punt – five shillings on Flight in the Melbourne Cup – at 13. His cousin gave him the tip and his SP bookie aunt refunded the losing bet out of respect for his age.

Born in Campsie, Sydney, in 1936, he was reared by his mother after his father died when he was seven. A 15-year-old Mordey arrived at *The Daily Mirror* newspaper in Sydney in the 1950s. It was a field for which he was well-suited and he soon became one of the town's best-known sportswriters and one of its most colourful characters.

Mordey's gambling was renowned. He won £10,000 ($20,000 after 1966's decimalisation) on a horse while a reporter for the *Mirror* – the equivalent of eight years' pay.

Colleague Jeff Collerson remembers when he, Mordey and Mordey's opposite from *The Sun* newspaper, E.E. Christensen, went to the races in France, where Mordey and Christensen were covering the 1972 Rugby League World Cup. Mordey wanted to bet, but none of them knew anything about the horses and they couldn't follow the money because there were no bookmakers. The trio tracked down the journalists' room.

'There were six blokes playing cards,' Collerson remembers. 'Mordey said: "Hang on, this will be tricky. There could be a few with no idea, how will we know which one to believe?"'

'Then Mordey, who'd been complaining about the price of food, had an idea. There was a very fat man in the room and Mordey said if he could afford food in this country, he must be rich and worth listening to.'

After fumbling through some schoolboy French – Mordey asked him for his 'les egg flips' – the man marked their selections and the trio set out to gamble. Mordey bet big and by the second last race was up $10,000. Knowing there was a race meeting the next day he asked Collerson, who was on holidays, to cover the next day's game as he planned to go to the races again with the well-fed Frenchman.

'He said: "Christensen will help you out and make sure you don't get scooped – you just write under my name,"' Collerson recalls. 'Anyway, he lost $10,000 on the last race and decided to cover the game instead of going back.'

Once Mordey bought a greyhound from Ireland and held a press function for it at the Souths Sydney Juniors league club where its photograph was taken eating lobster from a plate.

'It was Bill's idea and it got in all the papers, but then some nark got on to the club and they had to smash all their plates because of the health regulations,' Collerson says.

Mordey seemed to care little for money. Taking $10,000 to the Gold Coast to bet on a horse, he turned it into more than $100,000 at the casino before the race but came home without enough money to catch a taxi from the airport – the horse had lost.

Mordey gave up journalism after watching a boxing match staged by Grantlee Kieza in 1984 and decided it was the game for him. He began to promote Jeff Fenech and drew an Australian record crowd of 37,000 to Melbourne's Princes Park in 1992 to watch the Australian fight Azumah Nelson in the rain.

He took Jeff Harding and Kostya Tszyu to world titles, luring the Russian to Australia with the promise of a microwave oven.

An acrimonious split with Tszyu saw Mordey awarded more than $7 million in damages before he gave up the fight game to start up a horse stud with his wife in the Hunter Valley in NSW. The couple owned a 140-hectare property called Lurline Lodge, a former dairy farm he bought in 2000 with the dream of winning a Golden Slipper.

Bill Mordey is survived by his wife, Gwenda; children Karen and Craig; and three grandchildren.

The Australian, 27 April 2004